MODERN IRELAND SINCE 1850

Mark Tierney, OSB, MA

MODERN IRELAND SINCE 1850

Revised edition

Gill and Macmillan

First published in 1972 under the title
Modern Ireland 1850-1950
This revised edition first published in 1978 by
Gill and Macmillan Ltd
Goldenbridge
Dublin 8
with associated companies throughout the world
© Mark Tierney, 1972 and 1978
7171 0886 4
Print origination in Ireland by
Joe Healy Typesetting, Dublin

Front cover portraits (l. to r.)
Top Row: Davitt, Parnell, Redmond
Second Row: Carson, Pearse, Connolly
Third Row: Griffith, Collins, Cosgrave
Bottom Row: De Valera, Craig, Lemass
(all pictures by courtesy of Radio Times Hulton Picture Library)

All rights reserved.
No part of this publication may be copied,
reproduced or transmitted in any form or by
any means, without permission of the publishers.
Photocopying any part of this book is illegal.

Photocopying
prohibited
by law

CONTENTS

Preface to the revised edition — 1

Chapter 1	*Post-Famine Ireland, 1850-70*	3
Chapter 2	*The Land Question, 1870-1914*	26
Chapter 3	*Home Rule, 1870-1914*	42
Chapter 4	*The Ulster Question, 1850-1914*	63
Chapter 5	*Developing Nationalism, 1880-1914*	86
Chapter 6	*The Easter Rising and the new Sinn Féin, 1914-18*	113
Chapter 7	*The War of Independence, 1919-21*	140
Chapter 8	*The Treaty and the Civil War, 1921-23*	155
Chapter 9	*The Irish Free State, 1923-32*	183
Chapter 10	*De Valera in Power, 1932-48*	198
Chapter 11	*Coalition Governments and the new Fianna Fáil, 1948-66*	215
Chapter 12	*The Ulster Question and Northern Ireland, 1914-69*	227

Index — 239

To
COLM CROKER
Who helped so much

PREFACE TO THE REVISED EDITION

IT is now six years since *Modern Ireland, 1850-1950* first appeared. During that time, many books and articles have appeared, throwing new light on Irish history for the period after 1850. This second edition tries to take into consideration much of this recent scholarship. I have also tried to incorporate the suggestions of readers and friends, who kindly pointed out some inconsistencies and ambiguities in the first edition. I am most grateful to them all.

While this textbook is directed primarily to students of the higher and lower courses of the Leaving Certificate, it makes no claim to be a complete history of the period. It is rather meant to be a guide and a pointer, and in no way should it be treated as an encyclopaedia. It is to be hoped that students will read other textbooks, as well as some of the excellent histories and biographies of Irish interest in their school and local libraries.

Irish history since 1850 is a complicated and involved subject. To many people it appears as a jigsaw puzzle. There is the added difficulty that from 1886 on we are trying to work out two jigsaw puzzles. On the one hand we have the emergence of the Irish Free State, while on the other hand separate developments in Ulster leading to the establishment of Northern Ireland. Both are part of the history of modern Ireland.

The period covered in this new edition has been extended to bring it up to the end of the Sean Lemass era (1966) for the Republic of Ireland, and to the end of Captain Terence O'Neill's premiership (1969) for Ulster. It is not too much to hope that the book will be read with interest and profit by students north and south of the border. No matter how different our roots and traditions, we have more in common than the sharing of the same island.

I would like to thank all those who have helped with their time and advice in making this second edition possible. My debt to Mr Colm Croker cannot be measured in material terms. He has been at hand at all times, and exercised great skill in seeing this second edition through the press.

Mark Tierney OSB
Glenstal Abbey
Co. Limerick
1 May 1978

Chapter 1
POST-FAMINE IRELAND 1850-70

Agrarian society all over Europe was experiencing a social evolution in the middle of the nineteenth century. In France, Prussia, the Baltic countries and elsewhere age-old traditions were breaking down in the face of liberal economics and a growing humanitarianism. Reforms were being introduced by enlightened governments and implemented by benevolent landlords. Ireland, however, did not follow this general pattern.

In the 1840s Ireland had a population of almost 9 million, two-thirds of which depended entirely on agriculture. Ruled from England, and situated so near to the richest nation in the world, it was Ireland's misfortune that she was unable to cash in on the wealth of her sister island. Over and over again the British government failed to come up with a solution to Ireland's two greatest problems: overpopulation and poverty. The advice of the Devon Commission, which reported in 1845 that tenants should be given security of tenure, was ignored. No constructive emigration policy was adopted, and all that could be offered were some timid half-measures of land reform, public works and fiscal reform. When famine hit Ireland during the years 1845-49 government officials were unable to cope with the catastrophe, being limited by their lack of vision and unwillingness to rise above the economic conventions of their day.

Eventually they realised that their theories of political economy could not be applied to a nationwide emergency like the famine. But their belated extension of the Poor Law to meet the crisis put too much pressure on an already overstrained system; and it has been estimated that by 1851 one million people had died of starvation and disease, while another one million had been forced to emigrate.

Consequences of the Famine 1850-70

The Great Famine may be considered as a turning-point in Irish history. It is the 'great divide' which has left an enduring mark on the folk memory of the country. The pattern of social and economic life in Ireland underwent a number of profound changes, so that people's values also changed and they began to think in new ways about their problems and how they might be solved.

1. *Population decline:* The most significant long-term result of the famine was a *sustained* reduction in population, a trend which was not reversed until the 1960s (see figure 1). This steady decline was caused by the extinction and non-replacement of the lowest class of agricultural ten-

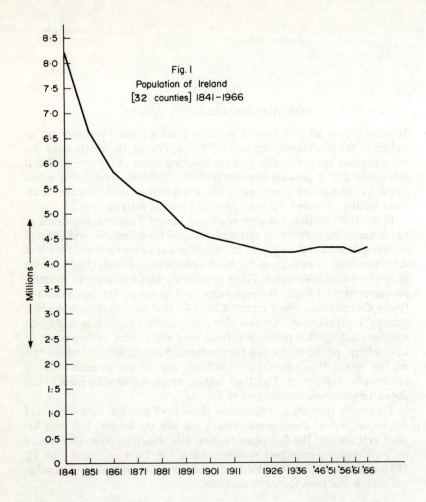

Fig. I
Population of Ireland
[32 counties] 1841–1966

ants during the famine, and by the new system of agricultural economy which emerged after the famine and which placed its emphasis on fewer and larger farms, fewer and later marriages, and emigration.

2. *The demise of the cottiers:* Perhaps the most immediately noticeable effect of the famine was the virtual destruction of the cottier class during the years 1845-65. The cottiers were at the lowest rung of the agricultural ladder, living in mud cabins and holding less than five acres; many of them had little more than a small potato patch on which to live. Their economy was a simple, non-monetary one, based on the potato, and their rent was paid either in the form of labour for the landlord or from the sale of a pig. It has been calculated that in 1845 there were approximately 300,000 cottiers in Ireland, nearly half of whom lived on

less than one acre. In addition, there were about 310,000 'small farmers' holding rather more substantial farms of between five and fifteen acres.

Already in the decade before the famine the demand for all Irish agricultural products had taken a downward trend. The farmers failed to see the writing on the wall and continued to rely mainly on tillage. Constant subdivision and the overcropping of the soil put an impossible burden on the available land, and the resulting distress was felt most acutely by those with the smallest holdings. The small farmers and cottiers were especially vulnerable during the famine because the 'quarter-acre clause' in the amended Poor Law excluded from 'outdoor relief' all those holding more than a quarter of an acre of land. Thus the cottiers, under threat of starvation, were induced to abandon their miserable holdings and seek refuge in the workhouse or in emigration. The famine got rid of those who had previously been able to live without money. It was precisely because they had no money that the cottiers were unable to survive the crisis. By 1851 their number had been reduced to 88,000, of whom only 38,000 held less than one acre, while the number of small farmers holding between five and fifteen acres had shrunk to 192,000. This sharp decline was to continue throughout the rest of the nineteenth century.

Agricultural labourers who held no land at all were a further category in the rural community who were badly hit by the famine. As they were paid wages in cash, and as there was always a demand for labourers on the larger farms, their class was not wiped out like the cottiers. But in the areas of greatest distress during the famine their plight was similar to that of the cottiers and the poorer small farmers. Their numbers fell from about 700,000 in 1845 to 500,000 in 1851, after which a more gradual decline set in.

Table 1.
Number of Agricultural Holdings in Ireland

	1841		1851		1871	
		%		%		%
up to 1 acre	135,314	(16.37)	37,728	(6.20)	48,448	(8.18)
1-15 acres	563,235	(68.15)	279,937	(46.04)	246,192	(41.54)
15-30 acres	79,342	(9.60)	141,311	(23.24)	138,647	(23.40)
over 30 acres	48,625	(5.88)	149,090	(24.52)	159,303	(26.88)
TOTAL	826,516	(100.00)	608,066	(100.00)	592,590	(100.00)

J. E. Pomfret, *The Struggle for Land in Ireland,* Princeton 1930, p. 42.

3. *The restructuring of the rural community:* Another consequence of the famine was that it brought about a transformation of the social structure of the rural community. The rapid fall of the population from 8½-9

million to about 6 million (a drop of some 30 per cent) in the period 1846-56 meant that there was a considerable reduction in the pressure of population upon the land. These years coincided with the repeal of the Corn Laws in England and the adoption of a policy of free trade in grain. The Irish farmers could no longer hope for non-competitive prices on the English market, and the only alternative was to change from tillage to pasture. A numerous tenantry had been an advantage as long as tillage was the mainstay of Irish agriculture, but the pasture system required larger ranch-type holdings which were not crowded with small cabins and potato patches. With this end in view, some landlords had already begun a campaign of clearances in the early 1840s, but it was the famine which was the really effective agent in clearing the unwanted people from the land. The balance now swung in favour of farms rather than smallholdings, and in favour of large farms rather than small ones. The number of farms of over fifteen acres rose from an estimated 277,000 in 1845 to nearly 300,000 in 1851; the most dramatic part of this increase was in the larger farms of over thirty acres, whose numbers soared from approximately 50,000 to 150,000 in the ten years 1841-51.

4. *The family farm: marriage patterns:* Those who remained on their farms were forced to change their way of life. It was no longer possible or permitted to subdivide the land. Instead there appeared the family farm, with all the members working on it, engaging in mixed tillage or livestock production. The changeover from subsistence to commercial farming brought prosperity to many. By combining dairying and grazing they could cash in on the upward trend in the market prices for butter and cattle. Agricultural wages also improved from a basic wage of 6d a day in 1840 to 6s or 9s a week by 1870.

The keynotes of the new system of agrarian economy were security, money, and the maintenance of the family farm — and with it the family's social status — intact. Money became an essential factor and was often hoarded under the bed in a tin box, and when a farmer married he now insisted on receiving a dowry with his bride. The ending of subdivision meant that the eldest son now inherited the whole farm, but he usually had to wait until middle age before he could get married and have the farm to himself. Gone were the early and improvident marriages of the pre-famine era. The younger sons of farmers had little hope of marrying since they did not inherit land; they had the choice of remaining as unmarried farm labourers or emigrating. Many farmers could save enough money for only one daughter's dowry, so their other daughters were forced to remain single too. Thus the new emphasis on security brought with it fewer marriages, later marriages, a lower birth rate, emigration, and a consequent steady decline in the population.

5. *Emigration:* Emigration was a constant feature of Irish life in the century 1850-1950. Although there had been a certain amount of emigration before the famine, it did not become a firm tradition until after

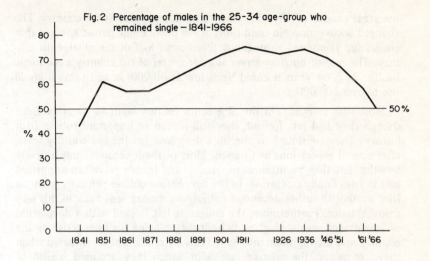

Fig. 2 Percentage of males in the 25-34 age-group who remained single — 1841-1966

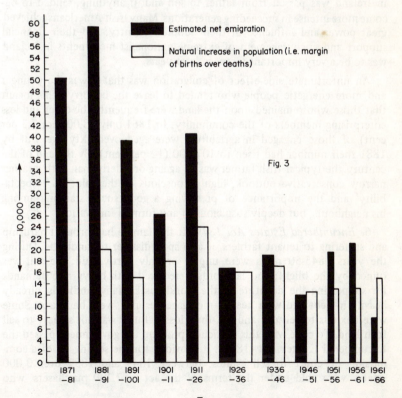

Fig. 3

the great exodus of 1848-55, when 2 million people left the country. The changed socio-economic conditions of the post-famine period ensured that emigration continued throughout the second half of the nineteenth century. The rate of outflow serves as a barometer of the country's economic health: in good years it could be as low as 30,000; in bad years it could rise to over 100,000.

Most Irish emigrants in the nineteenth century went to America. Even though they had left Ireland, they still played an important role in Irish history. They continued to cherish a deep love for the old country, even after several generations had passed. Most of them became comparatively wealthy, and their remittances to relatives and friends played an important part in Irish family budgeting. In the days before old-age pensions many an Irish mother or father depended entirely on money sent back in this way from America. Furthermore, the emigrants left Ireland with a deep sense of resentment against England, whom they blamed for impoverishing the country and driving them into exile. This bitterness was accentuated when they contrasted the relative ease with which they acquired wealth in America with their earlier poverty in Ireland. Their hatred of British rule in Ireland was passed from father to son and, if anything, tended to become more intense in succeeding generations. Many Irish-Americans achieved great power and influence in their adopted country, and their financial support and encouragement of extreme nationalist movements in Ireland was to be a very important factor in later years.

An unfortunate side-effect of emigration was that it was the younger and more energetic people who tended to leave the country. This meant that those who remained upon the land were frequently the older and less enterprising members of the community. In 1861 only 78,000 (or 7.3 per cent) of those engaged in agriculture were aged over sixty-five, but by 1881 their number had risen to 107,000 (12 per cent). By the end of the century the typical Irish farmer was an ageing or elderly man with a rather narrow conservative outlook, highly conscious of the value of 'respectability' and the importance of preserving a good social standing among his neighbours, but deeply suspicious of any form of innovation.

6. *Encumbered Estates Act 1849:* If the famine had brought hardship and suffering to tenant farmers, it also spelt disaster to landlords. During the years 1845-50 rents were unpaid or only partly paid; the soil was ruined by the blight; and landlords were faced with heavy rate demands for supporting the destitute in the workhouses. Many landlords, already heavily in debt and with heavily mortgaged estates, went bankrupt. Some were anxious to sell out and cut their losses. But it was not so easy to sell Irish land. To cope with this particular problem the government passed the Encumbered Estates Act (1849). It provided for the setting up of a commission or court to sell estates. Between 1849 and 1857 over 3,000 estates were sold under the terms of the act to 7,200 purchasers, who

paid a total of £20 million. By 1880 about a quarter of the land of Ireland (5 million acres) had passed to new owners.

The new landlords were hard-headed speculators who bought land on strict business terms, hoping for a good return for their money. The majority of them were native Irish Catholics of the same social origins as the tenants and they formed a marked contrast to the outgoing landlords of the Anglo-Irish Protestant gentry, whose feckless, easy-going ways and bad management had contributed to their ruin. From the tenants' point of view, the new landlords were worse than the old. They insisted on regular payment of rent, and many of them were 'graziers' who 'improved' their estates by clearing them of small tillage farmers in order to create large profit-making cattle-ranches. The tenant thus remained in constant fear of eviction, and throughout the second half of the nineteenth century his relationship with his landlord was of paramount concern to him.

A further effect of the Encumbered Estates Act was that it introduced an entirely new idea to the tenants. They had seen members of the old landed gentry replaced by successful businessmen of their own stock. They now realised that the seventeenth-century land settlement was not immutable and that further shifts in the structure of property-owning might be possible in future years. This thought, which was given an additional impetus by the theories of Fintan Lalor (see below), lay behind the land agitation which will be examined in the next chapter.

7. *The post-famine political climate:* We have already seen how emigrants to America harboured bitter recollections of the famine and its causes. For those who remained in Ireland the famine drew attention to a number of factors in Irish rural life which demanded reform: the injustices of the land laws; the low standard of living of the majority of those who formed the agricultural community (in 1871 there were still 118,000 single-roomed houses and 37,000 mud cabins in Ireland); the need for investment and improved techniques in farming; the absence of alternative work for those who were forced to leave the land; the inability of the British government to understand Irish problems and to cope successfully with a crisis.

In fact one of the few things in Ireland on which the famine had no effect was the system of government. The Union of Great Britain and Ireland emerged unscathed from the famine in spite of Daniel O'Connell's long campaign for its repeal. Ireland was still governed from Westminster through the Lord Lieutenant (or Viceroy), Chief Secretary and Under-Secretary, who from the headquarters of Dublin Castle directed an extensive civil service and numerous governmental boards and departments. The machinery of government extended to local level with such institutions as municipal corporations and poor law unions, while law and order was enforced throughout the country by Resident Magistrates and the Irish Constabulary (renamed the Royal Irish Constabulary in 1867).

The only significant political change that occurred in the decades before the famine was the achievement of Catholic Emancipation in 1829. As a result of this a small 'nationalist' caucus of Irish MPs had grown up in the Westminster parliament under the leadership of Daniel O'Connell. This embryo party was to grow in size and importance in the later nineteenth century until it was even able to exercise a decisive influence on English politics. Its existence and changing fortunes are of vital significance in Irish history in the seventy years after the famine.

O'Connell had always insisted on moderate constitutional methods to attain his party's objectives. He constantly opposed the use of physical violence. However, the terrible experiences of the famine years brought about a bitter hatred of British rule in Ireland and a desire to destroy it forcibly. This new militant nationalism expressed ideas of separatism, republicanism, social revolution and agitation for the redistribution of property. None of these ideas were new, but the earlier extremist movements which had attempted to achieve them had been largely conducted by middle-class intellectuals and had never received widespread active support. Now such ideas became popular among large numbers of Irish tenants and workers, and armed conspiracies, secret societies and agrarian outrages denote the constant presence or threat of voilence in the post-famine period.

The two nationalist traditions — the constitutionalist campaign for reform undertaken at Westminster, and the extremist campaign for revolution, including outbreaks of agrarian violence and plans for a large-scale military uprising — existed side by side in Ireland between the famine and the Treaty of 1921. The inter-relationship between these styles of nationalism was complex and was of immense importance at some of the most crucial phases of Irish history. But neither the MPs of the Irish Party nor the subversives of the IRB and the secret agrarian societies could hope to achieve any lasting results unless they had massive popular support in the country. And it was the bulk of the Irish people themselves who at certain critical times constituted the third and greatest of the nationalist forces in Ireland, wielding effectively the power of mass agitation or stolid resistance.

A similar duality was displayed by British governments, both Liberal and Conservative, in their approach to framing policies in reaction to the situation in Ireland. Some politicians favoured combating violence and outrage by ever harsher measures for the enforcement of law and order. Others believed that unrest in Ireland resulted from genuine grievances which should be investigated and redressed by parliament. As Ireland approached the 1880s, arguments for and against 'coercion' and 'conciliation' were heard with increasing frequency at Westminster as successive governments sought an acceptable balance between the two, sometimes even applying them both at the same time.

James Fintan Lalor

It was during the famine years that Ireland produced one of her greatest writers on social and economic problems, a man whose influence extends right up to the present. James Fintan Lalor (1807-49) was born in Co. Laois, the son of an O'Connellite MP. He had a passionate interest in the land question and dreamed of the day when the peasants would become proprietors of their own land. Lalor was a thinker and a theorist, but owing to poor health (he suffered from tuberculosis) and an early death, he did not make any great impact upon his contemporaries. However, he was a forceful writer, and in a series of letters to *The Nation* he outlined a number of economic principles which lived on after his death. He maintained that all title to land derived from the people, and that the restoration of the soil to the Irish peasantry was of more immediate urgency than the restoration of political independence. 'Beside the land question', Lalor declared, 'Repeal dwarfed down into a petty parish question.' In thus relegating Repeal to second place as a political objective Lalor incurred the hostility of the O'Connellite MPs.

Lalor's basic theories on land-ownership are admirably summed up in a passage in a letter written to John Mitchel's *Irish Felon* in 1848:

> The principle I state, and mean to stand upon, is this, that the entire ownership of Ireland, moral and material, up to the sun, and down to the centre, is vested of right in the people of Ireland, that they, and none but they, are the landowners and lawmakers of this island; that all laws are null and void not made by them; and all titles to land invalid not conferred by them; and that this full right of ownership may and ought to be asserted and enforced by any and all means which God has put in the power of man. In other, if not plainer words, I hold and maintain that the entire soil of a country belongs of right to the entire people of that country, and is the rightful property, not of any one class, but of the nation at large, in full effective possession, to let to whom they will, on whatever tenures, terms, rents, services, and conditions they will; one condition being, however, unavoidable and essential, the condition that the tenant shall bear full, true, and undivided fealty to the Nation, and the laws of the Nation, whose land he holds, and own no allegiance whatsoever to any other prince, power, or people, or any obligation of obedience or respect to their will, order or laws. I hold further, and firmly believe, that the enjoyment by the people of this right of first ownership in the soil, is essential to the vigour and vitality of all other rights; to their validity and efficacy, and value; to their secure possession and safe exercise.

It was the famine which forced Lalor to take up his pen. He believed that the landlord-tenant system was the source of all the evils in Ireland: famine, poverty, eviction and emigration. On behalf of the Irish peasant he demanded 'our fair share of Ireland, our fair share of the earth, a house to live in that no one can tumble down, a happy home, the necessities of life ... these we must have and security for all these'. To achieve his purpose, Lalor proposed what amounted to a 'no rent manifesto', in which he suggested that the tenants should organise a general strike against rent, and also refuse to pay poor rates. His proposals may be summarised as follows: (1) subsistence before rent, not vice versa; (2) strike against rent and eviction; (3) the money from withheld rents should be put into a local pool and used for community welfare.

These proposals contained the germ of two important new ideas. One related to *strategy:* the notion that tenants should combine in a well-directed mass organisation. The other concerned *tactics:* Lalor originated the concept of a 'land war'. These ideas were later developed and put into practice by Michael Davitt, who called Lalor 'the only real Irish revolutionary mind in the '48 period'.

Lalor is also important because of his influence upon later activists such as P. H. Pearse and James Connolly. They were attracted to Lalor by the passionate hatred for injustice which coloured his writings and led him to advocate extreme republican views in some of his later articles:

> Somewhere and somehow and by somebody, a beginning must be made. Who strikes the first blow? Who draws first blood for Ireland? Who wins a wreath that will be green for ever?

This kind of language was to be echoed by many of the leaders of the Easter Rising in 1916. Pearse wrote of Lalor: 'Tone sounded the gallant reveille of democracy in Ireland; the man who gave it its battle-cries was James Fintan Lalor.' Connolly wrote of Lalor that

> he died as he had lived, a revolutionary and a rebel against all forms of political and social injustice. In his writings we find principles of action and of society which have within them, not only the best plan of campaign for a country seeking its freedom through insurrection against a dominant nation, but also the seeds of a more perfect social peace of the future.

Lalor was a prophet, a man before his time. He was part socialist, part republican. He epitomised in his writings many of the national feelings of Irishmen in the second half of the nineteenth century. While he reminded his fellow countrymen of their allegiance to Ireland, and called for a 'social constitution', he was the great champion of agrarian reform. His dictum 'henceforth the owners of our soil must be Irish' was one which echoed in the hearts and minds of Irishmen until the land question was finally settled. However, one of the difficulties of Lalor was his failure to define 'the Irish people', and to indicate how the real owners were to come into their own.

The Tenant League 1850-59

The decade following the famine brought confusion and uncertainty into the lives of the tenant farmers. The threat of land clearance and eviction loomed large before them, especially on those estates which had changed hands under the Encumbered Estates Act. In 1849 17,000 families (90,000 persons) were evicted, and in 1850 the number rose to 20,000 (104,000 persons). In various parts of the south the more affluent tenants began to band together in small organisations in the hope of protecting themselves from arbitary eviction, while in Ulster a similar association of farmers began to press for the legalisation of the 'Ulster custom'.

According to the 'Ulster custom', tenants were not evicted so long as they paid their rents, and if a tenant decided to leave his farm, he was allowed to sell his interest in it. It is not surprising that farmers in other parts of Ireland cast envious eyes on the privileged conditions enjoyed by their counterparts in the north-east. However, the weakness of the 'custom' was that it was only a *custom,* not a law. Ulster tenants could be ejected just as easily as those in the south if their landlords so desired, and there was even a danger that landlords would circumvent the Ulster custom by raising rents to unreasonable levels so that even quite well-to-do farmers would be forced out of their farms.

In 1850 the several tenant protection societies, north and south, were drawn together into a single body, the Tenant League, founded by Charles Gavan Duffy, a former Young Irelander and close associate of Thomas Davis, and Frederick Lucas, an English convert to Catholicism who had come to live in Dublin, where he edited a newspaper called *The Tablet.* The basic aim of the Tenant League was to give the force of law to an improved version of the Ulster custom. Their particular demands were that (1) tenants should be assured of a fair rent, fixed by an impartial valuation, not by the landlord; (2) they should have security from eviction for as long as they paid their rents; (3) they should be able to sell their interest in their holdings for the best price they could get. These aims became famous as the 'Three Fs' (fair rent, fixity of tenure, free sale).

The Tenant League failed to obtain its objective and collapsed within a few years. There were several reasons why it did not live up to its early hopeful expectations: (1) Duffy and Lucas were strong constitutionalists and decided to embark on a purely parliamentary struggle. The fortunes of the Tenant League were therefore closely tied up with the Independent Irish Party which in 1851-52 was consolidating itself at Westminster. The party's subsequent ignominious disintegration (see below) had disastrous effects on the Tenant League. (2) By committing itself to a constitutional struggle the League failed to gain popular support on the extra-parliamentary level. When the parliamentarians failed them they had nothing left to fall back on. Furthermore, the League was not a mass movement; it drew its support from the wealthier members of the farming community, and its programme was geared to their interests. There was little attempt to extend its appeal to the mass of the smaller tenantry. The most important lesson of the Tenant League experiment was that a nationalist party at

Westminster was ineffective unless backed by a powerful and popular movement at home. (3) The League was opposed by Archbishop Cullen (see below), who considered that it was tinged with socialist doctrine. Cullen used his influence to induce many of the Catholic clergy to withdraw their support from the League. Both Duffy and Lucas became involved in an unseemly wrangle with Cullen, which did little good to the League. (4) The death of Lucas and the departure of the disillusioned Duffy to Australia in 1855 deprived the League of its principal driving forces.

The Tenant League's programme (the 'Three Fs') was embodied in a land bill introduced in parliament in 1852 by Sharman Crawford, an Ulster champion of tenant right. This bill was defeated. After the collapse of the Independent Irish Party a very different piece of legislation was enacted in 1860. Known as 'Deasy's Act', it confirmed the landlord as absolute owner of the soil and stipulated that all land must be held on terms agreed by contract between landlord and tenant. Since the tenant was in a very poor bargaining position, the act was entirely in favour of the landlord.

The Independent Irish Party 1851-59

After the death of O'Connell in 1847 the Irish Catholic MPs were without a leader and were absorbed into the Liberal Party. However, in 1850-51 a series of events occurred which caused them to reassert their separate identity and constitute themselves into a party. In 1850 the Pope decided to restore the Catholic hierarchy in England. This alleged 'papal aggression' provoked an outburst of anti-Catholic hysteria and led to the passage of the Ecclesiastical Titles Act (1851) which forbade Catholic prelates to assume territorial titles. The Irish Catholic MPs opposed the act and broke away from the Liberal government which had sponsored it. This group of MPs led by G. H. Moore, John Sadleir and William Keogh, became known as the 'Irish Brigade' or (in later years) as 'the Pope's Brass Band'.

The newly-formed 'Brigade' came to an agreement with the newly-formed Tenant League, and after the general election of July 1852 forty of its members reconstituted themselves as an Independent Irish Party. They pledged themselves to oppose any British government which would not repeal the Ecclesiastical Titles Act and enact the land reforms demanded by the Tenant League.

The party's high hopes were doomed to failure. (1) The combination of religious and agrarian issues proved divisive. Many of the supporters of land reform were Ulster Presbyterians who were unwilling to oppose the Ecclesiastical Titles Act. (2) The party was unfortunate in its leaders. Moore's volatile and undiplomatic personality made him unsuitable for reconciling the differences among his followers. He was eventually expelled from parliament in 1857 when it was found that his election had been due to gross clerical influence. Keogh was ambitious and self-seeking, while Sadleir was later proved to be a wholesale swindler. When the Conservatives fell from power in December 1852 the new Whig-Peelite coalition offered posts in the administration to Sadleir and Keogh. Both of them accepted, thereby breaking their pledge. Their dishonourable defection weakened the party's morale: by 1853 it had dwindled to 26 members, and by 1855 to 12. (3) Archbishop Cullen was suspicious of the Independent Irish Party because it had undertaken the cause of the Tenant League. He also disapproved of priests becoming involved in politics and in 1854 forbade them to do so. This deprived the party of some of its most influential supporters. (4) The party's pledge of 'independent opposition' proved to be a mistaken tactic in the circumstances of the time. Parliamentary politics in the 1850s were very unstable, neither party enjoying a firm majority. The Irish Party might have gained some of their demands by playing the English parties off against each other (as Parnell was to do thirty years later), but the pledge would not allow this. Eventually in 1859 half the members decided to take the more realistic line and break the pledge. This split the party and proved to be the final blow to its flagging morale.

By 1859 the Independent Irish Party was clearly defunct, having failed in all its objectives. Its history may have served as a cautionary lesson to a later generation of politicians, who were careful to avoid making the same mistakes. But for the time being the mass of the Irish people became disillusioned with the constitutional approach, so that, in the words of John Devoy 'the country became ripe for a physical-force movement'. When the Fenians offered a revolutionary solution to Irish problems they received a degree of popular support.

Fenianism 1858-67

After the abortive rising of 1848 many of its leaders fled to America or the continent, where they kept alive the tradition of physical-force nationalism. Two of them, James Stephens and John O'Mahony, were present in Paris during the 'days of the barricades' in the 1848 revolution, where they witnessed the successful use of force and became converts to the republican ideas of Lamartine. They then decided to establish contact with other revolutionaries and participants in the 1848 rising, both in Ireland and America, with a view to founding an organisation dedicated to the overthrow of British rule in Ireland. Accordingly O'Mahony departed for New York, while Stephens returned to Ireland.

For two years Stephens tramped on foot around Ireland, covering a total of 3,000 miles, making contact with secret societies and recruiting support throughout the country. He was a curious character, blending both vanity and charm; this latter feature immediately won him many adherents at this stage. His principal helpers were Thomas Clarke Luby,

John O'Leary and Charles J. Kickham (all former Young Irelanders) and Jeremiah O'Donovan Rossa, organiser of a thriving revolutionary group, the Phoenix Society, in Co. Cork.

Meanwhile in America the scholarly patriot O'Mahony was stirring up the revolutionary spirit among the hordes of famine immigrants. By 1851 there were about a million people of Irish birth in the United States. In New York the Irish community comprised 133,000 people in 1851, which was a quarter of the total population of the city. The New York Irish community formed a military organisation called the Irish Republican Union and had their own regiment in the New York state militia. The famous 69th Regiment was formed in 1851, with Michael Doheny as lieutenant-colonel. The Fenian flag was orange and green stripes, with thirty-two stars, representing the thirty-two counties of the Irish republic, while the stars and stripes signified for the first time the important role which America would henceforth play in Irish affairs.

Stephens kept in touch with his friends in America through their emissary Joseph Denieffe. Early in 1858 Denieffe arrived back in America with a message from Stephens to O'Mahony and Doheny in which he promised to raise 10,000 men, 1,500 of them armed, within three months, provided the Irish-Americans could supply the necessary financial backing. Stephens was disappointed by the small amount of money that was eventually collected, but he decided to go ahead, and on St Patrick's Day 1858 he inaugurated the Irish Revolutionary (or Republican) Brotherhood — better known as the IRB — in Dublin. On the same day O'Mahony founded a parallel American organisation which he called the Fenian Brotherhood. Historians generally refer to the members of both organisations in the early phase of their existence simply as 'Fenians' and to their ideology as 'Fenianism'.

Fenianism sought to establish an independent Irish republic by military force in the immediate future. It took as its motto 'Soon or Never'. It drew much of its ideology from the libertarian principles of the American and French revolutions and also revived the old revolutionary doctrine of Wolfe Tone and the United Irishmen. It stated that

> The Supreme Council [the eleven-member committee which directed the IRB] is hereby declared to be in fact, as well as by right, the sole government of the Irish Republic. Its enactments shall be the laws of the Irish Republic until Ireland secures absolute national independence.

The society was secret and oath-bound and was organised by means of an elaborate system devised by Stephens into groups or 'circles' of 820 men commanded by officers or 'centres'; Stephens himself took the title 'Head Centre'. A version of the oath written by Stephens in 1859 reads:

> I . . . , in the presence of Almighty God do solemnly swear allegiance to the Irish Republic, now virtually established; that I will do my utmost, at every risk, while life lasts, to defend its independence and integrity;

and finally that I will yield implicit obedience in all things not contrary to the law of God to the commands of my superior officer. So help me God. Amen.

A later version of the oath contains the pledge to 'take up arms, at a moment's notice' to defend the Republic.

It should be noted that Fenianism was essentially both autocratic and negative. The self-appointed Supreme Council was acting only on its self-created authority when it proclaimed a republic and declared itself to be the provisional government of the Irish people. Stephens referred to himself with pride as 'a provisional dictator'. Furthermore, the Fenians proposed no political programme outlining how an independent Irish republic should be governed; they were concerned solely with the destruction of British rule.

The movement got off to a slow start, partly because the financial help from America was not as great as had been hoped, and partly because there was an improvement in the Irish economy in the late 1850s. In the early 1860s, however, a series of bad harvests precipitated an agricultural crisis which gave a powerful impetus to recruiting. This trend was reinforced by the Fenian newspaper, the *Irish People,* launched in 1863, which provided a constant flow of propaganda on behalf of republicanism. The impassioned articles of Kickham, Luby and O'Leary aroused the hearts of many Irishmen to a bitter resentment against England.

While the leaders were mainly of a 'petty-bourgeois' background, rank-and-file Fenians came predominantly from the working classes, both urban and rural: small farmers, labourers, clerks, shop assistants and artisans. The movement was the first in Irish history to have such a widespread appeal at popular level. As John O'Leary said, 'Our movement was mainly one of the *masses,* not the *classes.*' By 1865 Stephens was to claim (somewhat optimistically) that there were 80,000 Fenians in Ireland and Britain. These men, whatever their true number, regarded themselves as forming the nucleus of a national army, and when the Irish Volunteers were formed in 1913 some of its most enthusiastic recruits were members of the IRB. One of the organisation's cleverest and most successful methods of increasing its power was its infiltration of other national movements; it later played a significant role in the Land League, the Gaelic League, the Gaelic Athletic Association, the Irish Volunteers and Sinn Féin, all of which to some extent served as 'fronts' for the IRB, which remained in the background and exercised a secret influence over them. In the late 1860s it even infiltrated the British army, winning over as many as 12,000 (again, an optimistic estimate) of the Irish soldiers. Much of this work was done by John Devoy, a cottier's son, a young man of great ability and forceful personality who had a long career ahead of him in America as the greatest of all the Fenians.

By the early 1860s Ireland seemed ripe for the promised uprising. But the American Civil War (1861-65) brought to a standstill the much-needed aid from America. Tensions between the Irish and American wings of the movement grew, O'Mahony calling for prompt action, and Stephens retaliating with demands for funds. When the Civil War ended, the American organisation itself divided, some members undertaking an abortive invasion of Canada using trained Fenian soldiers demobilised from service in the American armies, rather than following O'Mahony's policy of supporting direct action in Ireland. The clash of personalities and the struggle for power and for control of the organisation and its finances weakened it considerably. The Fenian system of recruiting gave ample opportunity for spies to infiltrate the organisation and led to the closing down of the *Irish People* in 1865. Stephens himself was arrested, though his escape was engineered shortly afterwards by Devoy. The movement also came up against clerical opposition, partly for the technical reason that the Catholic Church abhorred any society administering a secret oath. Archbishop Cullen was its chief opponent among the hierarchy, but it was Bishop Moriarty of Kerry who expressed clerical displeasure in the strongest language: 'Hell is not hot enough, nor eternity long enough, to punish these miscreants.'

The long-awaited rising was postponed to 1865, then to 1866. When it eventually occurred, in March 1867, it collapsed almost immediately, giving a great blow to the morale and prestige of the Fenians. It was only in the aftermath of an incident occurring in England that Fenianism received a solid boost. During an attempt to rescue some Fenian prisoners in Manchester in September 1867 a police sergeant was accidentally killed, as a result of which three Fenians, Allen, Larkin and O'Brien, were executed for his murder. This event shook Ireland profoundly and caused a massive upsurge of hostility against England; the 'Manchester Martyrs' became national heroes, and their last words from the dock, 'God Save Ireland', were enshrined in a ballad that became the unofficial Irish national anthem until 'The Soldiers' Song' replaced it after 1916. In December 1867 another attempt to rescue a Fenian prisoner resulted in an explosion at Clerkenwell prison, London, which killed several people and outraged English opinion, in spite of the fact that the Supreme Council was quick to condemn it. Thus the incidents at Manchester and Clerkenwell drove a deep gulf between the two nations. But they also had the effect of making many English politicians think deeply about the causes of such violence. Not the least of these was William Ewart Gladstone who became Prime Minister for the first time in 1868. In Gladstone's words, 'Fenianism brought home to Englishmen the vast importance of the Irish Question.'

Fenianism appeared to be a spent force after 1867, but it remained an integral part of the Irish political scene for the next fifty years. The American wing of the movement, disgusted by the vacillations and ineptitudes of 1867, deposed Stephens and the old leadership and created a new, independent organisation, Clan na Gael, which was guided by more capable hands, chiefly by John Devoy. Henceforth Irish-American nationalism became a vital force in Irish politics. In Ireland itself Fenianism continued in a low key until the early years of the twentieth century, keeping alive the republican faith and the tradition of revolutionary conspiracy. After the turn of the century it took on a new lease of life, and the 1916 Rising was planned and led by members of the IRB. Perhaps the best illustration of the continuity of the Fenian tradition is provided by Pádraic Pearse's oration at the grave of the old Fenian O'Donovan Rossa in 1915, when he declared: 'Life springs from death, and from the graves of patriot men and women spring living nations ... They [the government] have left us our Fenian dead, and while Ireland holds these graves, Ireland unfree shall never be at peace.'

Disestablishment of the Church of Ireland 1869-71

Gladstone formed his first Liberal administration in 1868 after a general election which had been fought under the slogan 'Justice for Ireland' and which gave him a majority of 112 in the House of Commons. He had for many years been formulating a policy for his 'mission to pacify Ireland', and the revolutionary agitation of the Fenians in the late 1860s had conditioned his colleagues and the country at large to accept that a series of reforms and concessions was necessary. The first plank in Gladstone's Irish programme was the disestablishment of the Church of Ireland.

The Church of Ireland was part of the Established Church. Its ministry received the official recognition and financial support of the state, which empowered it to collect tithes from Catholics and Dissenters as well as from its own members. Its ecclesiastical courts were recognised in civil law, its bishops were government nominees, and its privileged position was protected by parliament. Yet according to the census of 1861, which was the first to provide reliable figures relating to religious affiliations, the Established Church in Ireland had less than 700,000 members (more than half of them concentrated in north-east Ulster) out of a total population of over 5,750,000, of whom some 4,500,000 were Roman Catholics. These statistics showed that the Church of Ireland was not the church of the majority of the people of Ireland. Catholics naturally resented this state of affairs, and their feelings were additionally tinged with a degree of sectarian animosity towards Protestantism in general which was due to a massive Evangelical proselytising mission in Ireland, financed and directed from England, in the period 1850-70. With many English Liberal Nonconformists also opposing any kind of church establishment, the climate seemed favourable for Gladstone's proposed reform.

Gladstone introduced his Irish Church Bill to parliament in March 1869, stating that its purpose was 'to put an end to the establishment of the Church in Ireland, and to make provision in respect of the temporalities thereof, and in respect of the Royal College of Maynooth'. He assured his listeners that he did not wish to proceed 'in the manner which has been in fashion in various continental countries, where churches have been disestablished, religious orders abolished and members of them turned out of doors'. The bill involved both a disestablishment and a disendowment. It stated that on 1 January 1871 'the union of the Churches of England and Ireland was to cease'. Henceforth the Church of Ireland was to be a voluntary body, without any state aid. Its property was to be vested in a Temporalities Commission, and a Representative Church Body, composed of lay and clerical members, was created to take over the government of the Church and to take possession of its ecclesiastical property actually in use (churches, burial grounds etc.) and to purchase such secular property as it required from the Temporalities Commission. The remaining surplus was to be devoted to charitable and educational purposes. Tenants on church lands were to be enabled to purchase their holdings and would receive state loans for this purpose.

The provisions relating to the Church of Ireland constituted the major component of a package deal — the general disendowment of *all* religion in Ireland. Supplementary measures arranged for the discontinuance of the state grant to Maynooth College and the *regium donum* (annual state grant for support of the Presbyterian ministry). Both the Maynooth trustees and the Presbyterian Church received a lump sum in compensation (some £373,000 in the case of Maynooth). The Church of Ireland itself received about £10 million in compensation from the Temporalities Commission.

The bill met with fierce opposition, both within and without parliament, although it eventually passed both houses and was given the royal assent on 26 July 1869. Irish Protestants took alarm at its tone, and were afraid that its apparent attack on the rights of property might set a precedent. On the other hand, some Catholics were disappointed that the bill made no provision for the Catholic recovery of some of the old cathedrals of Ireland. Great interest was naturally shown in the church surplus fund and the ways in which it was to be used. Rumour had it that the total value of the property in the hands of the Temporalities Commission was £45 million, whereas £30 million was perhaps nearer the mark. Compensation and associated costs totalled £16 million, leaving a sum of about £13 million which between 1871 and 1923 was spent on relief of poverty, the endowment of higher education and the encouragement of agriculture and fisheries through the Congested Districts Board (see page 38).

Disestablishment had a number of consequences for the people of Ireland as a whole, as well as for the Church of Ireland itself. (1) It introduced an element of religious equality into the country, by ending the privileged position of the Church of Ireland. Henceforth there was to be complete state neutrality in the religious affairs of Ireland. (2) It was a clear breach of the Act of Union, article 8 of which provided that 'the continuance and preservation of the United Church as the Established Church of England and Ireland shall be deemed as taken to be an essential and fundamental part of the Union'. Disestablishment thus had enormous symbolic implications and set a precedent which was not forgotten. It was the first of a series of breaches which were to be made in the Union over the next fifty years. (3) It turned many Irish Protestants against the Liberal Party, and led them to see in Gladstone's policy a conspiracy to put an end to their ascendancy in Ireland. Some, like Isaac Butt, felt that Protestants might expect better treatment under an Irish parliament than from Westminster (see Chapter 3). (4) Disestablishment gave new life to the Church of Ireland. It presented Protestants with a challenge, and brought the laity more into Church affairs. It gave the Church of Ireland an opportunity to take a good hard look at itself, and within a few years it had produced a new and excellent constitution, as well as a revised and updated liturgy. (5) The provisions relating to the estates of which the Church of Ireland was the landlord were of considerable significance for the future. In the years 1871-80 over 6,000 tenant farmers took advantage of the terms of the act to purchase their holdings with state assistance. The act thus introduced the ideas of land purchase by the tenant and peasant proprietorship which were to occupy an important place in the great series of Land Acts initiated by Gladstone.

Cardinal Cullen and the Catholic Church 1850-78

The Catholic Church experienced many changes and adaptations during the years 1850-70. The link with Rome was firmly forged and established mainly through the person of Paul Cullen. Most of Cullen's early career had been spent in Rome, where he served for eighteen years as Rector of the Irish College. This was a very disturbed period in Italian history, during which the Church was under constant attack from radicals and revolutionaries. Cullen became a confirmed Ultramontanist, i.e. an upholder of the principle of absolute papal authority throughout the whole Church. He strongly opposed Gallicanism, which favoured a looser central discipline and allowed the Church to display distinctve national characteristics, even to the point of expressing independent opinions on matters relating to politics. Gallicanism in Ireland was most forcefully represented by the fiery nationalist, John MacHale, Archbishop of Tuam.

The Pope appointed Cullen papal legate and Archbishop of Armagh in 1850. On arrival in Ireland he held the first National Synod since the Reformation, which met at Thurles in 1850. Cullen presided over the assembly of bishops and imposed his Ultramontanist views on them. Under his influence the synod introduced stricter ecclesiastical discipline into the Irish Church and imposed many Roman customs not previously in force. By 1850 the Irish Catholic Church had stepped out of the penal days, and while she retained some customs of the post-Reformation era, these were now controlled and adapted to Roman canon law. In 1852 Cullen was made Archbishop of Dublin and in 1866 became the first cardinal to be created in Ireland. He was a great organiser and governor and remained the predominant figure in Irish church affairs until his death in 1878.

Cullen's attitude towards politics was determined by his Ultramontanism. He kept himself publicly aloof from the state authorities, declining to accept appointment to any of the government commissions on which his predecessor had served, and refusing to attend viceregal levees. On the other hand he opposed nationalist movements whose aims he considered not to be in accordance with the social teachings of the Church. In some cases he went too far, as when he attacked Gavan Duffy during the Tenant League campaign. He quite wrongly considered Duffy to be an Irish Mazzini, imbued with republican and revolutionary ideals. But if Cullen expressed disapproval of the Tenant League and its parliamentary ally, the Independent Irish Party, his sternest denunciations were reserved for the Fenians, whose subversive activities and avowed aim of overthrowing the existing authority by force of arms represented everything he had most hated and feared while in Italy. Cullen condemned the movement in a series of pastoral letters and excommunicated its members, but was ably answered by Kickham and O'Leary in the pages of the *Irish People*.

One of the most controversial issues in the post-famine years was that of priests in politics. Ever since the 1820s when O'Connell received the active support of the clergy in the struggle for Catholic Emancipation, it was an accepted fact of Irish life that priests should be involved in politics. They helped in selecting candidates at elections, canvassed voters and even organised the transport of electors to the polls. However, the practice led to some abuses, and there were justifiable complaints of clerical intimidation. Some priests also used the pulpit or altar for political motives. Cullen was particularly anxious that the Catholic clergy should avoid scandal, and he therefore took a firm line on the subject, in 1854 banning all clerical involvement in politics.

On the positive side, Cullen was not averse to the use of constitutional politics to improve the conditions of life of the Irish people and to advance the interests of the Catholic Church. He realised that the best means for doing so lay in maintaining a friendly relationship with the Liberal Party in England. Partly to fill the vacuum created at Westminster by the demise of the Independent Irish Party, and partly to encourage an alternative to Fenianism, Cullen gave his support to the National Association, founded in 1864. This body had a threefold programme: the disestablishment of the Church of Ireland, land reform, and state-aided denominational education (including assistance for the Catholic university, founded in 1854). The National Association never enjoyed widespread popularity, but it did succeed in keeping Irish grievances alive at Westminster during a rather fallow period, and Cullen lived to see the Church of Ireland disestablished and a start made in the reform of the land law, though Catholic university education was to be a vexed question which was not finally solved until 1908 (see pages 26 and 58).

Within the Catholic Church itself, as part of the 'Romanising' and updating policy, a number of new religious orders were introduced into Ireland in the 1850s, and when Pope Pius IX proclaimed the dogma of the Immaculate Conception of the Blessed Virgin, there was an upsurge in Marian devotion throughout Ireland. The second half of the nineteenth century was also a time when pulpit oratory and formal sermons drew large congregations to the churches. John Henry Newman's University Church in Dublin became famous for the sermons preached there not only by Newman himself, but by many other distinguished churchmen as well. The Dominican Fr Tom Burke (1830-82) was perhaps Ireland's greatest orator. Sermons lasted more than an hour and were talking-points among the people for days afterwards.

The years 1850-70 saw a great wave of church building throughout the whole country. In town and village the new Catholic church stood in contrast to the old Protestant church. Money for the new churches came from America and the colonies, although this spate of church building also gave evidence of the relative prosperity of the Catholic community in Ireland at the time.

The Railways

One factor which helped to bring prosperity to the country and affected life in Ireland during the two decades following the famine was the building of the railways. Besides giving employment, it meant that people became more mobile. By 1855 the main lines between Dublin and Belfast, Cork, Galway, Limerick and Waterford were finished, and a total of 1,000 miles of rail had been laid; by 1865 this figure had doubled. Most of the work was done under the direction of the great engineer William Dargan. The railways cut the cost and time of travel by more than half. Trains travelled at about twenty-five miles an hour in the 1860s. Thus, while the journey from Dublin to Cork took seventeen hours by the fastest coach, the train took only about seven hours and was also much more comfortable. The railways killed the passenger traffic on the canals and also the mail-coach on the roads.

The railways opened up a whole new world of tourism. New hotels were built to cater for travellers, and holiday resorts such as Killarney, Sligo and Kilkee grew in size and importance. The railways also brought about a revolution in the life of the ordinary people, especially in their diet and dress. After 1850 they began to substitute Indian meal and bread for potatoes, while tea became the most common domestic drink. Imported manufactured clothes, especially among women, now took the place of homespun clothes. Tobacco-smoking likewise became popular among men.

The railways helped in the growth and development of market towns. The years after the famine saw the countryside filled with commercial

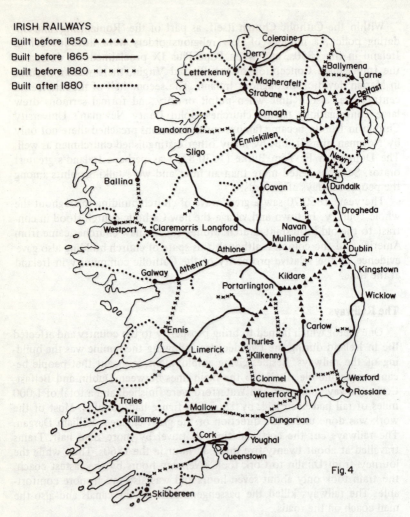

Fig. 4

travellers, who used the railways for personal travel and for sending goods to their customers. The post office also used the railways and did a growing business, thanks to mail order catalogues. The farmers also benefited by this new and quick means of transport. Cattle could now be exported conveniently from the remoter areas, and thus the railways helped to bring about the changeover from tillage to pasture.

In one way the railway system did a disservice to the country as a whole, in that it speeded up the rate of emigration, as more and more impoverished farmers took advantage of the cheap travel it offered to reach their nearest port. It also exposed local trades to competition from the big firms in Dublin, which, together with the easy transport of imported goods into the interior of the country, helped to close down many small industries in the provinces. The development of the railway network also meant that many small towns situated near it grew and prospered, while old commercial centres not in the vicinity of the railway declined in importance.

Talking Points

Chapter 1: Post-Famine Ireland 1850-70

1 Outline the main consequences of the Great Famine during the years 1850-70, with special reference to the agricultural classes.

2 What were the principles of economic and political thought proposed by James Fintan Lalor? Explain how he had such a profound influence on future Irish politicians and writers.

3 Explain the initial success of the Tenant League movement. How did the Sadleir-Keogh 'betrayal' cause the collapse of the Tenant League? What was the attitude of Cardinal Cullen to the League?

4 Assess critically the role which Fenianism played in Irish political life between 1858 and 1867.

5 What were the main reasons behind Gladstone's Act of Disestablishment of the Church of Ireland in 1869? How did the Church of Ireland benefit in the long run from this Act?

6 Discuss the changes which the introduction of the railways brought to Irish life during the years 1850-70.

Chapter 2
THE LAND QUESTION, 1870-1914

The 'land question' was nothing new in Ireland. It had its roots in a series of plantations and confiscations, and each succeeding century brought its own particular problems. The second half of the nineteenth century was no exception, only this time a combination of factors and personalities helped to make the protest a more serious one. It was not just a repetition of the Whiteboy agitation of the eighteenth century, but a radical and organised effort to solve once and for all the centuries-old dispute over land ownership. It was a shrewd combination of theory and practice, basing itself upon the theories of such writers as James Fintan Lalor and Henry George. The land question was not just limited to local agitation, but was raised to the level of a constitutional struggle, thanks to the interest and backing of Parnell and Gladstone. It was a multi-sided struggle, and lasted for some forty years. By 1914 the land question, in its fullest sense, had been solved.

The Land Act of 1870

Successive British governments had failed to provide any solution to the Irish land question in the post-famine years. It was left to the Liberal Prime Minister, W. E. Gladstone, to make the first serious attempt to do so. When taking office for the first time in December 1868, he said: 'My mission is to pacify Ireland.' He began by disestablishing the Church of Ireland, and then turned his attention to the land question. He introduced his first land bill to the House of Commons on 15 February 1870.

The bill was very much his own brain-child; as his biographer, John Morley, wrote, 'It was almost a point of honour in those days for British cabinets to make Irish laws out of their own heads.' But there were other reasons for Gladstone's intensely personal sponsorship of the legislation. He was aware that many members of his own party were opposed to the principle of land reform, and he feared that the involvement of too many people during the bill's preparation would lead to a major public debate which would jeopardise the bill's passage through parliament. Accordingly, Gladstone did not consult Irish opinion (which was not, in any case, effectively represented at Westminster at this time), nor did he set up a parliamentary committee to study the complicated Irish land system. He did, however, receive encouragement and advice from Fortescue, the Chief Secretary, and from John Bright, the Quaker MP for Birmingham, who was a confirmed advocate of peasant proprietorship.

Gladstone steered the bill through parliament with skill and determination. In order to deflate possible Liberal hostility, it was framed in cautious and moderate terms, and Gladstone constantly stressed its purpose as an instrument of 'pacification'. Many MPs voted for it because they believed that its acceptance in Ireland would reduce the influence of Fenianism.

The keynote of the Land Act was *tenant security*. Its main provisions were: (1) Wherever the Ulster custom (see page 64) already existed, it was given the force of law. (2) Tenants not protected by the 'custom' were to receive compensation for their improvements if they gave up their farms and (3) were to receive compensation for disturbance if evicted for any cause other than non-payment of rent. (4) A measure of land purchase was introduced, with two-thirds of the price loaned by the state. (This was the 'Bright Clause'.) Gladstone hoped that the act would mean the beginning of a new era in landlord-tenant relations, because it made unjust eviction cut both ways. While the evicted tenant would suffer the loss of his holding, the evicting landlord would also suffer by having to pay compensation. Unjust eviction would 'cut his hands with the sharp edge of pecuniary damages'.

In practice the act failed on almost every score. The Ulster custom proved extremely difficult to define: the onus was on the tenant to prove that it existed, and conflicting claims tended to be settled in favour of the landlord. No incentive was given to landlords to sell, as the Bright Clause had suggested. In fact only 877 tenants bought their holdings under the 1870 act. Furthermore, two large classes of tenants were excluded from the act: tenants who held leases of thirty-one years or more received no compensation for disturbance if their leases were not renewed, while the most distressed group of all, the tenants in arrears, could be evicted without compensation. The act depended almost entirely on its acceptance by the landlords and on the efficiency of the courts in giving decisions in disputed cases. But in fact the landlords showed little or no enthusiasm for it, while the complicated legal processes and the cost of using the courts proved a serious deterrent for the tenants.

The underlying reasons for the act's failure were: (1) It offered the tenant 'security' in the form of *compensation* for eviction, rather than giving him what he really wanted – security of *tenure*. However long his lease might be, he was still in danger of being driven from his holding. (2) It did nothing to restrict the landlord's power to raise rents, and for as long as he retained this ultimate weapon, he could defeat the act by driving any tenant into arrears.

But if it was a failure in *practice,* the 1870 Land Act was a considerable achievement in *principle* and marked a decisive step towards solving the Irish land question. In spite of its tentative approach and its limited provisions, the act established important precedents. It implied that the arrangement between landlord and tenant was no longer a purely private contract, as stated by Deasy's Act of 1860 (see page 14), but one which would be controlled by the state. In laying down standards of just dealing to be followed by landlords, the government declared itself responsible for the welfare of tenants. Future governments were to use and extend this new power, and the 1870 act was therefore a landmark in the kind of thinking that led to the Welfare State. Most significant of all, the British parliament had showed its willingness to limit the power of the landlords by introducing the idea of 'tenant interest' in its legislation. The Land Act thus not only struck a blow at the established landed interest but, like the Irish Church Act (see page 20) eroded the basis of the Union which was its guarantee.

Economic and Social Pressures, 1870-80

In the 1870s the small farmer began to feel the effects of the changeover from tillage to pasture which was the pattern of the post-famine era. His only hope of making both ends meet was by raising crops. Yet, between 1860 and 1870 the area under tillage declined by some 400,000 acres. This was due mainly to the increase in the number of large cattle ranches. Farm labourers were thus deprived of employment and there was little or no industry to absorb them except in north-east Ulster. Some sought seasonal work in England, but many were forced to emigrate for good. Others managed to hold on, relying on remittances from relatives in America.

Several factors entered the scene in the late 1870s which caused further economic depression in Ireland, England and Scotland. The development of American agriculture and transatlantic shipping brought American wheat to the European market, and the price of corn dropped everywhere. The importation of frozen meat from Australia and New Zealand also posed a serious threat to the Irish and British markets. Farmers in England and Scotland, as well as in Ireland, were affected by the resulting agricultural crisis and fell into arrears. Large tracts of arable land went out of cultivation everywhere, and there was a depopulation of the countryside. In Scotland there were scenes similar to those witnessed in Ireland, with landlords evicting their crofter tenants and turning their land into grouse shooting estates.

However, Ireland, being a predominantly agricultural country, was worse hit than England; in Ireland, furthermore, the agricultural depression was accompanied by a severe setback to industry as British manufacturers sought outlets in Ireland for surplus goods which had built up during a period of industrial recession. Many firms, even in Belfast, went bankrupt, and urban unemployment rose. This effectively closed one door to alternative employment for poverty-stricken farmers, while another was closed by the drying up of the demand for migrant labour on English and Scottish farms. Such work had previously enabled many families to stave off complete destitution during periods of hardship.

A series of bad harvests in the late 1870s also made life very miserable for the farming community. The value of crops produced in Ireland between 1876 and 1879 fell by some £14 million. The potato crop was especially hit by excessive rain. In 1876 Ireland had produced 4 million tons of potatoes worth £12½ million; in 1879 the total amount of potatoes came to just over one million tons and their value was less than £3½ million. Farmers were unable to pay their rents, more than half a million people were starving, and the number of families evicted increased to over 1,000 in 1879 and over 2,000 in 1880.

Under these circumstances violence and outrage became the order of the day. Cattle were maimed, haystacks and farmhouses burnt, landlords and their agents attacked. A state of emergency arose and conditions were ripe for revolution. The landlords were unable to meet the situation. Many of them were absentees and showed no personal interest in what happened to their tenants. Others were bankrupt or in financial difficulties, as the non-payment of rents and the drop in the export cattle and corn markets had ruined them. But the brunt of the suffering and misery fell on the

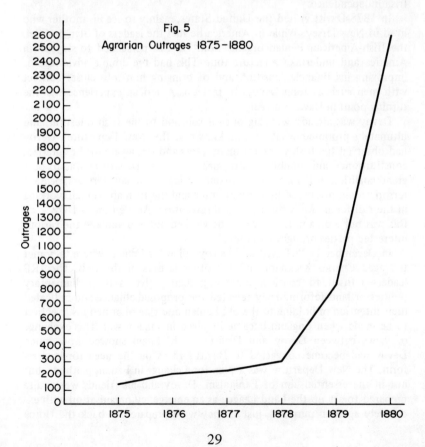

Fig. 5 Agrarian Outrages 1875-1880

tenant farmers and the labourers. They were desperately in need of money, and of an organisation to protect their interests.

Michael Davitt and the New Departure, 1878-79

Michael Davitt (1846-1906) was the son of an evicted Co. Mayo tenant farmer who emigrated with his family to Lancashire in 1852. When only eleven years of age the young Davitt lost his right arm in a cotton mill accident. This left him unfit for manual work, so he turned his energies to clerical work, journalism and the study of literature and history. He has given us a detailed account of his life in a number of books, among which are *Leaves from a Prison Diary* and *The Fall of Feudalism in Ireland*.

As a young man, Davitt joined the Irish Republican Brotherhood and was appointed organising secretary for the North of England division. He spent the years 1870-77 in prison, and on being released on ticket-of-leave, he rejoined the IRB and threw himself once more into the movement for Irish independence.

In 1878 Davitt visited the United States, mainly to see his mother who lived in New Jersey. While in America he met the leaders of Clan na Gael, the Irish-American Fenian organisation. He was persuaded to stay on in America and undertake a lecture tour. This had the double advantage of improving his financial position and of bringing him into closer contact with men such as John Devoy. In fact this American experience was the turning-point in Davitt's career.

Devoy was already working out his solution to the Irish question, and ultimately proposed what became known as the 'New Departure'. Devoy had observed the Irish scene for many years and was aware of the agrarian, constitutional and republican struggles. The New Departure was to be a grand coalition of Fenians and parliamentarians, of tenant farmers, peasant terrorists and priests, of the Irish at home and the Irish abroad, all working in their different ways for a political revolution. At the time — 1878 — all this was but a dream. It had yet to be worked out in detail and the various interested parties brought together.

In December 1878 Davitt and Devoy sailed for France, where they met the aged Charles Kickham and the other leaders of the IRB. The IRB leaders refused to consider extending their activities to parliamentary politics or land reform. They rejected the proposed alliance and indicated their intention of holding to the old Fenian doctrine of armed insurrection to be made when England became involved in a major war. This exchange of views between Devoy and Davitt and Kickham showed how much Devoy had become converted to Davitt's ideas on the need for land reform. The New Departure was a plan for a change in Fenian methods, but not in the essential aim of Fenianism. Devoy and his friends were quite prepared to set up the Land League as an emergency organisation with exclusively agrarian purposes, just as they were prepared to back the Home

Rule movement at Westminster; but these were seen only as steps on the long road to complete Irish independence.

Having failed with Kickham, Devoy and Davitt next turned to Parnell, the leader of the increasingly powerful radical section of the Home Rule League. Parnell was quite aware of the injustices of the Irish land system. As early as 1877 his mind was working towards the idea of peasant proprietorship as the only real solution. Speaking in Cavan in 1879 he said that he looked forward to the time 'when by purchasing the interests of the landlords, it might be possible for every tenant to be the owner of the farm which he at present occupies as tenant-at-will or otherwise'. Parnell was, therefore, very interested in the Devoy-Davitt plan. He saw that involvement in the land struggle would strengthen his hand and provide him with a wider audience for his ideas than the Westminster parliament. Thus he gave his tacit consent to the New Departure, which was an alliance between Parnell the parliamentarian, Devoy the Irish-American Fenian, and Davitt the Land League organiser, with the avowed purpose of obtaining justice for the Irish farmers.

The Land League, 1879

In the spring of 1879 Davitt visited his native Co. Mayo. He was appalled by what he saw: starvation, eviction, emigration and poverty. It was at this moment that he became convinced of the need to do something to help the victims of the Irish land system. In the light of his American experience and his talks with Devoy and Parnell, he realised that some combination of the farmers was necessary. On 20 April 1879 Davitt organised a demonstration at Irishtown, Co. Mayo, when 15,000 people and 500 green-bannered horsemen protested against the unjust land laws and demanded fair play for the tenants. As a result of this demonstration, the local landlord, a Catholic priest, Canon Bourke, reduced the rents by 25 per cent. Word soon got around of the success of the Irishtown meeting, and other demonstrations were planned. A great meeting was held at Westport on 8 June 1879, where the crowd displayed banners bearing the mottoes 'The Land for the People' and 'Down with the Land Robbers'. Parnell was the principal speaker at the Westport meeting. He told his listeners to 'keep a firm grip on your homesteads' and not to allow themselves to be dispossessed.

On 21 October 1879 Davitt founded the Irish National Land League in Dublin, with Parnell as president. The Land League, despite the involvement of some of its members in acts of violence, was essentially a moral force movement. It adopted a charter, containing seven points, and a declaration of principles. The main objectives of the League were (1) to prevent tenants from being rack-rented and unjustly evicted; (2) to press for legislation, so that the tenant farmers could become owners of their lands.

The Land League grew into an immense popular movement almost overnight. It provided the kind of protection and leadership which the Irish tenant farmers had needed for so long. The League made its appeal not only by words but also by deeds. Money poured in from America and also from England and the colonies. John Devoy issued a series of manifestoes to the Irish-Americans, one of which went as follows: 'Survivors of '47, does the memory of the hunger pang, the pestilence, the reeking emigrant ship and the ghastly fever shed, arouse no righteous indignation in your souls . . . Can you contemplate a repetition of these scenes?' Patrick Ford's newspaper, the *Irish World*, was another powerful force in whipping up enthusiasm in America for the cause of the Irish farmers. Extracts from it were printed in the Irish newspapers, especially in the *Irish Flag*, the *Freeman's Journal* and the *Nation*. Ford preached the doctrine of liberty and freedom. He asked: 'If the Irish in America can be free and equal to all the other races in the New World, why are the Irish at home acting and living as though they were an inferior race?'

The Land League taught the Irish farmers to stand on their own feet and assert their rights. Thanks to the American backing, a new spirit, a democratic one, entered the Irish scene. Such undemocratic behaviour as tipping the hat to their landlord and his agent was to be discouraged.

The Land War, 1879-82

Gladstone became Prime Minister for the second time in April 1880 and hoped to pass an emergency Land Bill through parliament that summer. When his proposals were defeated in the House of Lords, the Land League took the law into its own hands. Speaking at Ennis on 19 September 1880, Parnell declared:

> When a man takes a farm from which another has been evicted you must shun him on the roadside when you meet him – you must shun him in the streets of the town – you must shun him in the shop – you must shun him in the fairgreen and in the market place, and even in the place of worship, by leaving him alone, by putting him into a moral Coventry, by isolating him from the rest of his country as if he were the leper of old – you must show him your detestation of the crime he has committed.

The case of Captain Boycott, a Co. Mayo land agent, who was effectively put into this type of 'moral Coventry' and isolated by the local people until his nerve broke, was only one incident of the land war, which increased in intensity in the summer of 1880 and continued unabated until the 'Kilmainham Treaty' in 1882. Although the League's organisers officially condemned the use of physical violence, many of its members used the old Whiteboy tactics of cattle-maiming, night burnings, shootings and assassinations. Special land courts were set up to decide agrarian disputes. These

Land League courts worked as if the government courts did not exist. The tenants were encouraged to resist eviction. All in all the Irish country scene for the last six months of 1880 was not a pretty one, nearly 2,000 crimes being reported to Dublin Castle.

The government was at this time preparing a major reform of the land law, but Gladstone knew that it would receive little support unless immediate action was taken to restore order in Ireland. W. E. Forster, the Chief Secretary, therefore introduced a new coercion bill in parliament, which came into force on 2 March 1881 as the Protection of Person and Property Act. The parliamentary debate on the bill was long and bitter: Parnell's supporters used the tactic of obstruction (see page 45) to a greater extent than ever before, and the bill could only be passed after the rules of the House had been changed to make further obstruction impossible. One of the first actions taken by Forster after the fast reading of the new bill was to arrest Michael Davitt. The news caused scenes of uproar in parliament, and business could proceed only after the Home Rule MPs were ejected from the House. Many of Parnell's followers hoped that he would secede from parliament altogether and help promote a massive no-rent campaign in Ireland, but he decided to operate strictly within constitutional limits and to participate in the debate on the forthcoming Land Bill.

The Land League retaliated to coercion by putting on more pressure than ever. The worse the situation became, the more the League thrived and consolidated its position. Many Fenians now actively supported it, and money poured in from America. The Ladies' Land League was founded in Clonmel on 21 February 1881, with the express purpose of 'lightening the lot of those who may fall victim to the coercion act'. Here, for the first time in modern Irish history, the women of Ireland entered politics. They would remain a continuing influence for the next fifty years. Their diehard attitude is well illustrated in the resolution put forward at a meeting of the Ladies' Land League by Mary A. Crowley: 'We will never marry any young man who is not a Land Leaguer, but let him live and die an old bachelor, that he may be as tired of Skellig as we are of the English government.'

The Land Act of 1881

In April 1881 Gladstone introduced a Land Bill which he hoped would go a long way towards satisfying the demands of the Land League. It gave the tenant farmers the Three Fs: (1) fair rent, to be fixed by arbitration; (2) fixity of tenure, so long as the rent was paid; (3) free sale of his right of occupancy at the best market price; (4) a special Land Commission to be set up where rents could be fixed by judicial arbitration for a period of fifteen years. These four provisions established the principle of dual ownership and thus recognised the permanent interest of the tenant in his holding. (5) The government loan to purchasing tenants was also extended from two-thirds to three-quarters of the purchase money.

The Land Act became law in August 1881, and when it was published proved to be a very lengthy and complicated document. The Three Fs went a long way to meeting the tenants' demands. But if the government thought that the act would solve the land question and quell agrarian violence, they were seriously mistaken, since (1) not many tenant farmers could raise the capital to purchase their holdings and only a few hundred farms were brought under the new system; (2) more than half the tenants who had holdings of over an acre were excluded from its operation, the hardest hit being the 150,000 leaseholders and the 130,000 occupiers who were in arrears of rent; (3) the opposition of some of Parnell's party, especially John Dillon, to the Land Act created a problem; (4) the act was accompanied by a new coercion bill which aroused the anger of many who might otherwise have been prepared to give the Land Act a chance to prove itself.

Parnell's own reaction to the Land Act were dictated by his need to preserve unity among the many diverse elements of Irish nationalism. He could not afford to alienate moderate opinion either in parliament or in Ireland, yet it was equally vital to retain his grassroots agrarian support, as well as that of the Fenians and other extremists (e.g. Dillon). He therefore avoided condemning the act outright, but concentrated instead on emphasising its weakest points, such as the large number of tenants who were not entitled to benefit from it. He also launched an attack on the government's coercion policy through the medium of a newspaper which he founded in August 1881, the *United Ireland,* edited by William O'Brien, a Cork journalist, later an MP.

Parnell performed his delicate balancing-act between moderates and extremists with skill, carefully choosing his statements as occasion seemed to demand and according to the type of audience he was addressing. Immediately the Land Act became law he returned to Ireland and embarked on a series of speeches which suggested to the government that he was seeking to wreck the act. Gladstone was so incensed by some of Parnell's remarks that he said of him in a speech at Leeds on 7 October 1881: 'He desires to arrest the operation of the Land Act, to stand as Moses stood, between the living and the dead; to stand there, not as Moses stood, to arrest but to extend the plague.' Parnell replied two days later with a speech in Wexford in which he called Gladstone 'a masquerading knight errant who is prepared to carry fire and sword into your homesteads'. In the heated atmosphere of the time, it appeared to many people that Parnell was courting trouble and that he was trying to provoke Gladstone and Forster to order his arrest.

Parnell was arrested on 13 October and imprisoned in Kilmainham Jail, where he was later joined by Dillon, O'Brien and other nationalists. On 18 October they issued a 'No Rent Manifesto' calling on the tenant farmers to withold all rents from their landlords. It was nothing less than a call for a general strike against the payment of rent. However, it was denounced by several moderate nationalists and failed to receive general acceptance throughout Ireland. But it so enraged the government that Forster promptly suppressed the Land League. This, in turn, led to a new wave of violence and 'moonlighting' (i.e. the waging of agrarian vendettas by secret societies). The year 1881 ended with Forster as determined as ever to use coercion and to take the hard line with trouble-makers, but without any solution being found to the serious depression and suffering of the farming community.

The 'Kilmainham Treaty', 1882

Parnell's behaviour before his arrest may be partly explained by the fact that he had begun to lose interest in the land question for its own sake and that he was anxious to adopt a new approach to the problem of Irish independence. He seems to have regarded his period of imprisonment as marking the end of one phase of his political career and the opening of another.

By the spring of 1882 Gladstone was anxious to reach some kind of compromise. Parnell concurred, and in April 1882 they agreed to what has been called the 'Kilmainham Treaty'. By its terms, (1) Parnell was to be released and to use his influence to put down lawlessness; (2) coercion was to be relaxed; (3) leaseholders were to be admitted to the benefits of the Land Act and (4) protection was to be given to tenants in arrears.

The concessions gained by Parnell in the Kilmainham Treaty enabled him to end his active association with the land war without loosing his credibility in the eyes of most of the agrarian agitators. The 'treaty' thus brought the New Departure to an end and left Parnell free to concentrate on the struggle in parliament for Home Rule. He also showed his willingness to co-operate with Gladstone and the Liberal Party in furthering measures of general reform. This alliance with the Liberals was considered by some as a betrayal which made the Irish Party the puppet of the Liberals. Davitt considered the 'treaty' a surrender, but in the interests of unity did not make any protest. Instead he threw himself into his new plans for the nationalisation of the land of Ireland.

In America, the 'treaty' was considered by Clan na Gael as a sell-out. They were only half satisfied by Dillon's assurance when he visited America after his release from Kilmainham: 'Mr Parnell wishes — considers it best — that the movement in Ireland should be conducted on moderate lines till the present coercion act is exhausted. He believes that after the next election his power in parliament to resist coercion will be increased ten-fold.'

The Phoenix Park Murders, 1882

The Chief Secretary, Forster, likewise looked upon the Kilmainham

Treaty as a sell-out and he resigned in protest. He was succeeded by Lord Frederick Cavendish, who arrived in Dublin on 6 May 1882 to take up his duties as the new Chief Secretary. Lord Frederick was walking in the Phoenix Park with the Under-Secretary T. H. Burke, on the evening of his arrival in Dublin, when both men were stabbed to death by a group who called themselves the Invincibles. As soon as he heard of the Phoenix Park murders, Parnell denounced them and even told Gladstone that he was prepared to resign his seat in parliament, but was dissuaded from taking this step.

The Phoenix Park murders, followed immediately by a new coercion act, appeared to undo all the good achieved by the Kilmainham Treaty. But in fact Parnell's prestige increased rather than diminished. His offer to resign gained him the respect of British politicians; the reduction of rents which took place as a result of his co-operation with the government over the Land Act was seen as his own personal achievement; while his opposition to the coercion act united nationalist opinion behind him once again.

Irish National League, 1882

Parnell's position was now so secure that he was able to form a new semi-agrarian organisation to replace the proscribed Land League. The Irish National League differed from its predecessor in two important ways: (1) it was dominated by the Irish Parliamentary Party and was virtually under the control of Parnell himself, and (2) it relegated agrarian reform to second place behind the movement for Home Rule. The National League acted as a magnet for money donations, and it also proved an efficient agent for organising the selection of parliamentary candidates and enforcing unified party discipline throughout the constituencies (see page 47). Its success in the latter function was to be apparent in the results of the general election of 1885.

The Ashbourne Act, 1885

Gladstone and the Liberals fell from power in 1885. The new government, a Conservative one, adopted a policy of conciliation towards Ireland. Coercion was dropped and a new land bill was passed through parliament; it became known as the Ashbourne Act. By this act the government undertook to advance to the tenant the *whole* sum necessary for the purchase of his holding. The loan was to be repaid at the rate of 4 per cent per annum over a period of forty-nine years. In addition, the power and scope of the Land Commission established under the 1881 act was extended. The government made available £5 million for the purpose of land purchase, and so successful was the act that within three years 25,000 tenants had exhausted the loan fund and a further £5 million was provided.

The Plan of Campaign, 1886-90

Thanks to the Ashbourne Act of 1885, and also to the interest and hopes raised as a result of the Home Rule Bill in 1886 (see Chapter 3), there was a lull in the Irish land agitation. However, when the Home Rule Bill was defeated in parliament, the land war entered a new phase. On 23 October 1886 the nationalist newspaper, *United Ireland,* published an article entitled 'A Plan of Campaign'. It was a proposal for collective bargaining on individual estates. The chief architects of the Plan were Timothy Harrington, John Dillon and William O'Brien. Parnell refused to become involved in the Plan, as he feared it would alienate his Liberal allies.

The Plan of Campaign was to work as follows: tenants should demand a reduction in rent (called an 'abatement') from their landlord; if the landlord refused to co-operate, the tenants were to pay their rent, less the desired reduction, into an 'estate fund' managed by a committee of trustees appointed by the Plan's organisers. The 'estate fund' would be used for the benefit of those evicted by the 'crowbar brigade' (i.e. the 'emergency men' of the landlords Property Defence Association and the constables who performed the eviction). The Plan remained the chief weapon of the land agitators for the next five years. It was put into operation on 116 estates, mainly in the counties Limerick, Tipperary and Kerry. One famous case, on the Smith-Barry estate in Tipperary, led to the building of a substitute town, New Tipperary, by the Plan organisers.

In 1887 A. J. Balfour was appointed Chief Secretary. He adopted a policy of more rigid coercion than any of his predecessors and immediately introduced a crimes act (a particularly stringent form of coercion act) with which he hoped to defeat the Plan of Campaign. The Act was ruthlessly enforced; several Irish MPs and priests were imprisoned and harshly treated; and the worst incident occurred in September 1887 when police opened fire on a disorderly crowd in Mitchelstown, killing three people. As a supplementary tactic, British intrigue at the Vatican secured a papal rescript (i.e. an official directive in answer to an inquiry) condemning the Plan, but this was greeted with a respectful defiance by the majority of Irish bishops and clergy.

The Plan of Campaign, more than anything else, brought the plight of the Irish tenant farmers before the eyes of the world. It won the sympathy of the English working class, especially in mining districts, where trade unionists were combining in a similar manner in their own dispute with the bosses. The plan was seen, by Liberal MP's and English workers alike, as a form of legitimate strike, which was quite legal, possessing as it did the element of collective bargaining.

The Plan of Campaign survived the attempt to destroy it, and in doing so, proved to the landlords that the tenant farmers meant business and were determined, sooner or later, to own their holdings. In practical terms, the Plan's success may be measured as follows: tenants' demands accepted immediately on 60 estates; tenants' demands accepted after confrontation on 24 estates; successful resistance by landlords on 15 estates; deadlock on 17 estates.

The Congested Districts Board, 1892-1923

Balfour's coercive measures formed only one side of Conservative policy in Ireland. Influenced by Chamberlain's pamphlet, *A Unionist Policy for Ireland* (1888), the government adopted a general policy of 'killing Home Rule by kindness' (see Chapter 3) and pressed on with conciliatory land reform. Three new land acts gave greater security to tenants (1887) and granted more favourable loans for land purchases (1888 and 1891). The 1891 act provided £33 million for loans, but this was payable not in cash but in land bonds, which were liable to fluctuate on the stock market, few landlords were willing to sell, and only 47,000 farms were purchased under this act.

A much more important provision of the 1891 act was the setting up of a Congested Districts Board, consisting of the Chief Secretary himself, two Land Commissioners and five experts appointed by the government. A 'congested district' was defined as one in which the rateable value was less than thirty shillings per head of population. The Board was to be financed mainly out of the funds of the disestablished Church.

The government had already given much thought to the desperate problem of overpopulation and poverty in some of the remote parts of Ireland. The Congested Districts Board was to provide relief to the farming community in the designated rural areas in four ways: (1) to encourage and assist home industries by subsidies and technical instruction; (2) to improve the quality of agriculture by technical and monetary assistance; (3) to enlarge uneconomic holdings by land purchase; (4) to assist migration from impoverished uneconomic areas to newly enlarged holdings.

The working of the Board was hampered by lack of sufficient funds. Its original grant was £41,000 a year, and although this was increased to £250,000 in 1909 and to £530,000 in 1912, the Board was always short of money. However, during its thirty-two years of existence (1892-1923) it helped to develop cottage industries, the building of roads, bridges and harbours, started an Irish fishing industry, improved agricultural methods and provided advice on land purchase and settlement. Another by-product of Balfour's plans to relieve poverty in the west and south of Ireland was the construction of light railways. This had the advantage of giving considerable employment (some 16,000 people) and opening up remote areas to business and trade (see page 24).

The Co-operative Movement, 1894-

Alongside the government-sponsored Congested Districts Board, an independent and unofficial enterprise got underway in the 1890s and grew into the co-operative movement. The man behind this movement was Sir Horace Plunkett, an Irish landlord who had spent ten years ranching in America, where he had observed the beneficial effects of self-help and go-ahead farming methods. Comparing the lack of self-respect and the inability of the Irish farmers to make full use of their resources with what he had experienced in the New World, he realised that a whole process of re-education was required. Plunkett believed that the basic problem in rural Ireland was not political but social and economic. He wanted the Irish farmers to better themselves by cultivating their lands in the best possible way; he wanted them to stop acting as isolated units aiming at little more than subsistence; he wanted them to be aware of the national economy as a whole and to co-operate for its improvement as well as for their own. He hoped that in this way they would be able to compete successfully with their English, American and continental counterparts. He disapproved of agitation in any form, and looked for a peaceful solution to the Irish Question.

In 1891 Plunkett was appointed to the Congested Districts Board, and his first-hand experience of the conditions of the rural population in the west of Ireland moved him deeply. But he gradually came to see that no hope of economic revival could be expected from the British parliament, and in 1894 he founded the Irish Agricultural Organisation Society (IAOS). Within ten years it counted some 800 co-operative societies and had a trade turnover of £3 million per annum.

The IAOS caused a revolution in rural society, especially by the establishment of the creameries, which became the great focal points for the local farming community. The IAOS looked after the marketing of produce, the manufacture of butter (before this the farmers' wives had to churn their own butter), the supply of equipment and fertilisers, and, most important of all, provided credit through its land banks. Plunkett's prestige grew with the success of the IAOS, so that he was able to persuade prominent Unionists and Nationalists to come together to press the government for support, and in 1899 the Department of Agriculture and Technical Instruction was established, with Plunkett at its head. Under his prodding, the government gradually came up with more money and a large team of instructors travelled the country instructing the farmers in up-to-date methods of agriculture. Plunkett's ideas were also expounded in his journal, the *Irish Homestead,* edited by George Russell (better known as the poet and painter 'AE') and in his book *Ireland in the New Century* (1904), Plunkett saw agriculture as the basic occupation of the Irish people, but he also encouraged industries; in later years his belief that Ireland should constitute a single economy caused him to abandon his own Unionist principles and to advocate the inclusion of industrial Ulster in an independent Ireland.

The United Irish League, 1898

In spite of the work of the Congested Districts Board, there was still considerable dissatisfaction with the land situation in the west. In 1898 William O'Brien founded the United Irish League in Mayo to agitate for the redistribution of land so that all farms should be of reasonable size. The League spread rapidly and by 1901, with 100,000 members, it had become a national movement. Just as the political Home Rule campaign had been strengthened by its involvement in the land agitation in the 1880s so did it benefit similarly in 1900, when its differing factions were reunited through the impetus of the United Irish League (see page 56).

By this time the League was demanding the abandonment of the 'dual ownership' principle of the 1881 Land Act and its replacement by peasant proprietorship, brought about, if necessary, by compulsory purchase from landlords. There was a certain amount of boycotting and intimidation, and for a brief period it looked as though the large-scale unrest of the early 1880s would be repeated. But the landlords were willing to discuss compromise, and with the encouragement of George Wyndham, the Chief Secretary, their representatives met those of the tenants at a Land Conference in 1902. They formulated a massive land purchase scheme, which they submitted to Wyndham.

The Wyndham Land Act, 1903

The report of the Land Conference was to form the basis of the most effective piece of land legislation yet enacted. The Wyndham Land Act encouraged landlords to sell by stipulating high purchase prices (the government advanced £70 million for purchase loans) and gave them an additional incentive to sell *entire* estates by means of a special 12 per cent bonus payable on such sales. (Compulsory purchase, however, was not instituted until 1909, when an amending act sponsored by the Liberal Chief Secretary, Augustine Birrell, conferred power on the Land Commission and the Congested Districts Board to force landlords to sell.) Tenants were encouraged to buy by the favourable terms for repayment (by annuities at the low rate of 3¼ per cent over an extended period of sixty-eight years). Sales were authorised wherever the landlord and three-quarters of the tenants agreed on a price acceptable to the Land Commission.

The act and its 1909 sequel completed a social and economic revolution and changed the face of the Irish countryside. The pace of land transfer and subdivision of estates accelerated dramatically. By 1909 over 270,000 purchases had been negotiated, and a further 46,000 were pending. By 1921 over 9 million acres had changed hands and nearly 1½ million acres more were in the process of being sold.

Thus a series of land acts, from 1870 to 1909, brought about a change in the ownership of land in rural Ireland. It meant in practice an end to landlordism and the creation of a peasant proprietorship. Over the entire period a total of over 13 million acres had been transferred to 390,000 new owner-farmers. By the beginning of the First World War the Irish land question was satisfactorily solved. Although the farmers had to pay annuities to the British government, they had achieved their independence and could look forward to brighter days ahead.

There were considerable economic and social repercussions in the changeover from landlord ownership to tenant ownership. It gave the farmers a definite interest in maintaining peace, so that they could get on with the job of working their land. On the other hand it also proved to some of the physical-force people that 'outrage' had paid off, and that it was only by persistent use of force that any tangible results could be attained. Ultimately, the settling of the land question marked the appearance of a conservative bourgeois society in Ireland, which was such a marked feature of the first quarter of the twentieth century.

Talking Points

Chapter 2: The Land Question, 1870-1914

1. Explain the circumstances surrounding the passing of Gladstone's Land Act of 1870. What were its main proposals? Why did it fail to solve the Irish land question?

2. By the end of the 1870s, Irish tenant farmers were facing new difficulties. Show how Michael Davitt and the Land League tried to cope with these difficulties between 1879 and 1881.

3. In what way and for what reasons did Parnell involve himself in the land struggle during the years 1879-1882? Explain what was meant by 'the new departure'. What were the terms of the so-called Kilmainham Treaty?

4. Trace the later stages of the land war, with special reference to the Plan of Campaign. In what way did the approach of the Conservative government differ to that of the Liberal government over the land question?

5. Outline the work of the Congested Districts Board and the Co-operative Movement. How successful were they in bringing peace and prosperity to the Irish countryside?

41

Chapter 3
HOME RULE 1870-1914

It is impossible to understand the struggle for Home Rule in the late nineteenth century without referring to its antecedents in the previous century. Home Rule was, in fact, the revival of the struggle for legislative independence of the eighteenth century, the chief exponents of which had been Henry Grattan and Henry Flood, who in turn were influenced by the even earlier ideas of William Molyneux and Jonathan Swift. Just as in the days of Swift and Grattan an Irish 'patriot' party had sought to obtain political and economic independence, so in the last quarter of the nineteenth century Isaac Butt, Charles Stewart Parnell and John Redmond sought to remove the control of Ireland's internal affairs from Westminster to an independent Irish parliament.

The leadership in both centuries fell on the shoulders of Protestants and in each case it was the threatened loss of power and influence that stirred men to action. There was a growing conviction that England was incapable of catering for the needs of Irishmen and that some form of independent self-government was necessary if only for protective purposes. When Gladstone disestablished the Church of Ireland and encroached on the power of the landed class, many Irish Protestants and landlords took alarm and saw in his action a kind of conspiracy to encroach still further on their rights. They felt they could look after their own rights and affairs better than any Englishman. When the Secret Ballot Act was passed in 1872, it suddenly became possible for the ordinary people to act independently of their landlord. It was not such a great step further to seek for independence on the political level.

Home Rule in the 1870s and 1880s meant the demand for an independent Irish parliament. Although this demand was expressed through a political party after 1874, individual opinions as to the precise powers of the Irish parliament and the nature of its relationship to the Westminster body were to differ. Many of those who became involved in the struggle for it were more than simply Home Rulers. They also concerned themselves with the social and economic ills of the country and were closely connected with movements which were far more radical in their aims than the moderate campaign for a federal political solution. A man like John Dillon could be as much involved in the work of the House of Commons as he was in organising the Plan of Campaign in Co. Tipperary. This fusion of interests broadened the base of the Home Rule movement, so that the struggle at Westminster overflowed into the Irish cities, towns and countryside and became a burning issue in Ireland during the years

1870-1914. The extent and nature of the support it enjoyed at popular level is illustrated by a jaundiced remark of a Chief Secretary, A. J. Balfour, who declared that the Home Rule movement consisted of 'the old Fenian element which desires *separation,* and the agrarian element which desires or did desire *spoilation'.* Home Rule was *the* great political issue of the time. It brought Irishmen together, and also divided them. It produced one of the ablest of Irish politicians, Charles Stewart Parnell, and provided a series of headaches and heart-searchings for most English statesmen of the time. The man who gave the first impetus to the idea of Home Rule was Isaac Butt.

Isaac Butt and the Origins of Home Rule, 1870-74

Isaac Butt (1813-79) was the son of a Church of Ireland minister. He became a distinguished barrister and, after an early career as a university professor, sat as a Conservative MP representing an English constituency from 1852 to 1865. He then returned to Ireland, serving as MP for Youghal from 1865 until his death in 1879. On his return to Ireland Butt undertook the legal defence of Fenian prisoners, whose sincerity impressed him although he disapproved of their aims. This connection with the Fenians led him to champion an Amnesty Association in the late 1860s which had some success in campaigning for the release of jailed Fenians; it also made him think deeply about the problems that had caused Fenianism and about how they could be solved by constitutional reforms. At the same time, as a Conservative Protestant, Butt was uneasy at the disestablishment of the Church of Ireland, just as many of his co-religionists were uneasy at the 1870 Land Act. He began to consider the ways in which the Anglican and landed interests might be protected from further exploitation by British Liberal governments with their strong tinge of nonconformity and radicalism.

In 1870 the two strands in Butt's thought united in his outline of his proposed solution to the Irish problem: 'I have long since had the conviction forced upon me, that it is equally essential to the safety of England and to the happiness and tranquillity of Ireland, that the right of self-government should be restored to this country.' Accordingly he founded the Home Government Association in 1870 'to mobilise opinion behind the demand for an Irish parliament, with full control over our domestic affairs'. True to his basic conservative principles, Butt was proposing a form of federalism, i.e., a limited system of self-government, with a continued Irish representation at Westminster. Under this federal system, an Irish parliament would look after Irish affairs, but would leave to Westminster all questions affecting the crown, defence and imperial government. He proposed what might best be called a kind of conservative nationalism, and obviously had Grattan's parliament very much in mind.

The Home Government Association was essentially an 'umbrella' organisation, containing many disparate elements: disgruntled landlords and Protestants, tenant-right campaigners disappointed by the 1870 Land Act, Liberals, former Repealers and Young Irelanders, moderate nationalists, even a few Orangemen and Fenians. At first the association was dominated by Protestants, a circumstance which earned it the hostility of Cardinal Cullen, but it received new blood in 1873 as a result of the split between the National Association (see page 22) and the Liberals over the issue of Catholic education. The Catholic and nationalist elements now predominated in the enlarged organisation, and in 1873 Butt reconstituted it as the Home Rule League, with membership open to all who paid a subscription. He also established a Home Rule Confederation of Great Britain, which quickly came under the control of Fenians. These changes had scarcely taken place when parliament was suddenly dissolved and a general election held in 1874.

Table 2
The growth of the Irish Electorate 1832-1918

	1832	1851	1868	1885	1918
Electorate	92,141	165,246	225,551	742,120	1,936,673
Percentage of population based on the census closest in time to the appropriate franchise reform	1.2	2.5	4.2	14.3	44.1

B. M. Walker, *A Companion to Irish History, I*, Oxford, (in preparation). By kind permission of the editors of *A New History of Ireland*.

The Home Rule League in Parliament, 1874-79

The general election of 1874 was the first to be held since the secret ballot was introduced in 1872. Voters no longer feared to offend their landlord or his agent at the polls, and they elected, out of a total of 103 Irish MPs, no fewer than 59 Home Rulers, mainly at the expense of the Liberals, and including – for the first time in history – two tenant farmers. These MPs formed themselves into a parliamentary party, resolving to vote unanimously on the issue of self-government.

The figure of 59 MPs, however, gives an exaggerated idea of the strength of the Home Rule Party. Many of the members were essentially Liberals who had adopted the Home Rule label during the election solely in order to win votes, and in fact the number of genuinely committed Home Rulers was probably as low as twenty. The existence of the 'nominal' Home Rulers was to constitute a problem for the party leaders for the next decade. Butt was not a dynamic leader, spending very little time in the House of Commons, and he was unable to impose proper party discipline on his very mixed bag of followers, who took an independent line whenever it suited them to do so. As a result the Home Rule Party resembled not so much a real party as a mere pressure group.

The Home Rulers were also unfortunate in the overall result of the general election, which returned Benjamin Disraeli and the Conservatives to power. The new government was fully occupied with the unsettled international situation. There was far more interest in the rise of Bismarck's Germany and the Eastern question than in Irish Home Rule. In fact the Conservatives evidently considered that Irish affairs had had a sufficient airing during Gladstone's administration; now the House of Commons seemed indifferent, while the House of Lords was clearly hostile. Under these prevailing circumstances, the parliamentary tactics adopted by Butt were totally ineffective. In his reverence for the traditions of the House of Commons he favoured a 'gentlemanly' approach, suggesting his desired reforms to parliament in the form of bills — which were invariably rejected.

Eventually a few of Butt's less gentlemanly colleagues, exasperated beyond endurance by the futility of his methods, decided to take matters into their own hands. They initiated a policy of 'obstruction' by which they exploited the rules of parliamentary procedure to prevent the House of Commons from carrying on with its routine work. They did this by making extremely long and boring speeches on any matter which lay before the House. The first Irish MP to practise obstruction (in 1875) was J. G. Biggar, a Belfast provision merchant and a member of the IRB, who had entered parliament for the first time in 1874. At first Biggar pursued his wrecking policy single-handed, but he was soon joined by John O'Connor Power, another Fenian, and a handful of other MPs. On one occasion the little group forced the House to sit continuously from four in the afternoon until after six on the following evening. Another time Biggar used the rules of the House to compel the Prince of Wales to leave the public gallery during a debate. Butt was horrified and disowned such 'ungentlemanly' conduct, while the government, in impotent rage, had to content itself with sneering at the low social origins of the obstructionists. But no such slur could be cast upon their latest recruit, a young man of aristocratic bearing and descent — the newly elected member for Meath, Charles Stewart Parnell.

The Rise of Parnell, 1875-80

Parnell (1846-91) was first elected to parliament in the Meath by-election of April 1875. A Protestant landlord, the family estate was at Avondale, Co. Wicklow. His mother, Delia Stewart, was American, and his grandfather, Admiral Stewart, had fought against the English in the 1812 war. Parnell was only twenty-nine when he entered parliament. He received most of his education in England, and later on fell in love with an English woman, Mrs O'Shea. Yet he appeared to despise everything English and professed a personal hatred of England. Above all, he hated the way the English looked down on the Irish. Parnell visited America in 1871, and while there he suffered the indignity of being identified with the poor and despised Irish immigrants. His passionate pride and masterful personality were tempered by a remarkable self-control and reserve which made him appear an aloof and enigmatic figure, even to those who knew him best.

Parnell on entering parliament found that he could give vent to his anti-English feelings by joining Biggar in obstructing the work of the House of Commons. Not all the obstruction was negative. Biggar and Parnell were responsible for introducing valuable amendments to bills, as in the case of discipline in the army and navy. The obstructionists attracted considerable support in Ireland and in Fenian circles, and their popular prestige grew while that of Butt diminished. Parnell in particular caught the attention of the Fenians after his daring assertion in parliament in 1876 that the Manchester Martyrs (see page 18) had been no murderers. In 1877 Parnell replaced Butt as president of the Fenian-dominated Home Rule Confederation of Great Britain. When Butt died in 1879 Parnell was still not strong enough to succeed him as party leader, but after the general election of April 1880 more than half the Home Rule seats were held by the Parnellite wing and he was elected chairman of the Home Rule Party (by now also known as the Irish Parliamentary Party), a position he retained for the next ten years.

Home Rule and the Land Agitation, 1879-82

Since 1879 the emphasis had shifted away from Home Rule and towards the land question. For Parnell the years 1879-82 were mainly taken up with his work for the Land League and his involvement in the land war (see Chapter 2). But the land agitation had some important implications for the Home Rule movement and for Parnell's leadership of it. One of the items of the New Departure agreement between Devoy, Davitt and Parnell (see page 30) was that Irish MPs should drop Butt's plan for federal Home Rule and demand instead full Irish self-government. It was even suggested that Parnell and his followers should withdraw from Westminster and set up an Irish parliament in Dublin. Parnell considered such a step premature. The Irish people had first to be educated towards Irish independence. Patrick Ford, the editor of the *Irish World,* an American newspaper, recognised this fact, and he played a considerable role in converting Irish-Americans to Home Rule. Parnell followed this lead, and in August 1881 founded his own newspaper, *United Ireland,* which was edited by William O'Brien.

The value of the New Departure venture for Parnell, and of his involvement in the land struggle, lay in the fact that it won for him the sympathy and active support of Irish nationalists as a whole. At the same time it gave him a wider platform for his ideas than he would have got had he limited himself to the Westminster arena. As president of the Land League and chairman of the Home Rule party, he combined in his own person the leadership of the extra-parliamentary struggle (i.e., the land agitation) and the constitutional struggle. He wielded tremendous power and influence.

Parnell became the accepted leader of the Irish nationalist movement during the years 1880-82. Thanks to the considerable financial support from America (Parnell went to America in 1880 with John Dillon and collected more than £26,000), he could pose as the champion of the Irish underdog, while at the same time he could channel funds to support the Irish Parliamentary Party. Parnell always believed that the land agitation should serve as a means towards a much greater end — the achievement of Home Rule through the efforts of the Irish Party at Westminster. In 1880 he had declared: 'I would not have taken off my coat and gone to this work if I had not known that we were laying the foundation in this movement [the Land League] for the regeneration of our legislative independence.' In December 1882, therefore, when the suppressed Land League was replaced by the Irish National League (see page 36) he ensured that this new organisation was under the control of his party and that its primary objective was the winning of Home Rule.

The National League gave the party a full organisational machinery, extending to constituency level, and enabled its leader to take a tighter control of party discipline. By 1884 Parnell's authority was so secure that he was able to impose a party pledge, thereby welding the party into a single homogenous unit under his own command, and finally overcoming one of Isaac Butt's most besetting difficulties.

The English Liberals and Home Rule, 1882-85

The year 1882 was a turning point in every sense of the word. It marked the stage when Parnell withdrew his support from the revolutionary movement and strove instead to back reform. Many Irishmen, both in Ireland and America, remembered that 1882 was the centenary year of legislative independence won by Grattan for the Irish parliament. But neither Parnell nor his supporters in Ireland and America could achieve anything without the support of one or other of the two English parliamentary parties.

Gladstone's second Liberal administration was in power from 1880 to 1885. The Liberals had shown themselves far more receptive than the Conservatives to Irish demands, but this by no means closed Parnell's mind to the possibility of throwing his support behind the Conservatives if he thought more could be got out of them. His bargaining position was greatly improved by a massive franchise reform which was enacted in 1884; the Irish electorate was increased from 230,000 to over 700,000, and many Irishmen living in Britain now got the vote for the first time. This made it certain that the Irish Party would win more seats at the next election; it also meant that Parnell was in a position to influence elections in a number of British constituencies, since his loyal followers in Britain would vote for whichever of the two main parties he instructed them to support.

The Home Rule cause was also helped by the general climate of parliamentary politics in the 1880s. The debates in the House of Commons proved how much valuable time was spent on what was merely of domestic concern. Some English MPs considered that the removal of the Irish members from Westminster would be a good thing. They had come to look upon the Irish as 'dry rot in the House of Commons'. They hoped that if it were possible to get rid of the Irish, then parliament could get on with the job of governing the Empire.

At the same time in England there was a demand for some form of local government making itself felt in the growing centres of population. Cities such as Birmingham, Manchester and Liverpool were experiencing a second industrial revolution and were asking for freedom to control their own domestic affairs: lighting, water, sewage, roads, etc. Joseph Chamberlain, the MP for Birmingham and the leader of the Radical wing of the Liberal Party, proposed in 1884-85 what would nowadays be called a limited 'devolution' scheme, providing for the setting up of 'central boards' to deal with Irish, Scottish and Welsh affairs. Chamberlain did not wish to expel the Irish members from Westminster, but he did think that all purely domestic issues should be dealt with at local level and not take up the time of the imperial parliament. Parnell was prepared to approve of this scheme, but only as a step in the right direction, *not* as a final settlement. However, owing to a misunderstanding, Chamberlain was led to believe that it had Parnell's unqualified support, and he was extremely annoyed to find that this was not the case. This created a rift of ill-feeling between the Irish Party and the hitherto friendly English Radicals which was to have disastrous consequences when Home Rule was put to the vote in 1886.

The General Election and the 'Hawarden Kite', 1885

In June 1885 the tottering Liberal government fell, and a Conservative caretaker administration under Lord Salisbury took office until a general election could be held. The Conservatives were quick to angle for Parnellite support; they did not renew the 1882 coercion act when it expired; they passed the popular Ashbourne Land Act (see page 36); while the Irish hierarchy believed that the Conservatives would bring in a satisfactory education bill. Nor was it forgotten that Conservative legislation had a much better chance of passing through the Conservative-dominated House of Lords. More important still, the new Lord Lieutenant, Lord Carnarvon, was known to be a believer in federal self-government, which he had helped to establish in Canada in 1867, and at a secret meeting with Parnell he raised hopes that Ireland might soon be offered similar dominion status to that of Canada within the United Kingdom.

Parnell then turned to Gladstone, hoping that he would make an even more attractive offer. But Gladstone, although he had already privately become 'converted' to the belief that Home Rule was the answer to the Irish question, refused on principle to descend to a sordid bidding for votes. The Conservative-Parnellite alliance was therefore cemented, and Parnell instructed his supporters in Britain to vote Conservative at the general election in November 1885.

The election produced a sensational result: Liberals 335; Conservatives 249; Irish Parliamentary Party 86. The Liberal majority was 86, which was exactly the number of the unified, pledge-bound Irish Party, which was now victorious in every constituency in Ireland except in half of Ulster and in the University of Dublin. Parnell was now in a very strong position, although he did not hold a perfect balance of power: he could keep the Liberals in office, and he could keep either party out of office, but he could not keep the Conservatives in office against Liberal opposition.

Shortly after the election a second sensational event occurred. In December 1885 Gladstone's son Herbert, speaking to some newspaper reporters at the Gladstone family home at Hawarden, revealed the secret of his father's conversion to Home Rule. Gladstone had been guided in reaching his decision by religious and moral principles and by his anxiety to do the 'right' thing for Ireland. He considered that the Irish question was more than a mere party political issue, and indeed, at the very time that his son 'flew the Hawarden kite' he was taking the unusual step of indicating to the Prime Minister, Salisbury, that if the Conservatives introduced a Home Rule measure in parliament, he would support them.

Herbert Gladstone's indiscretion had the effect of bringing about a political realignment. It killed the Conservative-Parnellite pact, which had already been considerably weakened by the inconclusive election result and which, for the Conservatives, had in any case never been anything more than a vote-catching gambit. The Conservatives swung away from Home Rule, and Parnell threw his party's support behind Gladstone and the Liberals. When parliament reassembled in January 1886 and Salisbury outlined plans for a return to coercion, the Conservatives were thrown out of office by the combined Liberal-Parnellite vote. Gladstone then formed a ministry and announced his intention of bringing in a Home Rule bill.

The First Home Rule Bill, 1886

Gladstone presented the First Home Rule Bill to parliament on 8 April 1886. Its main provisions were: (1) the setting up in Dublin of an Irish parliament, consisting of two houses of 'orders', with control over domestic affairs; (2) the imperial parliament at Westminster should still have ultimate authority and retain control of all matters affecting the crown, defence, foreign relations, etc.; (3) Irish representation in the imperial parliament should cease; (4) the RIC to remain under imperial control for a time, but eventually to be handed over to the Irish executive; (5) Ireland should pay one-fifteenth of the United Kingdom's imperial expenses but should retain all her other revenue. In addition, though not a part of the bill, (6) in order to protect the landlords Gladstone outlined a gigantic land purchase scheme which would virtually buy out the entire landlord interest.

The bill was defeated on its second reading in the House of Commons on 8 June 1886 by 343 votes to 313. A group of 93 Liberal anti-Home Rulers (henceforth known as Liberal Unionists) voted against it. Gladstone at once called a general election on the Home Rule issue, the result of which showed clearly how much English public opinion was against granting self-government to Ireland: Liberals 191; Irish Parliamentary Party 85; Conservatives 316; Liberal Unionists 78. The Liberal Unionists therefore held the balance of power, and since it was their Unionism and not their Liberalism which counted on the Home Rule issue, they gave the Conservatives a clear majority. Gladstone had to resign, and Salisbury and the Conservatives returned to power.

There were several reasons why Gladstone's Home Rule Bill failed to receive acceptance in England. (1) Parnell had assured parliament that he would accept Home Rule as the final settlement of the Irish question. However, this assertion contrasted markedly with some of his earlier speeches in Ireland, such as his declaration that 'No man has a right to fix the boundary to the march of a nation. No man has the right to say to his country, "Thus far shalt thou go and no further." ' This appeared to many Englishmen to be sheer duplicity whose author was not to be trusted: Parnell's real opinion of Home Rule seemed to be that it was merely a stepping-stone to complete independence and the break-up of the British Empire. This view was held by most Conservatives and some Liberals. Gladstone had dispatched General Gordon to the Sudan and the death of Gordon at Khartoum in 1885 had caused a national panic and a loss of confidence in Gladstone's imperial policy. (2) There was a widely prevailing view that the Irish were unfit for self-government. This idea was based on a racial prejudice which saw the Celts as distinctly inferior to Anglo-Saxons. Such prejudice had been boosted in the preceding decades by the post-famine influx of Irish immigrants whose squalid living conditions and competition for jobs had generated bitter anti-Irish hostility. The Irish were commonly regarded as idle, ignorant, dirty, drunken, diseased, brutal, violent, treacherous, priest-ridden savages, and such a view was reflected in contemporary cartoons and caricatures which depicted the typical Irishman as a sub-human, ape-like creature, frequently shown in the act of shooting a defenceless landlord (of angelic aspect) in the back or maiming his cattle. (3) There was considerable opposition in and on behalf of loyalist Ulster to the threat that the north-east would come under the jurisdiction of a Dublin parliament. There were those, such as the Conservative Lord Randolph Churchill, who spoke of 'two Irelands' and said it was both unfair and dangerous to hand over one section (the Ulster Protestants) to another section (the Catholics). Loyalists of all classes expressed their opposition to Home Rule through the Orange Order, which now became very powerful (see Chapter 4). (4) Two sections of the Liberal Party broke away from Gladstone and voted against Home Rule. The right-wing old-style 'Whigs', led by Lord Hartington (whose brother Cavendish had been murdered in the Phoenix Park in 1882), had even refused to join Gladstone's government. The Radical wing, led by Chamberlain, had originally participated in the government, but for a complex variety of personal and other reasons Chamberlain later resigned and the Radicals withdrew their support from Gladstone. Chamberlain's defection was crucial to the thirty-vote majority which defeated the bill. Parnell himself had no doubt that Chamberlain was 'the man who killed Home Rule'.

The Home Rule crisis of 1886 had some important long-term consequences. (1) It split and weakened the great Liberal Party, so that except for a short period (1892-95) the Conservatives ruled Britain and Ireland for the next twenty years. (2) British as well as Irish politics were dominated until the early 1920s by the Irish question. In both countries people were divided sharply into the opposing Home Rule and Unionist camps, between which there could be no compromise. (3) If the Liberals were committed to Home Rule, Parnell and his party were also committed — for better or worse — to the Liberal alliance. Parnell could no longer play the two main parties off against each other as he had done so adroitly in 1885. The alliance thus limited the freedom of manoeuvre, not only of Parnell but of all subsequent leaders of the Irish Parliamentary Party. The events of 1890-91 were to show how devastating a price the party would have to pay for that alliance. (4) The crisis brought into prominence a resolute and intransigent minority in the north of Ireland who were determined to oppose Home Rule to the uttermost. A sinister development during 1886 had been the large-scale military drilling of Ulster loyalists, which indicated the lengths to which they were prepared to carry their resistance to Home Rule. Ulster Unionism constituted a serious problem to which no politician, British or Irish, could find a satisfactory solution, then or since.

The Special Commission, 1888-89

After the defeat of the First Home Rule Bill Parnell became even more than usually remote from the political scene. He was not in good health at this time, and he had also become increasingly involved in his relationship with Mrs O'Shea. He spent very little time in parliament and was constantly absent from meetings of the Irish Party. Yet he was careful to hold on to the party leadership and to maintain the alliance with Gladstone and the Liberals. Thus he refused to support the Plan of Campaign (see page 37); more and more he was turning away from the agrarian struggle and dissociating himself from any illegal activity.

It was an attempt to discredit the Home Rule cause and to link Parnell directly with criminal activity that brought him out of his semi-retirement. In March and April 1887 the London *Times* published a series of articles entitled 'Parnellism and Crime' whose object was to prove that Parnell and his followers were deeply involved in a revolutionary movement. The *Times* reproduced a number of facsimile letters, allegedly bearing Parnell's signature; in one of these letters, bearing the date 15 May 1882, the Irish leader excused and condoned the murder of T. H. Burke in the Phoenix Park which he had publicly denounced (see page 35).

Parnell immediately declared the letter a forgery and called for a public inquiry. The government set up a Special Commission to investigate the charges made by the *Times* against Parnell and his party. The commission sat for nearly two years and uncovered a wealth of data relating to Irish problems. A great number of witnesses were called to give evidence. In February 1889 one of the witnesses, a Dublin journalist, Richard Pigott, admitted to having forged the letters; he then fled to Madrid, where he shot himself.

Parnell's reputation was completely vindicated. He was cleared of all the charges made against him, and the *Times* paid a substantial sum of money by way of compensation. The closing months of 1889 marked the high point of Parnell's popularity. He received a standing ovation in the House of Commons, was presented with the freedom of the city of Edinburgh, and stayed as Gladstone's guest at Hawarden. He was the idol of London society and in Ireland he was hailed as 'the uncrowned king'. The stage seemed set for a revival of the Liberal-Parnellite alliance, with Home Rule for Ireland as its first objective.

The Fall of Parnell, 1890-91

In the midst of all these triumphs came a further and much more dangerous threat to Parnell's public career. In December 1889 Captain O'Shea filed suit for divorce from his wife, and cited Parnell as co-respondent. Parnell decided not to defend himself, and to most people it appeared as if the whole business was another trumped-up fabrication, like the Pigott forgery affair. Only this time Parnell was not innocent. He and Mrs Katharine O'Shea had fallen in love when they first met in 1880. By that time her marriage with Captain O'Shea was breaking down. From 1886 Parnell and Katharine O'Shea lived together.

Captain O'Shea was undoubtedly aware of the relationship between his wife and Parnell. To keep her husband happy, Parnell furthered O'Shea's political career and had him elected as an unpledged Home Ruler to the Galway City seat in February 1886, despite much angry opposition from his party. Why O'Shea delayed until December 1889 before seeking a divorce is not quite clear. One possible reason was the hope of obtaining a substantial sum of money from his wife, when her aunt, Mrs Woods, died. This wealthy lady had named Katharine as her heir, but would obviously cut her off without a penny in the event of a divorce. Mrs Woods, died in May 1889, and left her entire fortune to Katharine, but in such a way that her husband could not get his hands on it. O'Shea apparently resorted to blackmail, asking for £20,000 from his wife, but she refused to pay. It was after this rebuff that the irate husband went ahead with his suit.

The verdict of the divorce court was given on 17 November 1890, and Parnell was found guilty. It caused a sensation in England and Ireland. Victorian England was indulgent to those who kept their moral weaknesses out of the public eye. There is evidence that Gladstone and several of Parnell's colleagues had been privately aware of the affair for some years. Parnell's crime was that of having his indiscretions brought to public notice. But in the immediate aftermath of the lawsuit there was an immense upsurge of loyalty to Parnell in Ireland and the Irish Party, and he was unanimously re-elected chairman on 25 November. However, many of his followers changed their minds when it was learned that a strong Nonconformist pressure group in the Liberal Party had forced Gladstone to repudiate Parnell's leadership, and the Catholic bishops thereupon also declared against Parnell. On all sides there was a belief that the Irish leader would retire from public life, at least temporarily. Cecil Rhodes sent Parnell a cable from South Africa with the three words: 'Resign — marry — return'. But Parnell showed no intention of retiring. The question now was: could he be induced to abdicate the leadership of the Irish party, or would he have to be deposed?

A meeting of the Irish Parliamentary Party was held during the first week of December 1890, in Committee Room 15 of the House of Commons. Parnell presided and reiterated the viewpoint he had made in his 'Manifesto to the Irish People' of 29 November 1890: 'My position has been granted to me, not because I am the mere leader of a parliamentary party, but because I am the leader of the Irish nation.' The meeting was a very stormy one, and after long discussion as to whether the Man (Parnell) was more important than the Cause (Home Rule), the party split in two. Forty-four members sided with Justin McCarthy, the vice-chairman, and remained committed to the alliance with the Liberals; and twenty-seven sided with Parnell. Parnell was thus deposed from the leadership of the parliamentary party, but he refused to accept the verdict given against him. He was determined to appeal to the whole Irish nation in Ireland, England and America. He firmly believed that the Irish people would stand by him.

Thus he carried his campaign to Ireland and throughout 1891 fought three by-elections (North Kilkenny, North Sligo and Carlow). At times he *seemed* to be appealing to the old physical-force revolutionary tradition — and did in fact gain the support of Fenians and extremists — but such statements were always couched in ambiguous terms. In all three by-elections Parnell's candidate was defeated. He suffered every kind of indignity: mud-throwing, personal abuse, etc. But as far as he was concerned it was 'war to the death'. In June 1891 he married Katharine O'Shea, and even her request that he retire from public life was turned down. Eventually the strain of addressing meetings up and down the country proved too much for him. He likewise suffered the psychological disappointment of apparent betrayal by his former friends and colleagues. On 6 October 1891 he died at Brighton. He was only forty-five years of age. His funeral drew one of the largest crowds Dublin ever saw. But he left behind him a divided Ireland, those who called themselves 'Parnellites' and others who called themselves 'anti-Parnellites'.

Parnell's Achievement

Despite the fact that Parnell seemed an enigma to many of his contemporaries, his achievements were real and lasting. He provided firm leadership and drive during the exciting decade 1880-90. He brought Home Rule from being a vague aspiration to the forefront of national politics, both in Ireland and in Britain. He compelled both the English political parties and successive governments to recognise the importance of the Irish question and to declare their standpoint on it. By the creation of an efficient and disciplined party, ready and willing to work within the parliamentary limits, he proved that Irishmen were capable of ruling themselves. Above all, by bridging the gap between the forces of revolution and constitutionalism, and by harnessing the forces of mass agitation in the Land League, he made it possible for men of differing 'national outlooks' to come together and work for a common end. Even though the land question was not solved, Parnell's involvement in it during the years 1879-82 was a vital factor, and made it possible for future reforms to get under way.

Parnell was the architect of his own downfall. He signed his own political death-warrant by refusing to co-operate with the party during the critical time of the divorce dispute. His attitude was that of a 'loner' who was prepared to ignore the advice of his best friends. Because of the peculiar circumstances of his downfall and the tragedy of his death at a comparatively young age, a myth has grown up around his name, and the memory of the 'lost leader' of 1891 was to serve as a symbol around which could crystallise feelings of contempt for majority opinion, clerical influence, and 'politics' in general. Parnell was hailed as a champion by later national movements, and men of every political colour claimed him for their own. If Parnell appeared to later generations as a revolutionary, it was simply that his *words* were sometimes those of one, whereas his *actions* and *methods* were invariably those of a constitutionalist.

The Second Home Rule Bill, 1893

In August 1892 the eighty-three-year-old Gladstone became Prime Minister for the fourth time and at once set about framing a new Home Rule Bill which he introduced in parliament in February 1893. Like the First Home Rule Bill, it proposed that the Irish parliament should have autonomy in domestic affairs, while the imperial parliament should retain responsibility in all matters affecting Ireland as part of the United Kingdom. Once again the Irish parliament was to consist of two houses, in this case defined as a Legislative Council, containing 48 councillors elected for eight-year terms by voters with considerable property qualifications, and a Legislative Assembly, containing 103 members elected by the existing constituencies. Unlike the 1886 scheme, however, there was to be a continued representation of Irish MPs at Westminster. The financial clauses of the bill were found unsatisfactory by Irish members, as it was believed that Ireland was already overtaxed.

On 1 September 1893 the bill was passed by the Commons on its third reading by 301 votes to 267. But a week later it was thrown out by the House of Lords by 419 to 41. Opposition to the bill came from all quarters, especially Ulster (see Chapter 4) and Gladstone accepted defeat on the Home Rule issue as a sign that he should retire from public life. His successor, Lord Roseberry, realising that the Liberals' espousal of Home Rule was doing the party no good, soft-pedalled on the issue, and the divided Irish Party, their wounds still fresh from the split of 1890-91, found themselves in the doldrums at Westminster.

The Disunited Irish Party, 1890-1900

It took the Irish Parliamentary Party ten years to recover from the Parnell split. Between 1890 and 1900 there were no less than three groups: a small Parnellite rump led by John Redmond; a much larger body of anti-Parnellites led by Justin McCarthy (replaced by John Dillon in 1896); and a further anti-Parnellite faction, the People's Rights Association, formed by Tim Healy in 1897. In addition to the original split, the Home Rule cause was further weakened by the lack of interest shown by the Liberals after the defeat of the Second Home Rule Bill, and by personal squabbles among the anti-Parnellites — between clericalists and anti-clericalists over Healy's attempt to bring the party under priestly control, and between idealists and pragmatists over whether to support the Conservatives' measures of constructive Unionism (see below).

This state of affairs had a serious effect of the whole struggle for Irish independence. First of all, it meant that the Irish in America ceased to support the constitutional struggle. And as MPs did not receive salaries at this time, it caused great hardship to many of them. With the party funds at rock bottom, it was impossible to run proper campaigns at elections so that the impact of the party as a whole was limited. Secondly, many Irishmen became so disgusted with the divisions among the parliamentarians that they turned instead to the great cultural movement which began in the late nineteenth century and to minority nationalist organisations which proposed alternative means for solving the Irish question (see Chapter 5). Finally, the misfortunes of the Irish Party played into the hands of the Conservatives and Unionists, who wished to shelve for ever the idea of Home Rule.

William O'Brien's United Irish League, founded in 1898 (see page 40), rapidly became a popular national movement which could not be ignored by the parliamentarians. The League was an important factor in bringing Irish MPs to their senses and in putting new life into the Irish Party. By 1900 the main divergent groups united in self-defence against the League's challenge to their leadership and merged in a single Irish Party under John Redmond, who, although he lacked Parnell's dynamism and flair, was a competent leader dedicated to Parnell's objective of winning Home Rule with Liberal support. The League itself was brought firmly under the party's control and was made to serve as its national organising agency, in much the same way as Parnell's old National League.

Constructive Unionism, 1886-1905

Apart from the Liberal interlude in 1892-95, the Conservatives were in power from 1886 to 1905. When Salisbury and his colleagues took office they had no Irish policy at all, apart from their opposition to Home Rule and their determination to combat lawlessness with strong coercive measures. At the same time they recognised that genuine and justified grievances lay behind much of the unrest and agitation in Ireland, and that such grievances were in urgent need of reform. In seeking to work out a suitable Irish policy which would be positive in its aims without conflicting with the Conservative stance on Home Rule, they were greatly influenced by Chamberlain's document *A Unionist Policy for Ireland* (1888), which helped them to devise a project for constructive Unionism or, as it is more aptly known, 'killing Home Rule with kindness'. From a practical point of view, Ireland gained more benefits from the series of piecemeal reforms implemented by the Conservatives between 1886 and 1905 than she received from the Liberals during the entire period 1880-1918, with their concentration after 1886 on the noble but elusive ideal of Home Rule.

The Conservative government had barely come to power in 1886 when the Plan of Campaign was initiated in Ireland (see page 37). The new Chief Secretary, A. J. Balfour (appointed in 1887), fought the Plan with rigorous coercion, but he also sought to remove the causes of the distress which led to the agitation. His policy of conciliation and reform was continued by his two successors as Conservative Chief Secretary, his brother Gerald and George Wyndhan. The emphasis of this legislation was, of course, on agrarian conditions and land purchase (see outline on pages 38-41), but Gerald Balfour also carried through an important reform which gave Ireland what amounted to local Home Rule. Gerald Balfour's Local Government Act (1898) vested all local government in bodies elected on a popular franchise (which included women), namely, urban and rural district councils and county councils. These councils were made responsible for rates, roads, housing, public health, the poor law, etc. The act put an end to the old system of local government by Grand Juries, and thus struck a blow at the landed gentry who had controlled the Grand Juries for centuries. It taught the Irish the value of looking after their own affairs at local level. It was not such a big step from this to the ideas introduced by Sinn Féin. It enabled the nationalist majority, who of course dominated every council outside Ulster, to obtain useful administrative experience. The single-party control of the councils led to corruption and jobbery, but as a democratic experiment the Local Government Act stirred the waters of Irish social and political life and provided an added incentive for seeking complete self-government.

Arguments in favour of a 'devolution' scheme were briefly revived in 1904 following an initiative from a committee of Irish landowners, who proposed the creation of financial and legislative councils with extended local powers. However, the scheme encountered considerable opposition from hardline Conservatives and Unionists and was quickly dropped.

The Revival of Home Rule, 1906-11

The 1906 general election brought a landslide victory for the Liberals, giving them 390 seats in the House of Commons and a majority of 132 over all other parties combined (including the Irish Party). While they still retained the achievement of Home Rule on their political programme, the new Prime Minister, Sir Henry Campbell-Bannerman, lacked the old Gladstonian enthusiasm for the cause, and it was not forgotten that the House of Lords would certainly use its power of veto to quash Home Rule as it had done in 1893, bringing all Gladstone's work to nothing. In any case, the Liberal majority in the Commons was so secure that the party did not have to seek Irish support.

The Liberals' Irish policy in the years 1906-09 was in fact very similar in its operation to the Conservative plan for 'killing Home Rule with kindness'. They pressed ahead with a series of social and industrial reforms including old-age pensions, improved housing and schools and further agrarian reforms. Most important of all, the Chief Secretary, Augustine Birrell, succeeded in finding a solution to the long-standing problem of Irish university education; Birrell realised that a single university system would be unacceptable over the whole country, and his Irish Universities Act (1908) created two new universities, one (the Queen's University of Belfast) for the Protestant north, the other (the National University of Ireland, with colleges in Dublin, Cork and Galway) for the Catholic south. This arrangement, by giving effective control of the National University to the Catholic hierarchy, satisfied the severest critics of all previous legislation on university education.

Home Rule was not actually dropped, but it was left in abeyance, and the best that Birrell could offer was a scheme of 'devolution' in 1907. It was, in fact, very similar to the abortive scheme proposed under the Conservatives in 1904. Its purpose was defined as a 'means for associating the people of Ireland with the conduct of Irish affairs'. An 'Irish Council' was to be set up, but its terms of reference were so vague that Redmond rejected this watered-down version of Home Rule. From this time Redmond came under pressure on two fronts. Some of his colleagues wanted him to drop the Liberal alliance altogether; and frustration in Ireland at his failure to deliver Home Rule led to a strengthening of the new extra-parliamentary political organisations, including Arthur Griffith's little Sinn Féin party, which gave Redmond a fright by contesting a by-election in 1908.

It was not until the constitutional crisis of 1909-11 that an opportunity came of asserting the Home Rule cause with renewed vigour. Considerable tensions had built up between H. H. Asquith's Liberal government and the House of Lords over the latter's persistent use of the power of veto to reject or mutilate Liberal legislation. The climax came in November 1909, when the Lords rejected the budget drawn up by the Chancellor of the Exchequer, Lloyd George. Asquith now determined to seek the necessary power to curtail the power of the Lords and to make sure that they lost their absolute veto on legislation. Asquith called a general election in January 1910 on the issues of the budget and the Lords' veto and gave Redmond the reassurances on the speedy enactment of Home Rule that were necessary for his support.

The election result recalled that of 1885 − except that Redmond and his party held a truer balance of power than Parnell had enjoyed: Liberals 275; Conservatives/Unionists 273; Labour 40; Irish Parliamentary Party 71; Independent Irish Nationalists 11. All private attempts to resolve the crisis resulted in deadlock, mainly because the two big English parties could not reach a compromise on Home Rule, and a second general election was held in December 1910. The result slightly strengthened Redmond's position: Liberals 273; Conservatives/Unionists 273; Labout 42; Irish Parliamentary Party 74; Independent Irish Nationalists 9. The House of Lords was forced to give in and agreed to the curtailment of its own powers. Asquith's Parliament Act (1911) replaced the Lords' veto with a delaying power which allowed them to hold up a bill for two years, but when the bill was passed for the third successive year by the House of Commons it had to be accepted by the Lords.

It now seemed to Redmond and his friends that Home Rule for Ireland was at last within their grasp. The one great constitutional barrier to its enactment had been removed, and it seemed to be only a question of time before Ireland would have her own parliament. But in overcoming the constitutional crisis of the Lords' veto the government had sown the seeds of a much greater and more dangerous national crisis which was to take Ireland — and England too — perilously close to civil war.

The Third Home Rule Bill, 1912-14

On 11 April 1912 the Third Home Rule Bill was introduced in parliament by Asquith. Its terms were similar to those of the 1893 bill, offering Ireland a rather narrow measure of autonomy, retaining the link with Britain through the crown, and witholding from the Irish parliament control over revenue, coinage, postal services and even, for a limited time, the police. Such matters, together with those relating to foreign policy, defence, overseas trade, etc. were to be solely the responsibility of the imperial parliament, in which Irish MPs would continue to represent their country.

The parliamentary debates on the bill proceeded exactly as expected: the Liberals, urged on by the Irish Party, provided the necessary majorities; the Conservatives, urged on by the Irish Unionists, fought the bill at every stage; and the House of Lords, like the Irish obstructionists of old, used its delaying power to the full. The Lords gave their final rejection to the bill early in 1913; according to the Parliament Act, therefore, Home Rule would almost certainly come into force in the autumn of 1914.

The real contest, however, was not the parliamentary one, with its foregone conclusion, but the struggle which was fought out with mounting bitterness in the country at large. The ferocity of the conflict was due to the conviction of both Unionists and Nationalists that the moderate measure of self-government provided by the bill was only the first stage of a process which would end in the complete separation of Ireland from Great Britain and the Empire.

The opposition to Home Rule hinged on the Ulster Unionists. (The development of Ulster Unionism and the preparations for armed resistance are outlined in Chapter 4. We are here concerned specifically with their effect on the progress of the Home Rule legislation and its political background in Britain.) The vital questions in 1912-14 were: How far were the Ulster loyalists prepared to carry their unconstitutional campaign against an act of parliament? — and how far were the English Conservatives prepared to support them? The massive displays of anti-Home Rule solidarity in Ulster, the signing of the Solemn League and Covenant, and the formation and arming of the Ulster Volunteers were dismissed by Redmond as 'a gigantic game of bluff' which would collapse once Home Rule was in operation. Redmond was wrong: in conveniently ignoring the strength of loyalist sentiment in the north he was making the same mistake as every other nationalist leader since O'Connell. As for the English Conservatives, their leader, Andrew Bonar Law, a Canadian of Ulster Presbyterian ancestry who had replaced Balfour in November 1911, ranged his party solidly behind the Unionists. In July 1912, while the Home Rule Bill was being debated in parliament, Bonar Law addressed a huge rally of his supporters at Blenheim Palace. After referring to the Liberal government as 'a revolutionary committee which has seized upon despotic power by fraud', he went on to say:

> There are things stronger than parliamentary majorities ... If an attempt were made to deprive these men [the Ulster Unionists] of their birthright — as part of a corrupt parliamentary bargain — they would be justified in resisting such an attempt by all means in their power, including force ... I can imagine no length of resistance to which Ulster can go in which I should not be prepared to support them, and in which, in my belief, they would not be supported by the overwhelming majority of the British people.

Such language, amounting to a seditious incitement to rebellion, had not been heard on the lips of a responsible British politician for two and a half centuries — and it was all the more extraordinary in that it was uttered by the leader of the Conservative Party, which had always been regarded as the traditional upholder of law and order and the British constitution. Bonar Law also tried to persuade the king to resurrect ancient powers of royal prerogative, such as the royal veto, the dissolution of parliament and the dismissal of ministers.

If Redmond had underestimated his opponents, so too had Carson, the Unionist leader. Carson, a Dubliner by birth, personally regarded his leadership of the Ulster Unionists as a means by which the whole of Ireland might be saved from Home Rule. He believed that if he could secure the exclusion of even a portion of Ulster from the jurisdiction of the proposed Dublin parliament, then Redmond would quickly drop the whole scheme, since a self-governing Ireland without the support of Ulster industry would be in a very shaky economic position. Carson had, of course, failed to reckon with the determined spirit of Irish nationalism, which would never permit the Irish Party to abandon its long-sought-for objective at the final stage. Nevertheless, although Carson's emphasis on the all-Ireland dimension differed somewhat from that of his Ulster-born followers (who eventually induced him to play it down), his plans for making Home Rule impossible in Ulster were entirely endorsed by them. And it was this specifically 'Ulsterite' character of the anti-Home Rule movement that seemed for a time to provide a tiny gleam of light amid the gathering darkness which might guide an anxious government towards a compromise solution.

English politicians, alarmed by the increasing gravity of the situation, began to consider making some special provision for Ulster within the Home Rule Bill. Their object was not so much to make the bill desirable to both Nationalists and Unionists — since that was clearly impossible — but rather to make it *equally* undesirable, so that the tensions and resentments which threatened to explode in rebellion or civil war would be reduced on both sides. The first such proposal in parliament was made in June 1912 by a Liberal member, T. G. Agar-Robartes, who suggested that the four most Protestant counties (Antrim, Armagh, Down and Londonderry) should be excluded altogether from the Home Rule Bill. Thereafter intermittant negotiations took place between political leaders during 1912 and 1913, and a number of schemes were proposed: temporary or permanent exclusion of a varying number of counties; an offer to individual counties to opt out of Home Rule, temporarily or permanently; 'Home Rule within Home Rule' — a Belfast parliament subordinate to the Dublin parliament (Redmond's solution, totally unacceptable to Carson); complete permanent exclusion of the entire nine-county province (Carson's solution, totally unacceptable to Redmond). But by the beginning of 1914 all proposals for partition had been rejected by either the Unionists or the Nationalists, and all the discussions had resulted in nothing but exasperation and deadlock.

The 1914 Crisis

During 1914 the situation worsened still further. Two large private armies in Ireland were in the process of arming themselves. There were rumours of serious disaffection in the Regular Army, almost all of whose officers had strong pro-Unionist sympathies, and even more sinister rumours that Bonar Law was about to contrive the rejection by the House of Lords of the annual Army Act, without which the army could not be kept in existence to enforce the government's authority.

In March Asquith introduced the Home Rule Bill for the third successive year. He later tacked on an amending bill, which he had with difficulty forced Redmond to accept, by which individual Ulster counties would be able to opt out of Home Rule for six years. If Asquith thought this compromise would satisfy the Ulster Unionists, he was gravely mistaken: Carson rejected it outright, declaring, 'We do not want sentence of death with a stay of execution for six years.' He then returned to Ulster, while his ally, the obdurate House of Lords, busied itself in 'amending' the amending bill so that it embodied Carson's original proposal, the permanent exclusion of all Ulster.

The government then tried to make a show of force, only to find that the reports of strong Unionist feeling in the army were true. Fifty-eight cavalry officers at the Curragh military camp made it quite clear that they intended to resign rather than obey orders to coerce Ulster into accepting Home Rule. In fact the orders were never given, but the so-called 'mutiny' led to the resignation of the Secretary of State for War, J.E.B. Seely, and two generals.

By the summer of 1914 the Prime Minister, Asquith, found himself in an almost impossible position. On the one hand, he had promised Redmond that he would give Home Rule to Ireland; on the other, he could not ignore the growing threat of revolt in Ulster. The two Volunteer forces were fully armed and standing by, one to defend the Union against the Liberal government, the other with exact purpose undefined, but clearly acting as a counterweight to the UVF. As a last resort, the king summoned a conference to Buckingham Palace on 21 July 1914, bringing Redmond and Carson, Asquith and Bonar Law face to face. Three days later the conference broke down, having failed to reach any agreement on the partition of Ireland.

The maximum period by which the House of Lords could delay the passage of the legislation had almost expired. In recognition of the urgency of the situation, Asquith dropped his amending bill, and the unaltered Home Rule Bill was due to be enacted in two months' time, with the crisis still unresolved and civil war apparently imminent. But on 4 August 1914 the First World War broke out, and the question of Irish independence suddenly had to give way to the still more urgent one of national safety. Thus, while the Home Rule Bill received the royal assent on 18 September 1914, it was accompanied by two emergency provisos: (1) that the act should not come into operation until after the end of the war; (2) that it should not come into operation until parliament had an opportunity to make special amending legislation for Ulster.

By the end of the war the situation in Ireland had changed to such an extent that the new act had lost all its meaning. Redmond, like Parnell before him, was thus thwarted of his ambition to lead the Irish people into the promised land of Home Rule.

Talking Points

Chapter 3 : Home Rule 1870-1914

  1. Analyse the progress of the Home Rule movement under Isaac Butt, during the years 1870-79.

  2. Outline the political career of Charles Stewart Parnell between 1879 and 1891, with special reference to the struggle for Home Rule.

  3. Write an essay on Gladstone's involvement in Irish affairs during the years 1885-93.

  4. What were the main elements contained in the programme of Constructive Unionism proposed by the Conservative government between 1886-1905?

  5. Give an outline of the main phases and problems surrounding the passage of the Third Home Rule Bill 1912-14.

Chapter 4
THE ULSTER QUESTION, 1850-1914

At its simplest, the Ulster question in the nineteenth and twentieth centuries might be phrased as follows: How and why did the majority of people living in north-east Ireland become so bitterly opposed to the aspiration for self-government held by the nationalist majority throughout the country? And how should the problems raised by this fundamental difference of opinion be dealt with?

The problem is a complex and many-sided one, containing a number of important subsidiary questions, some of which we will examine later. It had three main branches: economic, political and religious (or sectarian). The economic and political factors first came into prominence during the nineteenth century, while the origin of Ulster's religious difficulties can be traced back to the beginning of the seventeenth century. Indeed, some historians would go back even further, claiming that Ulster was at all times a place apart. During the Middle Ages the old Gaelic way of life was preserved almost intact in the province, and, in contrast to the rest of Ireland, anglicising influences touched only a very small portion of it. Constant migration across the narrow sea-passage to and from Gaelic Scotland also helped to give the area a distinctive character. There is even a firm tradition, confirmed by archaeology, that part of Ulster was an independent power base in prehistoric times, and there are legends of a great war fought between Ulster and the south, when Cuchulain (ironically, a British mercenary) defended the north against Queen Maeve and the 'men of Ireland'.

However, the modern Ulster problem undoubtedly originated in the early seventeenth century, when the area was systematically colonised by English and Lowland Scots settlers. The new settlers were Presbyterian or Anglican in religion, the former outnumbering the latter. No common ground developed between the planters and the dispossessed native stock, with their Catholic faith and pre-medieval Gaelic social order. By 1640 there were thus 'two breeds and two creeds' in Ulster, and the rivalries and misunderstandings between them created tensions which time failed to heal. The religious aspect of the problem involved not just church affiliation, but also much wider disagreements over principles, values and modes of thought between members of communities with very different outlooks.

Ulster's legacy from the seventeenth century was a population divided on a religious basis into Protestant and Catholic communities. By 1886, the majority of Protestant Ulstermen were firmly convinced that their destinies — indeed, even their survival — were inextricably bound up with

Britain. During and after the crisis brought about by the First Home Rule Bill, the Unionists' struggle to prevent the implementation of Irish self-government was conducted on the political plane. But before examining the political developments of the period 1886-1914 it is necessary to trace the economic and religious factors which lay behind the emergence of Unionism as a fully fledged political force in 1886.

Economic Factors 1800-1914

The Industrial Revolution

By 1850 the English Industrial Revolution was extending into Ulster, particularly into the Lagan valley and the city of Belfast, which came to have far more in common with the great industrialised cities of the north of England than with the towns in the south of Ireland.

A combination of favourable circumstances helped to bring prosperity to Belfast and its hinterland. (1) Land: Its geographical position, the resources of the Lagan valley, and the fact that the so-called 'Ulster custom' (fair rent; free sale and fixity of tenure) was upheld throughout the north-east, helped to keep the farming community content. (2) Labour: The Famine had not been so great a catastrophe as elsewhere in Ireland, and emigration was not on so wide a scale. There was thus a population expansion and a ready supply of labour. (3) Capital: The availability of money from investments and savings and the development of an efficient banking system created a climate favourable for industrial expansion. English businessmen, particularly from Liverpool, were attracted by Ulster's industrial potential and provided much of the necessary financial backing. (4) Free trade: Large-scale industry received a major boost through Britain's adoption of free trade in 1846. This gave Ulster industrialists unlimited access to the British free trade area, enabling the easy importation of raw materials and providing profitable international outlets for manufactured goods. (5) Industrial tradition: Since the early eighteenth century Ulster had a considerable reputation for the production of fine linen, which was widely carried on as a cottage craft. The Industrial Revolution, therefore, got off to a good start in a highly receptive society which was already accustomed to thinking in industrial terms. The traditional skills and techniques set a standard which was not lost in the mechanising process, and the high quality of finished goods became a hallmark, not merely of the linen industry, but of all Ulster industry and thus helped to ensure its success. (6) Enterprise: Ulster Protestants, like their seventeenth-century ancestors, tended to be shrewd, hard-headed and progressive, and firm believers in the Victorian principle of 'self-help'. They welcomed the Industrial Revolution and were quick to turn it to their advantage. Thanks to the initiative and business acumen of a number of remarkable personalities, a thriving industrial and commercial community was built up in the north-east.

Linen

By 1850 a vigorous linen industry was centred around Belfast and the Lagan valley. In the 1820s and 1830s steam-powered machinery was introduced for spinning the flax into yarn, and shortly after the famine, mechanical looms, also powered by steam, were invented. The mechanisation of the two processes of linen production brought the industry out of the cottage, with its spinning-wheel and hand loom, and into the big factory. In 1851 there was only a single power loom in Belfast, and 21,000 people were engaged in full-time employment in the manufacture of linen; by 1861 the number of power looms had risen to 6,000 and was still increasing, while the number of workers was over 40,000. The American Civil War (1861-65) brought a boom to the linen industry in Ireland. The import of raw cotton from America to England was curtailed, and the Irish linen mills increased fourfold, such was the demand for linen products. Greater and greater reliance was placed on the importation of cheap flax from Europe. By the year 1900 there were 31,000 power looms and 828,000 power spindles in operation in north-east Ulster, and the number of full-time workers stood at over 60,000.

Besides Belfast, the main centres of the linen industry were Lurgan, Dungannon, Ballymena and Derry. In Derry a subsidiary shirt-making industry had grown up, expanding from five factories in 1850 to thirty-eight by 1902, employing 18,000 full-time workers as well as another 80,000 privately-owned sewing-machines in the surrounding countryside. Only a very small proportion of the linen was actually sold in Ireland; the main markets to which the northern businessmen directed their attention were Britain, the colonies and the United States.

Two-thirds of those employed in the linen mills were women, and about a quarter of the labour force was made up of children. Up to the end of the nineteenth century conditions of work were very hard. The hours of work per week were limited to fifty-six by the Factory Act of 1879. Children even as young as eight years of age began work at 6 a.m. and after six hours in the mill, covered with dirt and steam, went off to school for a few hours. The mills were over-heated and under-ventilated, so that many workers suffered from bronchitis and other chest diseases. As late as 1867 Belfast had a higher death rate than any other town in Ireland. It was only after 1900 that women were given special treatment and consideration.

Wages for work in the linen mills were only 5s a week in 1850, rising to 11s 6d by 1900; women engaged in shirt-making in Derry were paid about 9s a week in 1900. Trade unions developed slowly in Ireland and were barely tolerated in the second half of the nineteenth century. They provided conciliation machinery for industrial disputes, but the workers were not sufficiently organised to use strike action until the twentieth century. Unemployment was always a serious problem, especially as there were more workers than jobs available. In Belfast this could be offset by the shipbuilding industry, which increased the likelihood of employment for the male members of the family. But Derry had no such large-scale alternative, and in many families the women and girls were the sole breadwinners. With the ever present threat of destitution, such workers could easily be exploited by their employers, and wages in Derry were thus lower than those in Belfast.

Shipbuilding

Belfast's second major industry was the construction of iron ships. In the 1850s the Belfast Harbour Commissioners straightened the channel of the Lagan and reclaimed a strip of land, on which was then constructed an artificial island called Queen's Island. This contained a patent launching slip and sites for building large ships.

The man who revolutionised shipbuilding in Belfast was Edward Harland. He designed and produced ships which were built with iron and later steel. The days of the old sailing boats had gone. Harland was the pioneer of the long narrow-beamed ship, built with an iron deck, which was capable of cutting through the waves, not just over them. The first Belfast-built liner crossed the Atlantic in 1871. Harland was a brilliant engineer, and his ships were not only strong and seaworthy but could carry more cargo and passengers than other ships, while at the same time they were economical with fuel.

The fortunes of Harland's company were assured in 1858, when he recruited a Liverpool engineer of German origin, G. W. Woolf, who successfully captured many large orders for the firm, especially from the famous White Star Line. Another remarkable figure connected with the firm was W. J. (later Lord) Pirrie, partner from 1874 to 1904 and sole director from 1904 to 1924. Under Pirrie's able management the firm specialised in large transatlantic liners and also developed profitable lines in manufacturing ships' engines and in maritime transport.

By 1914 the Belfast shipyards of Harland & Woolf were the largest in the world, and one-quarter of the total shipping tonnage of Great Britain had been built there. The 75,000 ton sister-ships *Olympic* and *Titanic* (the latter of which sank on its maiden voyage in 1912) were the largest ships yet built. Over 12,000 men were employed in the shipyard, while a second big firm, Workman & Clark, established in 1879, had a payroll of 10,000.

Since most of the ships were for export, the Belfast businessmen had to look outside their own island to an overseas market for their wares. Similarly, the raw materials necessary for the construction of ships, e.g. iron and coal, had to be imported in huge quantities from Britain. Belfast's commercial contacts were, therefore, with Clydeside and Merseyside and the north of England rather than with the small trading centres of Ireland.

Other Industries

Linen production and shipbuilding generated many subsidiary servicing industries alongside them. Since both the main industries were fully mechanised, there was a constant demand for machinery, steam engines, factory equipment, etc., and numerous engineering works were set up to supply these needs. Other servicing industries included iron foundries, the manufacture of heating and ventilating equipment, and rope-making. There were twelve rope-works in Belfast in 1860.

Once the north-east had become established as a major industrial centre, other industries also began to spring up: considerable employment was provided by carpentry, dyeing, button-making, tobacco-manufacturing, distilleries and flour mills. Belfast and Derry were the two main centres of industry and they attracted much capital from England. We find joint-stock banks in existence in the 1850s. By the end of the nineteenth century, the economic link between England and Ulster was firmly established.

Growth of Belfast

Belfast and Derry were the only urban centres in Ireland which experienced any real growth in the half-century after the famine. Belfast expanded at a particularly rapid rate, its population rising from 75,000 in 1841 to 100,000 in 1851, and reaching 350,000 in 1901. Its harbour was completed by 1849 and its port soon outclassed Dublin in volume of trade. By the end of the nineteenth century many streets had been widened, new bridges built over the Lagan and better roads constructed. The development of a wide network of railways in the 1850s helped to extend business and trading facilities. Horse trams came into use in Belfast in the 1870s. It has been calculated that they carried 2 million passengers in 1880, 10 million in 1890, and over 20 million in 1904. The horse trams brought about a major social change, in that people could now live at a distance from their work. Electric trams were introduced in 1905.

As more and more jobs became available in the developing industries there was a great influx of people from the countryside. In an effort to provide accommodation for these new industrial workers, rows of stereotyped dwellings were built around the factories and mills. These were exactly similar to the houses being built in all the big industrial cities in the north of England — small, cramped, two-storey boxes, built with little regard for sanitation or comfort. However, depressing as they were, they had three advantages: they were new, they were soundly built according to government-controlled standards, and they were designed as single-family units. Belfast was thus spared the horrors of the Dublin slums, where dozens of families crowded haphazardly into big tenement houses which had been built in bygone days for people of a different social standing. In 1892 a series of Housing of the Working Classes Acts did something to improve the living conditions of urban workers, but even then gas and water supplies were not always available.

As the mid-nineteenth century was a period of sectarian strife, Catholic and Protestant workers were encouraged to settle in separate parts of the city. The main Catholic area was the Falls Road in the western part of the city, and the main Protestant area was the Shankill Road, slightly to the north of the Falls. Elsewhere in the city the working classes were segregated into other smaller enclaves. Almost one-third of the population of Belfast were Catholics, and the parts of the city where they lived and worked became ghettoes out of which they seldom ventured and into which Protestants seldom came. The gulf between the two communities was thus maintained, they were unable to establish any kind of social contact with one another, and efforts to organise the working-class as a whole into labour movements or trade unions were very rare and were invariably doomed to failure.

The economic origins of Ulster Unionism

When the question of Irish Home Rule came up in 1886, 1893 and 1912, the northern industrialists opposed it. They saw Home Rule as a threat to their prosperity, which depended on free trade. They knew well that an independent Irish parliament would want to abolish free trade and introduce a system of protective tariffs in order to safeguard the agricultural economy of the other three provinces. This seemed a poor exchange for the loss of the important trading connections which the Union had given them. It would, they were convinced, spell economic disaster and the death of industry in the north. These economic factors helped to shape the political climate and led to the firm stand taken by the Ulster Unionists against any move to introduce self-government for Ireland. This orthodox Unionist view is well represented by a postcard, dated 1912 and labelled 'Belfast under Home Rule', which shows one of the city's principal streets deserted and overgrown with grass, while a large 'To Let' notice is seen hanging on the City Hall.

The health of the northern economy also had a profound social effect. Industrial advancement benefited both the employers and the employed. Similarly, in the rural parts of the province the 'Ulster custom' and the relatively prosperous condition of the peasantry, together with the improvements brought about by the late nineteenth-century land reforms (which were secured largely as a result of southern nationalist agitation, but which, of course, applied throughout the whole country), enabled good relations to be maintained between landlords and tenants. This social harmony on the urban and rural scenes ensured an almost complete absence of class conflict in Ulster — a factor which was to have immense significance, since it helped to weld Ulster Unionism into a coherent, homogeneous force deriving enormous strength from the unity of support it received from all classes within the Protestant community.

But it was not only the Ulster Protestant industrialists, workers and farmers who were determined to maintain the link with England. English businessmen had a vested interest in Ulster and felt that they had staked a claim there. Close business alliances had been formed between companies in England and Ulster, and everything seemed to be working to their mutual profit. Home Rule was seen as a threat to a financially rewarding partnership.

The difference between the economic doctrines of free trade and protection was so profound, the link forged between Ulster and England was so strong, and the determination of all classes in the Protestant community to maintain industrial growth in the face of the Home Rule menace was so resolute that by the 1880s Ulster's economic identity had become clearly differentiated from that of the rest of the country. The economic partition of Ireland was a reality long before political partition came into existence.

Nationalist reactions

Apart from their belief in a protectionist economy rather than a free-trade one, Irish nationalists had other reasons for regarding the industrialisation of the north-east with disfavour and even with indignation. This was partly due to the ideological clash between traditional Catholic and Protestant outlooks on life. Many Irish Catholics, with their ideal of a simple, self-sufficient pastoral and agricultural economy, condemned the industrialisation of Ulster and the planter virtues of thrift, progress and self-help as the manifestations of a society corrupted by gross materialism, lust for wealth, and excessive urbanisation. In bringing its economy into line with that of Britain, Ulster seemed to have renounced its Irish identity and cast its culture into the hated British mould, so that it was now the antithesis of everything that was holy, peasant, Irish and Catholic. Protestant Ulstermen, of course, took a totally different view of these matters: they measured holiness by a different standard, they despised Catholic peasants, and they were proud of the special connection they had built up with Britain.

Catholic criticism of the flourishing northern economy was also tinged by a degree of sheer envy. This was particularly true in Ulster itself, where the two communities lived side by side and where it could plainly be seen that the big profits and the best jobs went to the Protestants. The more wealthy and prosperous their Protestant neighbours and masters became, the more the Ulster Catholics were made aware of their own poverty, and they developed a deep sense of grievance at the second-class status to which they felt they had been relegated. Ulster Protestant sensibilities were keenly conscious of their feeling of hostility — indeed, they were inclined to overestimate its strength — and the old 'siege mentality' was thus reinforced. Protestants were convinced that they must be constantly prepared to defend themselves, their property and the thriving economy which they had built up by their own enterprise and hard work.

Religious Factors, 1800 – 1914

The deep religious divisions in Ulster life dated back to the original plantation and the century of turbulent history which followed it. Open animosity was less rife in the eighteenth century, since Catholics were powerless to challenge the Protestant supremacy, and there was probably a greater degree of good-neighbourliness in day-to-day life, particularly in rural Ulster, than is generally realised. But on the deeper levels of social intercourse there was still strict segregation between the two communities. Mixed marriages did occasionally take place, but they were regarded with extreme disfavour by both groups and were too infrequent to allow any chance for the evolution of an integrated society. Although the descendants of both the original settlers and the old native population did in time develop certain peculiarly 'Ulster' characteristics in common, the distinguishing labels 'Protestant' and 'Catholic' were the real determinants of a person's social identity. Such labels had a *tribal* rather than a purely theological significance, and the tribal taboos or conventions which governed social behaviour were so strong that they became the dominant differentiating factor in all fields of social activity, including politics, so that during and after the nineteenth century it is most unusual to find a Protestant who is not a Unionist or a Catholic who is not a Nationalist. Perhaps the most striking illustration of the solidity of the Protestant-Unionist and Catholic-Nationalist identifications was to be provided during the debate on the Government of Ireland Bill in 1920, when Carson and Craig, the Unionist leaders, carried out a detailed *religious* headcount of all the inhabitants of every townland in the counties of Cavan, Monaghan and Donegal in order to discover whether it would be possible to include these counties within the new state of Northern Ireland without impairing the overall Unionist majority.

Political power of Catholics

The nineteenth century was an age when great advances were being made throughout Europe towards religious toleration and political democracy. These trends were reflected not only in general social attitudes, but also — and perhaps more importantly, from a practical point of view — in legislation. In Britain three major reforms were enacted which, although designed for the United Kingdom as a whole, had their most decisive impact in Ireland, where they effectively brought about a redistribution of political power in favour of Catholics, which in turn led to far-reaching changes in the pattern of political activity in Ireland. (1) The Catholic Emancipation Act (1829) gave Catholics the right to sit in the Westminster parliament, formerly a strictly Protestant preserve. This made possible the formation of a small body of Irish Catholic MPs who would advocate nationalist causes. (2) A series of franchise reforms (see Table 2) by reducing the property qualifications of electors, extended the suffrage to the poorer classes. This process of democratisation of the franchise, culminating in the Representation of the People Act (1918), led to the rise of the Labour Party in Britain, while in Ireland, by giving a proportionately much greater degree of political representation to the Catholic-Nationalist majority in the population, enabled an increasing number of Nationalist MPs to consolidate their position at Westminster. (3) The Ballot Act (1872) introduced a system of secret voting and thus made it possible for the poorer sections of the electorate (in Ireland almost entirely Catholic nationalists) to vote freely for the candidates of their choice without fear of intimidation or retaliation from their landlords or employers.

Most Irish Protestants viewed these developments with growing dismay. The strength of the newly enfranchised Catholic opinion in Ireland resulted in four-fifths of the parliamentary seats being held by Home Rulers by the last quarter of the nineteenth century. Protestants believed that if the nationalist demand for Irish self-government was met, not only would Protestant ascendancy be gone for ever, but that it would be replaced by a new and possibly virulent Catholic ascendancy. The only sure bulwark against such a prospect was the maintenance of the Union; even if the Irish nationalist majority sent a full quota of Home Rule MPs to Westminster, they would always be in a minority in the United Kingdom parliament.

The fact that by the late nineteenth century Home Rule was clearly the desire of the majority of the Irish people was less important to Irish Protestants than their belief that 'Home Rule is Rome Rule'. The Protestant community had viewed with increasing unease the vigorous new spirit of Irish Catholicism in the years following Emancipation. For as long as the Catholic Church had been a penalised, semi-underground institution it had been regarded as relatively harmless, but after 1829 it seemed to be coming out into the open with a new and aggressive force and to be making a determined bid for power. Large numbers of new Catholic churches and cathedrals were built. Following their victorious campaign for Emancipation Catholics continued to engage in organised action and to openly press further demands, such as tithe reform and Repeal of the Union itself.

Ulster sectarianism, 1829-50

The tithe war of the 1830s was the occasion of frequent clashes between Catholic and Protestant groups, the latter fighting to retain Protestant supremacy in the form of the Established Church's right to exact cash payments from Catholics. The Church Temporalities Act (1833), which reduced the Established Church's revenue, and the Tithe Rent-Charge Act (1838), which attempted to take the sting out of tithe payment, were resented by Protestants, while they did little to conciliate Catholics.

The principal organisation through which Protestants expressed their determination to preserve their heritage was the Orange Order, which had become very widespread by the 1830s. Orange demonstrations and processions took place regularly in Ulster, where marches made provocative displays of Protestant solidarity and Protestant supremacy. Many of the Orange processions were deliberately planned to pass through Catholic areas, with the result that they were often accompanied by rioting and bloodshed. The worst of these clashes occurred on 12 July 1849 at Dolly's Brae, near Magheramayo, Co. Down, where an Orange parade, accompanied by police and military, forced its way through a Catholic townland, killing and injuring many of the inhabitants who were trying to prevent its passage.

Although it escaped the worst ravages of the famine, urbanised and industrialised Ulster entered the second half of the nineteenth century with its savage animosities unresolved and its two communities as far apart as they had been two centuries earlier.

Ulster sectarianism, 1850-1914

A number of events after 1850 seemed to confirm Ulster Protestants' worst suspicions that a monstrous plot against them was being concocted in the Vatican. The pope's restoration of the English Catholic hierarchy in 1850 and the consequent formation of a party of Irish Catholic MPs at Westminster (see page 14) led to an almost hysterical outcry against 'papal aggression' and to a 'no popery' campaign which was felt in Ulster. The strong anti-Protestant line taken by Archbishop Cullen and his Ultramontanist reorganisation of the Irish Catholic Church after the Synod of Thurles in 1850 (see page 21) also seemed to constitute a threat by introducing a more direct form of papal influence into Ireland. Cullen's attitude was largely dictated by his natural desire to combat a massive Evangelical Protestant mission in the distressed areas of the west which enjoyed a short-lived success during the 1850s. Many of the converts – popularly known as 'perverts' or 'jumpers' – were intimidated and forced to emigrate, and Ulster Protestants felt that they could expect the same treatment if Catholicism extended its power into the north. Protestant fears were further aroused by the leading role in local political activity assumed by priests during and after the 1850s, including some, such as the notorious Father Pat Lavelle of Partry, Co. Mayo, who were known to have contacts with Fenians. It was widely believed in Ulster that political leaders like Butt and Parnell were mere puppet figureheads and that the real power in nationalist politics was wielded by clerical magnates, such as Archbishops MacHale and Croke, in the interests of the pope in Rome.

In the prevailing atmosphere of mutual dislike and distrust between the two segregated communities, violence became a constant feature of life in Ulster, particularly in the rapidly expanding city of Belfast. Twelfth of July celebrations were invariably accompanied by disturbances, often involving loss of life. The mid-Victorian period was also the golden age of Evangelicalism, which had a powerful impact on the Protestant community in Ulster, culminating in a great religious revival in 1859. Unfortunately Evangelicalism emphasised those very aspects of Protestantism which were most opposed to Catholicism; much of the preaching was of an emotional and somewhat intemperate character and had an immense popular appeal, many thousands gathering to hear the impassioned sermons of powerful preachers such as the Rev. Thomas Drew, Grand Chaplain of the Orange Order, and the Rev. Hugh ('Roaring') Hanna, a fiery Presbyterian minister. The fact that sermons were frequently delivered in the open air or on street corners served as an additional provocation to the Catholic community and strained religious tensions dangerously close to breaking-point.

Later events which helped to accentuate sectarian animosity in Ulster included the disestablishment of the Church of Ireland in 1869, which was seen as yet another victory for the militant and menacing forces of Rome. The *Ne Temere* decree (1907), which pressurised the Protestant partners in mixed marriages to bring up their children as Catholics, seemed to be final proof of what Ulster Protestants had long believed — that the pope was perpetually scheming to acquire new subjects and to extend his power throughout the world.

Finally, and on a more general level, it should be noted that by the 1880s, sectarian rivalry had become such an ingrained feature of Ulster life that it formed a persistent undercurrent in the political campaigns for and against Home Rule. The Orange Order generated considerable mass emotion, much of it of a sectarian nature, among the rank and file of Ulster Unionists, and it provided a platform for the more extreme Protestant elements to voice their religious fears. Unionists were quick to realise the value of appealing to their co-religionists in England and Scotland. As one of their spokesmen said, 'I think that if we can stir up the religious feeling in Scotland, we have won the battle.'

Political Factors, 1886-1914

Despite the economic and religious factors which formed the background to the Ulster question, it was on the political plane that it manifested itself to the world at large. Before 1886 the political side was only apparent from time to time and was mainly connected with the shift in the balance of political representation in favour of Catholics which we have already examined. After 1886, when the Home Rule proposal was actually laid before parliament, politics, both at parliamentary and grassroots levels, became the vital, constant and obvious factor. It is possible to distinguish five separate reasons why the majority of people in the north-east supported the Union for purely political motives.

Fear of the Unknown

It was widely believed by Unionists that the very moderate measure of self-government proposed in all three Home Rule Bills was regarded by nationalists as merely the first stage in a long-term programme designed to achieve the complete severance of Ireland from Great Britain and the Empire. What life would be like in the new separatist state was anybody's guess, but Unionists took the gloomiest possible view of their prospects. Their jobs, their property, their liberty — even their lives — seemed to be in the gravest danger. In contrast to such imagined horrors was the solid and comfortable existence of the Union, the maintenance of which seemed to be the only sure guarantee of their continued security. Unionists condemned Home Rule not only for what it was, but even more for fear of what it could become. The idea that Home Rule was only an interim arrangement was an underlying feature of all the other Unionist objections to it listed below.

Opposition to the Parnell movement
The rise of Parnell and his powerful Nationalist Party brought about a confrontation between Unionists and Home Rulers in Ulster. It seemed to many that the control of Ireland's political destinies was about to be put into the hands of a man, who, though a Protestant, was an ultra-nationalist. The people of the north-east had good reasons for distrusting Parnell. His association with the Land League and the American Fenians, as well as the duplicity which became apparent when his statements in the House of Commons were compared with his speeches in Ireland, made him appear unscrupulous. They could not accept him as *their* political leader.

Distrust of Gladstone and the English Liberals
They blamed Gladstone for disestablishment, for widening the franchise so that the Catholic lower classes got the vote, and for introducing his Home Rule Bill without consulting public opinion in northern Ireland. They feared that he planned a complete sell-out, and suspected that he had become the tool of Parnell. As one commentator put it, "Mr Parnell, whether Mr Gladstone knows it or not, is the keeper of Mr Gladstone's conscience.'

Sense of belonging to a great empire
The Ulster Unionists were loyal to Britain, because they appreciated the advantages which this connection brought them. They felt that they belonged to a vast and powerful empire, and support for any move which might eventually result in cutting themselves off from this imperial heritage seemed a betrayal of their best interests. There was no guarantee that a self-governing Ireland would provide such a boon, or that an Irish parliament could be as efficient and honourable as Westminster.

Fear of violent revolution
Ulster Unionists were appalled by the violence that had been practised since the 1830s by opponents of the Union. The land war, the Irish-American dynamite campaign and, most of all, the Phoenix Park killings, had a profound effect upon the people in north-east Ireland. They refused to distinguish between the various types of nationalism, regarding them all as tarred with the same brush; and they were, therefore, equally opposed to the moderate constitutional campaign for reform and to the Fenian-republican principles of ending the Union by force of arms. Furthermore,

even on a non-political level, life in southern Ireland was marked by a high incidence of crimes of violence, e.g. the Maamtrasna murders in 1882. Unionists were shocked by the viciousness and brutality which seemed so rife in the south and were convinced that in a self-governing Ireland power would sooner or later be seized by a gang of savage thugs and murderers. (This idea is comparable to the popular English belief — see page 50 — that the Irish were unfit for self-government.) Not only would Home Rule mean Rome Rule, but it would eventually lead to republican rule, a reign of terror, and ultimately chaos.

Table 3
Distribution of unionist seats in Ireland by area at four general elections, 1885 - 1918

	1885	1892	Dec. 1910	1918
Ulster (9 counties)	16	19	18	23
Dublin City and County (inc. TCD)	2	4	3	3
Rest of Ireland	0	0	0	0
Total	18	23	21	26
Total number of Ulster seats (9 counties)	32	32	32	38
Total number of seats in Ireland	103	103	103	105

Aspects of the Ulster Question after 1886

Developments after 1886 brought into prominence certain aspects of the Ulster question which became dominant themes in the conflict between Unionism and Nationalism. Unionism was by no means confined to Ulster: it existed as a minority political creed throughout the entire country. Furthermore, although many Unionist leaders spoke of Ulster as if it were solidly Unionist, they were well aware that at least half the population of the nine-county province was strongly opposed to Unionism. The counties of Monaghan, Cavan and Donegal were overwhelmingly nationalist, parts of Londonderry, Fermanagh, Tyrone, South Armagh and South Down also had nationalist majorities, and even in the Unionist heartlands of Antrim, North Down and the city of Belfast, there were several pockets of non-

Unionists. We shall see below how the Ulster Unionists dealt with their southern allies during the crisis of 1912-14, while Chapter 12 demonstrates how they have never succeeded in solving the problem of the anti-Unionists in their midst.

Unionists assumed that a self-governing Ireland could not exist as a viable economic entity without the support of Northern industry, and that by standing firm against Home Rule they could force their opponents to abandon their campaign. In holding such views they not only overestimated their own importance but also gravely underestimated the strength of nationalist sentiment.

Nationalists on their part underestimated the strength and intransigence of their opponents in Ulster. This misapprehension may to some extent be due to the new pattern of political representation following the 1885 election, which resulted in nationalist victories in just over half the Ulster constituencies. But Nationalist leaders had traditionally shirked the realities of the Ulster situation and had often taken the easy way out of the problem by simply ignoring it. Few nationalist politicians had any constructive ideas on the Ulster question.

As a result of the events of the years 1885-86 Home Rule was suddenly transformed from a vague possibility into the most vital and urgent issue of the day. Since the principles of Home Rule and Unionism were diametrically opposed, there was no opportunity either for moderate middle-of-the-road opinion or for compromise. From 1886 onwards Ireland was divided into two hostile and irreconcilable camps.

In the south, outside Ulster, Unionists were a tiny minority and, except in Dublin and a few other centres, scattered in small pockets over a very wide area. Southern Unionists were almost entirely drawn from the upper classes (landowners, businessmen, professional men, government officials etc.) and their dependents (agents, gamekeepers, clerks, coastguards etc.). They tended to be extremely wealthy and were politically influential out of all proportion to their numbers. They had very close ties with the British Conservative Party and with the House of Lords. Too weak numerically to block Home Rule, they channelled their political activity and considerable financial resources into an effective campaign in Britain, persuading English voters that Home Rule would be fatal for the Empire as well as for Ireland. Their tenacious struggle to maintain the Union was fought on a single front, that of constitutional parliamentary politics.

In Ulster, on the other hand, the Unionist population was large enough to form a vital and self-contained community which ranged across the entire social spectrum. Unionism, and in particular Orangeism, by uniting all social classes in pursuit of a common objective, obliterated class conflict (a development which ran counter to the general European trend of growing working-class agitation).

Unlike the southern Unionists, those of the north knew that if the worst came to the worst they could hold their territory and prevent Home

Rule from operating in a large part of Ulster. But no one at the end of the nineteenth century dreamed that the independent course taken by Ulster Unionists would one day result in the partition of the country.

After 1886 Ulster Unionists expressed their opposition to Home Rule in four ways. Two of these were traditional: a parliamentary fight at Westminster, and outbreaks of sectarian rioting. The other two were new developments: the formation of a well-directed network of local and provincial organisations to co-ordinate all aspects of the campaign, and organised preparation for armed resistance should Home Rule actually be enacted. Military drilling by anti-Home Rulers in Ulster, ostensibly for the purpose of self-defence, began in 1886 and was resumed at all moments of crisis thereafter.

The 1886 Crisis and the Orange Card

The result of the 1885 general election and the announcement of Gladstone's conversion to Home Rule came as a heavy double blow to those who wanted to maintain the Union. The election result showed just how much of a minority they were: of 103 Irish seats they won only a total of eighteen, of which sixteen were in Ulster (just half the provincial total of thirty-two), while only two were in the south (Dublin University). The Prime Minister's action in giving top priority to Home Rule in his government's legislative programme meant that the long-dreaded threat was now actually in the process of materialising.

The immediate reaction of the anti-Home Rulers was to close ranks and to set about organising the machinery of opposition and resistance. The trend towards organisation had already been begun by the southern Unionists with the formation in early 1885 of the Irish Loyal and Patriotic Union (renamed the Irish Unionist Alliance in 1891), a small but wealthy and influential body, most of whose efforts were to be devoted to propagating the Unionist argument in Britain. Ulster Unionists were quick to follow this example by establishing their own local organisation, the Ulster Loyalist Anti-Repeal Union, at the beginning of 1886. This association had great success in rallying support on the home front, largely because of its quite unabashed appeal to the sectarian prejudices of Protestants. At the same time the eighteen MPs constituted themselves as a parliamentary party, which was, of course, dominated by the Ulster members. The Unionist Party was led for nearly twenty years by E. J. Saunderson, an ultra-Protestant landlord from Cavan and a convinced believer in the necessity for a trained Ulster army to hold the north against Home Rule.

The birth of Unionism as a highly organised political force was presided over by the most influential of all its organisations, the Orange Order. After nearly fifty years in the doldrums, the Order began to revive during the Land League agitation, and in 1886 it was recognised as a perfect readymade instrument for uniting all sections of Unionist society in a confident and coherent front against the common enemy which threatened them. The Orange Order suddenly became respectable and the upper and middle classes flocked to it in their thousands. Noblemen, landlords, clergymen, lawyers, doctors, merchants, businessmen and industrialists joined forces with small farmers, labourers, factory hands, shipyard workers and shopkeepers, and the Orange spirit of fraternal equality of all members helped ensure that class differences would never split the ranks of orthodox Unionism.

These events were followed with interest by the Conservative Party in England, who saw the situation in Ulster as one which might be exploited to their own advantage. If the Ulster Unionists showed that they were prepared to stop at nothing to prevent Home Rule, then the anti-Home Rule and anti-Liberal argument would have a much greater impact on the realistic English. If the Unionists successfully resisted a majority parliamentary decision in favour of Home Rule, then the authority of the Liberal government would collapse and it would be forced out of office. The Conservatives, therefore, did all they could to encourage the Ulster Unionists to prepare for unconstitutional action.

The alliance was confirmed during the visit to Belfast of Lord Randolph Churchill, a leading Conservative, in February 1886. Churchill stated privately: 'I decided some time ago that if the G.O.M. [Grand Old Man, i.e. Gladstone] went for Home Rule, the Orange card would be the one to play.' In public he assured his Ulster audience that if they found themselves forced to make a lone stand to defend Ulster from its enemies, 'there will not be wanting to you those of position and influence in England who are willing to cast in their lot with you – whatever it may be'. And as the debate on the Home Rule Bill neared its climax Churchill coined the slogan 'Ulster will fight and Ulster will be right.'

The Orange card was played in the British, not the Irish, political game. Churchill's warlike slogan was intended for use in England, not in Ireland. Ulster Unionists did not need an Englishman to tell them either that they were right or that they would fight. Of course, it was undoubtedly comforting for them to know that they had friends in England, and English votes were certainly necessary if Home Rule was to be defeated in parliament. But Ulster Unionists knew that it was not in parliament but in Ulster itself that the real issue would be decided. They knew that they could make a Home Rule Act unworkable without any help from their English supporters. Ulster needed the Conservative Party far less than the Conservative Party needed Ulster. Southern Unionists, on the other hand, isolated and thinly scattered throughout strongly nationalist areas, realised that parliamentary politics – and therefore the Conservative alliance – was their only hope. They did all they could to develop their links with the Conservatives and to promote their cause with the English public in a series of pamphlets, newspaper articles and speeches.

In the event, Home Rule got no further than the House of Commons in

1886; the moment of supreme crisis was averted for the time being, and Ulster Unionists were not given the chance to demonstrate the strength of their organised resistance. But the crisis of 1886 had forced them to provide themselves with the machinery of opposition and defiance. And what had been used once could be used again. The Unionists dug their heels in and, having successfully weathered the 1886 storm, felt that they could offer similar if not even more powerful opposition should another occasion arise. They maintained their high degree of organisation, extending it and improving its efficiency over the following decades, and creating new political bodies and alignments whenever occasion seemed to demand it.

Ulster Unionist Groups, 1893-1910

The Ulster Unionists were given another scare in 1893, when Gladstone introduced his Second Home Rule Bill. Preparations for armed resistance were resumed and were given an additional impetus by the establishment of the militant Ulster Defence Union, in which, as might be expected, Colonel Saunderson was a leading light. However, the Unionists in Ulster now showed a greater willingness to secure the rejection of Home Rule by constitutional methods. The success of the bill in the House of Commons, followed closely by its defeat in the House of Lords, taught the Unionists two things: first, that they had a permanent ally of the utmost reliability in the upper house; and secondly, that the single weak point of their own organised defences was revealed as the lack of really powerful political clubs in Ulster, capable of swaying public opinion in Ireland and England and throughout the English-speaking world. They accordingly set about building up an extended network of Unionist Clubs for this purpose, thereby bringing their tactics more into line with the southern Unionists of the Irish Unionist Alliance.

With a Conservative government in power between 1895 and 1905, the Unionists had little to fear. They offered little or no opposition to the policy of 'killing Home Rule with kindness'. The only real crisis occured over the 'devolution' scheme of 1904-05, proposed by an independent group of southern Unionists and enjoying the backing of the Chief Secretary, George Wyndham (see page 57). The scheme was a relatively moderate one, giving Ireland 'some say in the control and conduct of her own affairs' and was seen in the eyes of its backers as a compromise solution which could be accepted by nationalists in place of full Home Rule, and, therefore, as an extension of the 'killing by kindness' principle. But Unionists in the north regarded *any* meddling with the constitutional connection between Britain and Ireland as little short of rank treachery. All the strength and bitterness of northern intransigence came into action against the 'devolution' proposal. As a result, the scheme was quickly dropped and Wyndham was forced out of office. The incident serves to illustrate the 'siege mentality' of the northern majority community; in reasserting

'No Surrender' as the warcry of orthodox Unionism they showed that they were prepared to take their own route into the political future.

The devolution scare led directly to the foundation of a new organisation, the Ulster Unionist Council, formally constituted in 1905. Its purpose was to tighten and co-ordinate all Unionist activity in a specifically Ulster context. It linked together the local and provincial organisations, the Orange lodges and the Unionist Parliamentary Party, and in 1911 it was enlarged to include the Unionist Clubs and the militant Derry Apprentice Boys. It framed the policy of the parliamentary party and acted as a watchdog on its performance at Westminster.

The return of the Liberals to power in 1905-06 was not immediately followed by any threat to the Union (see page 57). But the constitutional crisis of 1909-11 gave ominous signs that the battle between Home Rule and Unionism was about to enter a new and more alarming phase.

The Immediate Origins of Crisis, 1910-11

The two general elections of 1910, which lost the Liberals their absolute majority in the House of Commons and gave the balance of power to Redmond and the Irish Party, once more raised the spectre of an impending Home Rule Bill. The Parliament Act of 1911 (see page 58) which removed the House of Lords' power of veto, introduced a new degree of intensity into the crisis, since it ensured that once the forthcoming Home Rule Bill had been passed by the combined Liberal-Nationalist majority in the Commons, it would only be a matter of time until it became law. From now on, therefore, any effective resistance to Home Rule would have to be conducted on the unconstitutional, illegal plane.

Ulster Unionists left the world in no doubt that they were prepared to launch a massive rebellion. They had the good fortune at this time to acquire two leaders who had exactly the right qualities of capability, courage and charisma which the situation demanded. These two men, who shared the heavy responsibility for leading the north into armed resistance against the government and the Irish nationalists, were Sir Edward Carson and James Craig.

Sir Edward Carson

Carson was born in Dublin in 1854. After a successful and lucrative career as a barrister, both in Ireland and England, he entered politics and became Unionist MP for Dublin University. By 1910 he was a prominent figure in British political life. In February 1910 Carson was elected leader of the Irish Unionist parliamentary party, and from then on he threw himself wholeheartedly into the campaign against Home Rule, first in parliament, then increasingly, after September 1911, in Ulster itself, where his extraordinary qualities as leader of a popular mass movement became apparent.

Carson's entire political career was dominated by the idea that the Union must be maintained for Ireland as a whole. He regarded the opposition which he led in the north simply as a means for blocking Home Rule, believing that if Ulster stood firm against the scheme, it would have to be abandoned in the rest of the country. Carson's essentially southern view of priorities was not shared by his followers in the north, who held that the preservation of Ulster's integrity must be the overriding — as well as the most realistic — consideration. However, Carson was wise enough not to draw attention to differing viewpoints and concentrated instead on rallying support into a firm united front, with himself as the figurehead of resistance. His powerful and incisive speeches were carefully contrived pieces of acting which electrified his vast audiences, boosting their morale and fortifying their determination to persevere in their dangerous enterprise.

James Craig

Carson's right-hand man was born in Belfast in 1871, the son of a millionaire industrialist. After a spell of distinguished service in the Boer War, he entered politics in 1906 as Unionist MP for East Down. Unlike Carson, Craig seemed to personify the spirit of Ulster intransigence. His rock-like impassivity, his stubbornness and his unflinching courage were a constant inspiration to his fellow-Ulstermen. A tireless worker, he possessed a considerable flair for administration, and it was under his able guidance that resistance to Home Rule was mustered and organised into a concerted campaign, mainly through the Orange lodges and the Unionist Clubs.

Organising Mass Resistance, 1911-12

The first phase of the Ulster Unionists' campaign against Home Rule began with Carson's return to Ireland after the passage of the Parliament Act in August 1911. The new act had made the parliamentary progress of Home Rule virtually a foregone conclusion, and although Carson continued to contribute to the Home Rule debate at Westminster, his purpose in doing so was merely to gain tactical advantages. His real work lay increasingly in Ulster.

The popular mass movement was launched on 23 September 1911 with a monster rally held in the grounds of Craigavon, Craig's home just outside Belfast which he had thrown open to the public for the occasion. A crowd estimated at as many as 100,000 gathered to hear Carson proclaim: 'We will yet defeat the most nefarious conspiracy that has ever been hatched against a free people ... We must be prepared, in the event of a Home Rule Bill passing, with such measures as will carry on for ourselves the government of those districts of which we have control. We must be prepared ... the morning Home Rule passes, ourselves to become responsible for the government of the Protestant province of Ulster.' Two days later the Ulster Unionist Council set up a committee, headed by Craig, 'to frame and submit a Constitution for a Provisional Government of Ireland, having regard to the interests of loyalists in the other parts of Ireland.' It will be noticed that the committee's terms of reference, unlike Carson's speech, applied to the whole of Ireland. Yet this was little more than an empty form of words, for Craig and his colleagues knew well that they could not force a government of their own making on the nationalist south. Carson's speech displayed the true nature of Unionist power politics. The process of abandoning the southern Unionists had begun.

All these activities had the full and open support of the British Conservative Party and its new leader, Andrew Bonar Law (see page 60), who were bitterly resentful of their severe parliamentary defeats and loss of power during the 1909-11 constitutional crisis. Bonar Law, like Lord Randolph Churchill before him, decided to play the Orange card. Visiting Belfast in April 1912, on the eve of the bill's introduction in parliament, he attended a huge semi-military demonstration at which he told his 100,000 listeners that the Conservative Party would support them to the bitter end and that millions of Englishmen regarded the Unionist cause as 'the cause of the Empire'. While the support and encouragement of the Conservatives were welcomed by Ulster Unionists, Carson for one had no illusions as to the real motive behind them: nine years later he was to admit: 'I was only a puppet, and so was Ulster, and so was Ireland, in the political game that got the Conservatives into power.'

The Solemn League and Covenant, 1912

The series of demonstrations and monster meetings continued throughout 1912, raising anti-Home Rule feeling to a high peak and vividly expressing the strength and solidarity of Unionist resistance. This phase of the campaign reached its climax on 28 September 1912, when Craig and the Ulster Unionist Council arranged a number of simultaneous rallies throughout the province at which over 200,000 male Unionists signed the following pledge (a differently worded version being signed by an even greater number of women):

ULSTER'S SOLEMN LEAGUE AND COVENANT

Being convinced in our consciences that Home Rule would be disastrous to the material well-being of Ulster as well as of the whole of Ireland, subversive of our civil and religious freedom, destructive of our citizenship and perilous to the unity of the Empire, we, whose names are underwritten, men of Ulster, loyal subjects of His Gracious Majesty King George V, humbly relying on the God whom our fathers in the days of stress and trial confidently trusted, do hereby pledge ourselves in solemn Covenant through this our time of threatened calamity to stand by one another in defending for ourselves and our children our cherished position of equal citizenship in the United Kingdom and in using all means which may be found necessary to defeat the present conspiracy to set up a Home Rule Parliament in Ireland.

And in the event of such a Parliament being forced upon us we further solemnly and mutually pledge ourselves to refuse to recognise its authority.

In sure confidence that God will defend the right we hereto subscribe our names.

And further, we individually declare that we have not already signed this Covenant.

GOD SAVE THE KING

The signing of the Covenant had the effect of convincing many English Liberal politicians that Home Rule could never be applied to Ulster. Some suggestions had already been made during 1912 for a separate provision for Ulster under the forthcoming act, and soon speculation about the possibility of some form of partition became more common.

The Rise of the Ulster Volunteers, 1913-14

Both Carson and Craig realised that the situation called for more than mere meetings, demonstrations and speeches. Fighting talk must necessarily be backed up by a show of physical force, and if a provisional government was to be declared, it must have some kind of army to enforce its authority. It was Craig himself who realised that the Orange Order could provide a framework for an Ulster citizen army. Even as early as 1911 some Orangemen had been secretly drilling and at the famous Craigavon rally on 23 September a trained contingent of Orangemen from Co. Tyrone paraded and attracted considerable attention by their smart appearance and the precision of their marching. Early in 1912 it was discovered that the law permitted any two Justices of the Peace to authorise drilling and other military operations 'for the purpose of maintaining the constitution of the United Kingdom as now established.' This was a godsend to Craig and his fellow-organisers, and soon licences were being issued all over Ulster permitting small local citizen armies to parade.

In January 1913 the Ulster Unionist Council met and decided that all these small local groups should be organised into one efficient body, to be known as the Ulster Volunteer Force. Recruiting was to be limited to 100,000, and only those who had signed the Covenant were eligible. A retired Indian army general, Sir George Richardson, was appointed commander of the Ulster Volunteer Force (UVF), and set up his headquarters in the Old Town Hall, Belfast. By the end of 1913 the UVF had grown into an efficient and formidable army with its own communication system.

It was prepared to seize and control all important roads, harbours and railways in Ulster and enforce the authority of the Ulster Unionist Council, which in September 1913 had formally reconstituted itself as the prospective provisional government of Ulster.

But the UVF was an army without arms. All the men had were wooden batons and dummy rifles, a drawback which occasioned a good deal of nationalist derision. Obviously they needed weapons, for the force was committed to making 'an armed resistance' to the imposition of Home Rule on Ulster. For some time individual Volunteers had been smuggling arms and ammunition into Ulster, but the force was still only partially and unsatisfactorily equipped when, on 5 December 1913, the government banned all importation of arms into Ireland. However, the Ulster provisional government had already established a 'defence fund' for the purchase and transportation of a single massive consignment of high-quality arms from Germany. The sum of £1,000,000 was subscribed with astonishing speed. The plans of the actual operation were kept a close secret, however, and the entire mission was entrusted to a Unionist zealot, Major Fred Crawford, who had already achieved a certain notoriety as a successful arms smuggler.

The 1914 Crisis

By the spring of 1914, with the Home Rule Bill in the process of passing through parliament, it was clear that everything depended on whether or not the Ulster Volunteers would be fully armed in time to mount a successful resistance to the act. By mid-April Richardson and his staff had made careful and far-seeing plans for the landing and dispersal of the weapons using motor-cars lent for the purpose by wealthy Unionists in all parts of the province. The entire operation went off without a hitch on the night of 24-25 April, the main consignment landing at Larne and two smaller ones arriving at Bangor and Donaghadee. The total shipment consisted of 35,000 rifles and 5,000,000 rounds of ammunition. (Compare these figures with those of the Irish Volunteers' gun-running at Howth, page 116). It is significant that the sheet of detailed instructions issued to all the participants included the warning: 'Sir Edward Carson is particularly desirous that no trouble should arise. Arms are therefore not to be carried; a determined attitude will probably overcome any possible show of interference by the police.' In fact the plans worked out so well that the arms were distributed before the police could step in, and the government was powerless to take any action against anyone who had taken part in the affair. The gun-running, occurring only a few weeks after the Curragh incident (see page 61), seemed to show that the illegal army in the north had the monopoly of military power in Ireland.

To most observers in the summer of 1914 it seemed that Ireland was on the verge of civil war. The provisional government in Ulster stood fully prepared and ready to take over the administration of the province as soon as the Home Rule Bill reached the statute book and became law. The Ulster Volunteers stood fully prepared to provide the necessary military backing for the authority of the provisional government. The Ulster Unionists were in a very strong position, and they contemptuously rejected all the last minute efforts of Asquith and the Liberals to reach a compromise (outlined at the end of Chapter 3). And when the Buckingham Palace Conference broke down in July the Unionists were more determined than ever to stand by the Covenant they had signed.

Civil war was averted only by the outbreak of European war on 4 August 1914. The Ulster Volunteers enlisted in the British army almost to a man and were allowed to keep their separate identity as the 36th (Ulster) Division. They fought with conspicuous bravery on the western front, suffering enormous losses at the Battle of the Somme in 1916. Meanwhile, Home Rule was shelved for the duration of the war. The crisis had been postponed, but the Ulster question still remained unsolved.

Talking Points

Chapter 4: The Ulster Question, 1850-1914
   1 Explain the origins and development of 'the Ulster Question' up to the first Home Rule crisis of 1886.
   2 What were the chief economic factors which made Ulster different from the rest of Ireland during the years 1850-1914? Explain the economic developments in the two large Ulster cities of Belfast and Derry.
   3 What exactly was meant by the saying 'Home Rule is Rome Rule'? How well founded were the religious fears of Ulster Protestants vis-a-vis an all-Ireland parliament in Dublin?
   4 What were the main political factors which constituted the Ulster question between 1886 and 1914?
   5 What role did the Orange Order play in bringing together all Ulster Protestants in the struggle against Home Rule? How did the English Conservative Party co-operate in helping Ulster Protestants?
   6 Show how and why the Ulster Unionists found it necessary to introduce a strong military organisation to deal with the third Home Rule crisis, 1912-14.

Chapter 5
DEVELOPING NATIONALISM, 1880-1914

Irish Nationalism: Three Versions

Nationalism, which became the dominant force in Irish politics in the second half of the nineteenth century, has a history which stretches back to the Confederation of Kilkenny in the 1640s. Since then there have been three main strands in its development. The first of these stemmed from the writings of Swift and Molyneux and the speeches of Grattan and Flood and reached its climax in the struggle for legislative independence which was brought to a successful conclusion by a party of aristocratic 'patriots' at the end of the eighteenth century. The second, originated in the separatist ideals of the United Irishmen in the 1790s, was revived again in the 1840s by the Young Ireland movement, whose members, like the United Irishmen, were mainly middle-class intellectuals. The third manifested itself in the great drive towards democracy and the supremacy of majority opinion which was started by Daniel O'Connell in his Emancipation and Repeal campaigns.

Nationalists of all three traditions were in agreement about their basic aims. They all maintained that Ireland was a separate and distinct nation and that the Irish people therefore possessed the right of self-determination, i.e., the control of their own affairs through their own government and parliament. However, there were fundamental and irreconcilable differences between the three outlooks. First of all, they could not agree about the degree of self-determination they required, or about the exact extent of the power to be held by the Irish parliament. The 'patriots' of Grattan's parliament wished to preserve the link with Britain through the crown; the United Irishmen and Young Irelanders wanted to break that link and so achieve absolute independence; O'Connell's personal views in this respect were similar to those of the eighteenth-century parliamentarians, but his successors may be divided into constitutionalists, who were prepared to accept a much more limited measure of self-government (Home Rule) as an interim practical proposition, and extremists, who tended to favour complete separation.

The most fundamental difference of all — the one which provides the real distinction between the three traditions — lay in their totally conflicting definitions of the 'Irish nation' and the 'Irish people'. The 'patriots' of Grattan's parliament assumed without question that the 'Irish people' consisted *only* of the Protestant Anglo-Irish community. They thus formed an exclusive upper-class oligarchy which, while adopting a generally benevolent attitude towards Catholics and their demands for reform, was firmly bent on maintaining the minority Protestant ascendancy. This view was challenged by the United Irishmen and the Young Irelanders, both of whom envisaged a genuinely pluralist society consisting of *all* the inhabitants of the country. Wolfe Tone and the United Irishmen stressed the *religious* unity of this society, in which Catholic, Protestant and Dissenter would share equally the 'rights of man'. Thomas Davis, the principal thinker and spokesman of Young Ireland, based his appeal on the evidence of ancient Irish nationality revealed by his reading of history and placed his emphasis on the *racial* unity which would result from a fusion of all the ethnic groups which contributed to the Irish population, from the early Celtic invaders to the most recent English, Scottish and Huguenot settlers.

Both Grattan's and Tone's definitions of the 'Irish nation' were eventually to be eclipsed by another concept which won a much wider acceptance. The most lasting effect of O'Connell's victorious campaign for Emancipation was the sense of common identity, achievement and purpose which it gave to Irish Catholics. Under the guidance of the Liberator they had been led out of the penal era and set free from their depressing and demoralising past. Their self-respect and self-confidence were restored. They now realised (like the Confederates in the 1640s) that they formed the largest single grouping in Ireland, and that if they continued to act in unison and press for full majority rights, there was no end to what they might accomplish. It was only a short step from this feeling to the belief that it was they *and they alone* who constituted the true 'Irish nation'.

The Gaelic Nation: 'Irish Ireland'

During the period 1870-1914 there were two more developments which not only seemed to confirm the Catholic-Irish identification, but which added a new dimension to it. First of all, nationalist aspirations rapidly progressed to the forefront of the political arena, both in Ireland and at Westminster. Irish self-government became the most burning political issue of the day, and nationalist politicians were constantly at work pressing home their demands and hammering out a solution to the Irish question. But not all Irishmen supported the demand for self-government; indeed, some of them were passionately opposed to it. It seemed to many nationalists that, in denying Ireland's right to nationhood, such men had forfeited their right to belong to the Irish nation. Indeed, it was even argued that, since they were bent on promoting British interests in Ireland, they had no right to call themselves Irishmen at all. Virtually all the Unionist anti-Home Rulers were Protestant Anglo-Irishmen and Ulster Scots, and by redefining them merely as expatriate 'Englishmen' and 'Scots' respectively, nationalists introduced a negative, exclusive racial element into their definition of the 'Irish people' and thus struck another blow at Thomas Davis's theory.

The second development enabled many Irishmen to assert their nationality in a more positive way. It took the form of a great 'cultural revolution' which emphasised every characteristic which contributed a unique and distinctive quality to Irish life and civilisation. Ireland became the breeding-ground of a new spirit, of new doctrines and new organisations. They seemed to fill a vacuum and contained the ripening forces of future political action. The basic assertion of this new nationalism was that Ireland was racially and culturally different from every other nation — particularly the English nation — and that therefore, the Irish people were capable of and entitled to complete autonomy and independent self-government. This new kind of thinking was by no means a peculiarly Irish phenomenon. Similar movements were being experienced in Bismarck's Germany and in several other eastern European countries at this time. Even in Ireland the birth of cultural nationalism owed a good deal to the enthusiasm of the Irish in America.

The resurgence of national consciousness was not simply a matter of 'politics' — whether Sinn Féin, Home Rule or revolutionary separatism. Political nationalists became aware that their thinking must undergo a transformation at the very deepest level — that political independance was worthless unless it was accompanied by an authentic independence of mind and spirit and by a full realisation of the essential 'Irishness' which determined their own and their nation's identity. This new mode of thought exalted the concept of a free and honourable Gaelic nation and found its fullest expression in the philosophy of 'Irish Ireland'.

'Irish Ireland' was not an organisation, nor was it a national movement except perhaps in the very widest sense of the term. It was a stimulating doctrine which attempted to reveal the hidden sources from which the lifeforce of true Irish nationality should spring. Under its inspiring influence many new organisations and movements were set in action with the object of forging a new Irish nation in which perfect Gaelic culture and civilisation would flourish and in which the rights and dignity of its members would be upheld. All aspects of human endeavour were employed for this purpose: social, cultural, economic, political and military. (The principal organisations and movements which were influenced by 'Irish Ireland' ideas are described in the remainder of this chapter.) In insisting on the essentially *Gaelic* nature of the nation, the 'Irish Ireland' philosophy was clearly based on racialism.

An idealised version of Gaelic civilisation was also promoted; by the early twentieth century many Irishmen were making a conscious effort to spend much of their leisure time in what they believed was the traditional Gaelic manner: their sports and pastimes, their speech, even their clothes reflected this new trend, and peasants in the depressed areas of the west, who were commonly supposed to represent the traditional Gaelic way of life in its purest form, suddenly found that they had become objects of extraordinary interest.

The philosophy of 'Irish Ireland' found its cleverest and most forceful champion in D. P. Moran, a brilliant journalist whose career extended from the 1890s to the 1930s. In a long series of skillfully argued articles in his famous weekly journal, *The Leader,* Moran effectively demolished Thomas Davis's vision of the Irish nation. Unlike most other nationalists, Moran was not afraid to follow his ideas through to their logical conclusion or to face the more unpleasant aspects of his theories. He had no qualms at all about his essentially racialist approach: 'The foundation of Ireland is the Gael,' he declared, 'and the Gael must be the element that absorbs.' All those who were descended from immigrants or colonists from Britain in the seven centuries since Strongbow's invasion were thus excluded from the Irish nation unless they had clearly been 'absorbed' in this way. Protestant Anglo-Irishmen, in particular, had no right to call themselves Irishmen: instead Moran dubbed them 'West Britons', alien interlopers who were trying to foist their debased culture on the Irish people. It is highly significant that Moran's sharpest invectives were directed not against Orangemen or absentee landlords, but against those Anglo-Irishmen like Parnell or Sir Horace Plunkett who had become involved in public life or who worked to advance the nationalist cause. The Irish nation, Moran maintained, must rid itself of the corrupting influence of these men. Moran also condemned Irishmen who showed no patent evidence of their nationalism, denouncing them as 'shoneens', renegades and Castle Catholics.

The Gaelic Athletic Association

In the early nineteenth century every European country — including Ireland — had its own traditional sports and pastimes which were practised with a great deal of enthusiasm but in an extremely haphazard and disorganised manner. During the course of the century, however, Europeans began to take sport much more seriously. Elaborate rules were drafted for each game, local clubs and nation-wide leagues and associations were established, proper sports grounds were laid out, and in many prestigious schools and colleges athletic ability was valued as highly as academic ability. This minor revolution was particularly thorough in England, affecting every level of society from the upper-class public schools to the industrial towns of the north. It brought about a 'cult of athleticism' which glorified physical health and strength and 'team spirit'.

These new developments made their way from England to Ireland. But they affected only the sports and games of English origin, which were carried on in Ireland by the Anglo-Irish gentry and the police and military of the British 'garrison'. Traditional Irish games, such as hurling, Gaelic football, handball, hammer-throwing and stone-casting, were still played up and down the country by the ordinary people, though the informal matches were frequently disorderly and sometimes led to faction-fights.

There was no central body to control discipline, organise competitions and draw up rules and regulations. By the 1870s there was a growing tendency for Irishmen to take up the English games made popular by the 'garrison' and organised according to the rules of the Irish Amateur Athletic Associations, an Anglo-Irish body dedicated to maintaining English standards. Interest in Ireland's national sports began to decline, and it seemed that they were in danger of dying out altogether. Furthermore, some Irishmen who wanted to play the 'garrison' games found themselves faced with a social problem. Many of the clubs were exclusive and snobbish bodies which maintained that organised sport was a recreation fit only for gentlemen: they refused to consider admitting working-class members.

It became clear that what was needed was a second nation-wide organisation which, by bringing unity and order into traditional Irish sport, would help to revive it. By encouraging its members to take a pride in their national sporting heritage, it would also instil a sense of cultural superiority which would balance that of the amateur Anglo-Irish cricketers and rugby-players, who were, according to *United Ireland* in November 1884, 'people hostile to the dearest aspirations of the Irish people'. With these ends in view, a group of interested sportsmen met in Thurles on 1 November 1884 to found the Gaelic Athletic Association, a purely Irish-based and Irish-controlled body. While the GAA was the brain-child of Michael Cusack and P. W. Nally, the principal members of the founding committee were Michael Cusack, Maurice Davin and J. K. Bracken. In order to give the new association some kind of status, Cusack invited Parnell and Davitt to act as patrons, along with the nationalist archbishop of Cashel, T. W. Croke. Croke was particularly enthusiastic about the new association, keeping a careful watch over its progress and helping to settle many of the disputes that troubled its early years.

The success of the GAA surpassed its founders' wildest dreams. Within an amazingly short time it spread through the south and west of Ireland. It was Ireland's first popular cultural organisation, and no subsequent movement exceeded it in size, and few have inspired such dedication and enthusiasm among their members and supporters. In a number of important ways it had a tremendous impact on the life of the nation during the thirty years 1884-1914.

First of all, the GAA acted as a de-anglicising force by its determined effort to sponsor native Irish games and discourage English games. It furthered the idea of separateness and showed Irishmen that in their physical recreation and sports they could assert their 'Irishness' and at the same time express their disapproval of English games. It applied the principle of the boycott to sport, rigidly banning two groups of people from its membership: the RIC and soldiers who comprised the security forces of the 'garrison' and any Irishmen who played — or even watched — English games. The GAA had no use for 'shoneens' who believed in a mingling of cultures; it thus fostered a spirit of exclusive elitism as surely as the sports clubs of the Anglo-Irish ascendancy. While this undoubtedly preserved the purity of the Gaelic tradition, it also nurtured divisions within Irish society as a whole.

Secondly, the GAA helped to build up a healthy and vigorous Irish manhood. In glorifying physical prowess, it gave greater currency to the idea that physical force might be used to achieve desired objectives. In many ways athletic training was identical with military drill, and, in common with similar athletic movements in England, France and Germany, the GAA established a strong connection between organised sport and militarism. It gave the young men of Ireland a feeling that they belonged to a vigorous and disciplined body through which they could express their loyalty and patriotism. In 1891 two thousand hurlers formed a guard of honour at Parnell's funeral, shouldering their hurleys like rifles and marching in military formation through Dublin. The authorities in Dublin Castle were aware of the quasi-military atmosphere of the association, and were extremely concerned about it.

These two characteristics of the GAA led directly to a third. The IRB realised that this nation-wide association of healthy young men dedicated to nationalist ideals was a potential recruiting-ground for their republican army. In fact it might even be said that this was one of the reasons for the association's establishment in the first place, for four of those on the seven-member founding committee were Fenians. Its ranks were infiltrated by Fenians from the very start, and by 1887 they had taken over almost complete control of the organisation. Trusted GAA members were sworn into the IRB, and in later years large numbers of Irish Volunteers were enlisted through the GAA branches. Many of those who fought in the Easter Rising had first learned to drill in the hurling or football clubs. Thus the GAA acted as a kind of bridge between the Fenianism of the 1867 tradition and the new IRB movement which planned and engineered the 1916 Rising.

Fourthly, by basing its club organisation on parish and county units the GAA gave birth to a new local spirit in rural Ireland. It acted as a major revitalising force in localities which were suffering from the acute social depression resulting from famine, emigration, eviction and agrarian distress. Thanks to the GAA, a new focus was given for local enthusiasm and for pride in one's county or parish; the local curate was often the chief sponsor, manager or coach of the parish team. The GAA thus helped to give a new lease of life to the almost moribund Irish countryside.

Finally, the association was one of the first great democratic movements in modern times, completely controlled by Irishmen and extending its appeal throughout the entire nationalist population. The GAA was constantly in the public eye. Its matches and meetings were fully reported in local and national newspapers and became topics for much discussion. Unlike most nationalist organisations, it required no great sacrifices on the part of its members and supporters. It was both easy and enjoyable to express one's patriotism by playing football or hurling or by supporting one's local team. By attending the exciting All-Ireland Final one could feel that one was participating in the most important regular national event of the year; the finals themselves became occasions for massive ritual displays of nationalist fervour and emotion. The overwhelming success and popularity of the GAA seemed to show that, once the dead wood (in the shape of the 'garrison' and the 'shoneens') had been cut away, the Irish nation could be seen as a vibrant and potent force, deriving immense strength and vitality from the united allegiance of its members.

The Gaelic League

At the beginning of the nineteenth century there were between two and three million native Irish speakers. But during the course of the century, there was a gradual decline of Irish as a spoken language. This was due to a combination of several factors. (1) English was the language spoken in most of the towns and cities; it was the language of pulpit, platform and parliament, of politics, commerce and progress. Many people felt that Irish was an antiquated survival in a modern world and that it had outlived its usefulness. The most prominent native Irish speaker in nineteenth-century Ireland was Daniel O'Connell, yet he too turned his back on it and used his great influence to promote the spread of English, saying: 'Although the Irish language is connected with the many recollections that twine around the hearts of Irishmen, yet the superior utility of the English tongue, as the medium of all modern communication, is so great that I can witness without a sigh the gradual disuse of the Irish language.' Irish came to be associated with the economically backward, poverty-stricken peasant communities of the west. If anyone from such a background wanted to better his condition in life, the first thing he had to do was to break away from his environment and learn English. Many native speakers became ashamed of their language and compelled their sons and daughters to learn and speak English for their own good. (2) Stanley's Education Act (1831) stipulated that all teaching in the newly-established National Schools should be done through the medium of English. (3) The Great Famine and the subsequent wave of emigration fell heaviest on the Irish-speaking districts, so that the population there declined more rapidly than elsewhere. (4) There was virtually no printing in Irish. The printed word, in newspapers, books and all public notices and signposts, came to the people in English. (5) English was required for all jobs which offered good prospects, especially in the civil service. (6) There was no adequate attempt to encourage bilingualism.

Yet there were several people who had an enthusiastic interest in the Irish language. But until the final decades of the nineteenth century the majority of these men were scholars who studied Irish in much the same way as they might have studied Latin or Greek. The work of such scholars as John O'Donovan and Eugene O'Curry was concentrated on ancient Irish literature and was carried on mainly under the auspices of the Royal Irish Academy and Trinity College.

There were others who were more interested in Irish as a living, spoken language of everyday life and who worked hard to prevent its extinction. They believed that a native tongue was one of the chief badges of a national identity, and that if Ireland was to be truly a nation, the Irish language must be revived throughout the whole country. Thomas Davis maintained: 'A people without a language of its own is only half a nation. A nation should guard its language more than its territories — 'tis a surer barrier, a more important frontier, than mountain or river.' This view was also held by the early Fenians, who actually made an attempt to start Irish classes among their supporters. John Devoy said: 'The intention to restore the language was as strong among the Fenians as that of establishing an Irish Republic.'

The work of two men in particular in the second half of the nineteenth century gave an added incentive to the restoration of the Irish language. One of these was Douglas Hyde (1863-1949), who was reared at Frenchpark, Co. Roscommon, where his father was the local Protestant rector. A fluent Irish speaker, Hyde believed that if a new Ireland was ever to be constructed, the Irish language must be considered one of 'the bricks of nationality'. In an important lecture delivered in 1892, entitled 'The Necessity for de-Anglicising Ireland', Hyde urged Irishmen to stop aping English manners and customs. His fellow-worker was Eóin Mac Néill (1867-1945), who was born in Co. Antrim, and became an Irish scholar as well as an internationally renowned authority on early Irish history. He appealed to the young men of Ireland 'to strike a blow for Irish' by speaking it, and 'if you cannot learn it, you can at least stand up for it'. It was Mac Néill who suggested to his friend, Hyde, that they establish a Gaelic League to help revive interest in the Irish language.

The Gaelic League was established in Dublin on 31 July 1893, with Hyde as its first president and Mac Néill as vice-president. Its fundamental principle was the uniting of all Irishmen in a love for the native language of their country. Its own main objectives were (1) the preservation of Irish as the national language of Ireland and the extension of its use as a spoken tongue, and (2) the study and publication of existing Gaelic literature and the cultivation of a modern literature in Irish. Hyde and Mac Néill were soon helped by a third Irish enthusiast, Father Eugene O'Growney (1863-1899), the editor of the *Gaelic Journal.* Father O'Growney was Professor of Irish at Maynooth College, and his *Simple Lessons in Irish,* as well as his other publications, proved invaluable to the Gaelic League.

Hyde had no interest in politics, maintaining that Ireland's cultural regeneration was far more important than Home Rule or separatism or any other political creed. Under his influence the Gaelic League was declared to be a non-political and non-denominational body, and in its early years it numbered several Anglo-Irish Unionists among its members. Within twenty years it had spread throughout the whole of Ireland, while branches were also established in Britain, America, Australia and New Zealand. The success of the League was due mainly to the dedicated workers who acted as organisers. By 1900 the League had a force of twenty full-time organisers or *timirí*. The *timire's* job was to address meetings, teach classes in Irish and share his enthusiasm for the Irish language with all those with whom he came into contact. These *timirí* travelled about the countryside on bicycles and were often referred to as 'men on wheels'. One of the most famous was Tomás Bán Ó Cohchenainn, a native of Inishmaan in the Aran Islands. Through its organisers the Gaelic League stirred up a great enthusiasm for learning Irish; by the early twentieth century it had become almost a craze. The League's impact was greatest in the towns and cities; it was less strongly supported in the rural areas.

The League established its first college for the training of teachers of Irish at Ballingeary in 1903. By 1915 there were nineteen such colleges, and they had about 2,000 students. The Gaelic League provided one of the most extensive and successful schemes of adult education in Ireland; they were also pioneers in new language techniques. From 1898 on they published a weekly bilingual journal *An Claidheamh Soluis*, edited by Eóin Mac Néill.

In 1897 the League held an all-Ireland *Oireachtas*, or festival of Irish culture, which became an annual event. Prizes were offered for Irish speaking, writing, dancing, music etc. The League also sponsored local *feiseanna*, mainly held on a provincial or county basis. The success of the League is seen from the statistics of its membership and the number of its branches. By 1908 there were about 600 branches in Ireland.

One of the objects of the League was to encourage the teaching of Irish in the schools. In 1893 less than 1,000 students were taught Irish in the National Schools throughout the whole country. The Irish Christian Brothers proved very successful and enthusiastic teachers of Irish. (Among their pupils was Pádraic Pearse, who became one of the leading figures in the Gaelic League and eventually editor of *An Claidheamh Soluis* from 1903 to 1909.) By 1910, thanks to the Gaelic League, over 50,000 children were learning the language, and in 1909 the League eventually succeeded in having Irish used in the new National University and made an essential subject for matriculation to it.

The League sponsored the writing and producing of Irish plays. The first Irish play staged under its auspices was called *Tadg Saor*, written by An tAthair Peadar Ua Laoghaire. Hyde's play *Casadh an tSúgáin* was first performed at the Gaiety Theatre, Dublin, in 1901. It was through the League's influence that from 1903 St Patrick's Day was observed as a general holiday in Ireland. It also organised the first national parade in Dublin on St Patrick's Day. Thanks to its campaign in 1905, the GPO was forced to accept mail addressed in Irish, an incident which became known as 'the Battle of the GPO'.

Like most of the cultural movements in Ireland at this time, the Gaelic League was infiltrated by members of the IRB. P. H. Pearse, who was himself recruited into the IRB in 1913, stated publicly in 1914: 'We never meant to be Gaelic Leaguers and nothing more than Gaelic Leaguers.' He looked upon the founding of the Irish Volunteers in 1913 as being 'the second phase in the revolution which the Gaelic League had initiated', but which it could never by itself accomplish. Sean Mac Diarmada, Tom Clarke and other Gaelic Leaguers began to consider the possibility of amending the League's constitution. Their chance came at the Ard-Fheis in Dundalk in July 1915, when it was proposed that the Gaelic League 'shall devote itself to realising the ideal of a Gaelic-speaking and independent Irish nation, free from all subjection to foreign influence'. Hyde resigned his presidency in protest, as he could not accept the political overtones in the phrase 'an independent Irish-speaking nation'. Mac Néill was elected president in his place.

By the beginning of 1916 the League was more than a mere vehicle of a language revival movement and had turned its energies into working for a free and independent Ireland. Its new watchword, 'Ireland not free only, but Gaelic as well; not Gaelic only, but free as well', showed how completely it had rejected Hyde's original idea of involving all sections of society in a love for the language, accepting instead the narrower 'Irish Ireland' definition of Irish nationality. The League was thus one of the major stepping-stones on the road to the 1916 Rising. The majority of those who fought in the Easter Rising were members of the Gaelic League. Indeed, some of the Easter rebels, such as Éamon de Valera, were at that time far more interested in the Irish language than in Irish independence.

The Literary Revival

The political aspects of the remarkable literary renaissance which began towards the end of the nineteenth century are extremely significant. The renaissance made a vitally important contribution to the awakening of national consciousness which was occurring at the same time. Ireland already had a considerable reputation for the fine literature in the English language which had been produced by Anglo-Irish writers such as Swift, Goldsmith, Sheridan, Burke, Charles Lever and Maria Edgeworth, or, in later years, Oscar Wilde and Bernard Shaw. However, the group of late nineteenth-century writers, although they came from the same Anglo-Irish stock and produced literature of equally high quality, were different in one important respect. Their work was inspired by a deep love for their country; it was essentially Irish, both in subject matter and interpretation; and as well as being *of Ireland*, it was *for Ireland*.

Most of the Anglo-Irish writers were not directly concerned with political nationalism, though some of them may have had separatist sympathies, and the most renowned of them, W. B. Yeats, was influenced by the old Fenian leader John O'Leary and was even for a time a member of an IRB circle. Many of the themes of their poetry, stories and plays were taken from the ancient past. Drawing on Ireland's rich treasury of legend and saga, they portrayed a noble and heroic civilisation to which its posterity in a less glorious age could look back with pride. They also shared the interest of the Gaelic 'Irish Irelanders' in the old traditional culture which was still to be found in the west of Ireland. Dramas based on Irish folktales or depicting the way of life of the peasantry formed a significant part of the Abbey Theatre's repertoire.

Yeats, Synge, Lady Gregory and the other Abbey playwrights and writers of the literary revival were not only inspired by a sense of Irish nationality; they also inspired it in others. They created a vision of an Ireland which had once been a great and illustrious nation and which would, by a process of spiritual regeneration, be great again. In Yeats's play *Cathleen Ní Houlihan* (1902), Ireland was symbolically personified as an old woman who is rejuvenated into a beautiful young girl 'with the walk of a queen' and who urges her brave young men to take up arms on her behalf. This play aroused the deepest emotions of patriotic fervour in its audiences, and many years after 1916 Yeats was to ask himself:

> Did that play of mine send out
> Certain men the English shot?

In spite of all this, the literary revival was not really a part of the 'Irish Ireland' movement. In the first place, the majority of the writers were Protestant Anglo-Irishmen, a fact which effectively excluded them from the narrow 'Gaelic and Catholic' definition of the Irish nation. 'Irish Irelanders' were profoundly suspicious of such people and angrily questioned their right to act as the intellectual mentors of the people. Secondly their literary output was entirely in the English language: this offended 'Gaelic' purists, who deplored the idea of a literature which could be Irish in inspiration and English in expression. Finally, all the writers of the revival were determined to maintain their individual artistic integrity: they refused to employ their talents merely for the purpose of serving the cause of nationalism. They wanted freedom to express life as they saw it, freedom to write as they pleased.

These aspects of the revival brought the Abbey playwrights, in particular, into conflict with advanced nationalists of the 'Gaelic and Catholic' tradition. Yeats's play *The Countess Cathleen* (1899), which describes how a noblewoman sells her soul to save her people from famine, appeared to strict Catholic sensibilities to be a blasphemous glorification of spiritual 'souperism'. D. P. Moran denounced it as 'one of the most glaring frauds that the Irish people have ever swallowed'. J. M. Synge, who, like most of the Anglo-Irish writers, had strong connections with the west of Ireland

and an intimate understanding of its people, also fell foul of the 'Irish Irelanders' when he attempted to present a realistic picture of peasant life as he knew it. His plays *In the Shadow of the Glen* (1903) and *The Playboy of the Western World* (1907) showed that Irish peasants could be just as selfish, brutal and immoral as city dwellers — or even Englishmen. This contrasted sharply with the idealised image of the Irish peasant which was so dear to the hearts of the 'Irish Irelanders'. Nationalists of his tradition found Synge's play's grossly offensive, and the first performances of *The Playboy* were accompanied by riots in the theatre, and during the play's American tour John Devoy interrupted a performance by jumping to his feet, cursing and swearing at the actors and shouting 'That's not Irish!' Thus did the voice of Gaelic Ireland raise its protest at the presumption of those Anglo-Irishmen who dared to bring the Irish people face to face with themselves.

Sinn Féin: The First Phase

As the nineteenth century drew to a close, a number of factors and events helped to instil a spirit of self-reliance into the hearts of many Irish people. First of all, there was the celebration of the centenary of 1798, which revived the ideas of Wolfe Tone and the United Irishmen. Anyone who reads through the mass of papers in Dublin Castle for the year 1898, will realise that this was a difficult year for the government, with trouble coming from all quarters. Secondly, the Local Government Act of 1898 (see page 57) gave Irishmen their first real taste of governing themselves. It was not such a great step from looking after their own affairs at county level, to aspiring to rule themselves at national level. Thirdly, the Boer War (1899-1901) in which some Irishmen fought on the side of the Boers against the British, gave Irish nationalists a chance to express their anti-English feelings. It also served as an opportunity to take a few practice shots at the English, in preparation for the day when Ireland would rise in arms against England. Finally, both the parliamentary campaign for Home Rule and the revolutionary conspiracy to establish a republic had fallen on very hard times in the 1890s. The Irish Party seemed unable to recover from the Parnell split, while the IRB seemed to be a spent force, committed to an impossible objective, which was, in any case, too extreme for the average Irishman. Many disillusioned nationalists were ready to consider alternative versions of Irish independence, to discuss alternative strategies and to adopt new modes of thought. Out of all this there emerged a movement for Irish independence, called Sinn Féin, which expressed and fostered a new spirit of nationalism.

Arthur Griffith (1871-1922), the founder of Sinn Féin, was born in Dublin. He worked for a short time as a printer, but in 1896, owing to a trade depression, he emigrated to South Africa. While there he organised the Irish Transvaal Society to celebrate the centenary of 1798. Soon afterwards he returned to Dublin and in partnership with his friend Willie Rooney, started a newspaper called the *United Irishman*. Money for the paper came from Clan na Gael, and its political slant was expressed in a leading article: 'We accept the nationalism of '98, '48, and '67 as the true nationalism'.

Griffith's privately-held political views differed from his publicly advocated policies. His personal preference was for complete separatism, even republicanism; in fact he joined the IRB and remained a member until about 1910. But he knew that these ideals did not command widespread support, and he also realised that moral force was a more potent and effective weapon than physical force. He therefore worked out a compromise between the Home Rule and IRB positions which he hoped would win greater public acceptance.

What Griffith proposed was that the Irish MPs should simply withdraw from Westminster and refuse to co-operate with the British government. The Irish people should then elect a Council of Three Hundred to act on their behalf and to take over control of the newly-established county councils. In this way the national ideal of 'an Irish state, governed by Irishmen for the benefit of the Irish people' could be quickly and effectively achieved, and Griffith was convinced that once the British government was confronted with this *fait accompli*, it would accept that it no longer possessed a mandate in Ireland and would peacefully withdraw. The constitutional arrangement between Ireland and Great Britain which had operated in the time of Grattan's parliament (1782-1800) could then be restored: the country would be governed by the King, Lords and Commons of Ireland, the link between the two countries being preserved through the crown alone. Griffith hoped that his advocacy of the principle of a dual monarchy would help him in persuading the more moderate Home Rulers to adopt moral force methods. Perhaps the most attractive aspect of the whole operation was that in winning her national independence for herself Ireland would recover her self-respect: she would be truly a nation once again — through her bold initiative, not as a result of servile and undignified begging at Westminster by 'a body of green-liveried henchmen of the British connection'. In order to prove that such a programme was feasible, Griffith pointed to the example of the Hungarians who in the 1860s had walked out of the Austrian imperial parliament in Vienna; in 1867 they had secured recognition from Austria as part of a constitutional settlement known as the *Ausgleich*, which established a dual monarchy for Austria and Hungary. In 1904 Griffith outlined his proposals in a pamphlet entitled *The Resurrection of Hungary*, which had a very wide circulation.

Griffith did not limit his plans to the achievement of political independence, but also proposed an economic programme for Ireland, involving the development of Irish industries behind a barrier of protective tariffs. A self-governing Ireland would thus be free from foreign — especially British — competition and would be able to utilise its natural resources for its own benefit so that the country would eventually become as self-sufficient as possible. He urged Irish businessmen not to invest in British enterprises but to put their money to work in Ireland to produce a buoyant home economy. In all this, Griffith was following the principles outlined by the German economist Friedrich List in a book called *National System of Protection*. Griffith had observed the industrial revolution achieved in Bismarck's Germany and the role which protectionism had played in this revolution. Although Ireland was an agricultural country, Griffith did not think it should be satisfied with being a merely agricultural economy. He saw the good work being done by Sir Horace Plunkett's co-operative movement, but he felt that Ireland must develop industries to survive in the twentieth century.

In 1900 Griffith founded Cumann na Gaedheal (not to be confused with the political party of the same name founded in 1923), a loosely-knit umbrella organisation advocating a wide range of cultural objectives and aiming in general 'to advance the cause of Irish independence by cultivating a fraternal spirit among Irishmen'. It promoted a 'buy Irish' campaign and translated the Gaelic League's de-anglicisation doctrine into economic terms. In 1903 Griffith set up another organisation, the National Council, whose original purpose was to protest against the visit of Edward VII to Ireland but which was kept in existence after the royal visit. The National Council served as a nationalist talking-shop where the members of various small societies could meet and exchange their views. It attracted many of the leading intellectuals of the time, among them W. B. Yeats, Maud Gonne and Edward Martyn — its first chairman — and also a number of Fenians.

Fenians were also behind a new network of societies, known as Dungannon Clubs, in the north of Ireland. The first of these were established in 1905 by two energetic young members of the IRB, Bulmer Hobson and Denis McCullough. Their objective was 'to educate the Irish people in the principles of independence' on a non-sectarian basis. Although the clubs were not secret organisations and were set up independently of the IRB, they embraced the fundamental IRB principles of full separatism and republicanism. Unlike Griffith, they had no wish to revive Grattan's parliament, and they had no use at all for the concept of a dual monarchy. However, some of their ideas, such as an Irish secession from Westminster, the value of moral force, and the importance of industrial growth, had remarkably close parallels in Griffith's thinking. It is not surprising, therefore, that the two groups of societies, centred in Belfast and Dublin, were drawn towards each other.

At a convention of the National Council held on 28 November 1905, Griffith elaborated his proposals in a comprehensive policy statement. The phrase 'Sinn Féin' (meaning 'ourselves') was suggested by Máire Butler, a Gaelic Leaguer, as a suitable name for the new brand of nationalism, and it was also proposed to bring all the independent clubs and societies under one organisation. By 1908 the amalgamation of Cumann na nGaedheal, the National Council, the Dungannon Clubs and many other nationalist groups was completed, and the name Sinn Féin was given to the newly-incorporated organisation. John Sweetman was elected first president, with Griffith and Hobson vice-presidents. Other prominent members were Seán Mac Diarmada, W. T. Cosgrave, Seán T. O'Kelly and the Countess Markievicz. A constitution was drawn up, asserting that the main object of Sinn Féin was 'the re-establishment of the independence of Ireland ... the creation of a prosperous, virile and independent nation'. The importance of de-anglicisation was stressed: 'Our declared objective,' said Griffith, 'was to make England take one hand away from Ireland's throat and the other out of Ireland's pocket.' Appended to the constitution was a fifteen-point programme outlining the practical steps by which Ireland's political independence and economic prosperity might be secured: protection for industry and commerce; the development of mineral resources; the establishment of a consular service, a mercantile marine, a national bank and stock exchange, a civil service, arbitration courts, and a national insurance system; control of transport, waste lands and fisheries, reform of education and the poor law; non-consumption of articles paying duty to the British exchequer; withdrawal of voluntary support to the British armed forces; and non-recognition of the British parliament.

Almost at once an opportunity arose for Sinn Féin to turn itself into a political party and put its policies to the test of public opinion. In 1908, C. J. Dolan, a disillusioned Home Rule MP, resigned his North Leitrim seat and contested it again on a Sinn Féin platform. He polled a quarter of the votes — quite a creditable performance for a newly-formed party, though the votes cast probably represented personal support for Dolan, who was well known and well liked in his old constituency. But in fact the North Leitrim by-election marked the high-water mark of Sinn Féin's appeal in its first phase (1908-16). The little movement thereafter ran into difficulties and its progress was marred by four particular problems.

First of all there was Griffith's personality. He was a very difficult man to get on with. He fought with Hyde over the place of the Irish language in the national struggle, and with W. B. Yeats on the role which the National Theatre should play in modern Ireland. He likewise fought with James Larkin, fearing lest the trade union movement would kill the country's struggling industry and trade. Griffith was jealous of D. P. Moran, whose newspaper *The Leader* was more successful than his own *United Irishman* (renamed *Sinn Féin* in 1906). As P. H. Pearse once wrote to him, chiding him on this matter: 'You were too hard. You were too obstinate. You were too narrow-minded. You were too headstrong. You did not trust your friends enough. You preferred to prove to the world that no one else was right except yourself.' Griffith conceived an inexplicable loathing for some of the people who were trying to work with him, such as the Countess Markievicz. In short, he was the very last man to make a success of leading a co-ordinating umbrella movement which aimed to reconcile different facets of nationalism and which relied on the goodwill of a wide variety of people.

The second difficulty was caused by this specifically 'umbrella' quality of Sinn Féin. Griffith attempted to make his ideas attractive to the broadest possible spectrum of nationalist opinion. But in thus co-ordinating support, it was impossible to co-ordinate the ideals of a dual monarchy and an Irish republic, Grattan's parliament and complete separatism. Sinn Féin's official pronouncements were, therefore, couched in vague and ambiguous terms; it seemed to be too theoretical, too hesitant about declaring its basic standpoint, and too reluctant to face up to a number of important issues. Like Parnell, Griffith attempted to harness the forces of different nationalist traditions; unlike Parnell, he was essentially a propagandist, not a skilful political manipulator.

Thirdly, the two moribund nationalist movements from which Sinn Féin hoped to wean support for its own alternative policy both began to take on a new lease of life at about the very time of Sinn Féin's foundation. In the years after 1906 the IRB was undergoing a process of revitalisation (see below), and while it was not its policy actively to oppose different versions of nationalism, it remained totally committed to its objective of achieving an Irish republic by force of arms. Sinn Féin was increasingly infiltrated by IRB members who used it as a facade behind which they could secretly work to their own ends. Griffith seemed unaware of the activities of this element within his group, thus making it easy for the IRB to build up a hard core of physical-force nationalism within Griffith's moral-force movement. Furthermore, the Irish Parliamentary Party also staged a dramatic comeback after 1909 and seemed at last to be on the point of winning its long-sought-for objective (see page 57-62). To most Irishmen it seemed thoroughly absurd at this juncture to ask the Irish MPs, as Griffith did, to withdraw from Westminster: Home Rule in the hand was worth more than any amount of moral force or visionary *Ausgleichs* in the bush.

Finally, the struggling movement encountered severe financial difficulties. Griffith's attempt to turn *Sinn Féin* into a daily paper in 1900-10 was a costly and discouraging failure, draining the organisation of its much needed funds.

As a result of these drawbacks. Sinn Féin was condemned to remain a minority movement operating on the sidelines of the Irish political scene. In fact the only really successful thing about Sinn Féin was its name. Griffith continued to preach his doctrines and thus kept the catchy title of his organisation constantly before the Irish public. 'Sinn Féin' became a household phrase, although few people bothered to find out what ideas lay behind it. More significant still, the name caught on in Dublin Castle, whose authorities were apt to describe *all* active nationalists as 'Shinners'. This development, revealing nothing more than the colossal ignorance of the government about what was going on in Ireland, was in itself unimportant before 1916. But when the Irish Volunteers were dubbed the 'Sinn Féin Army' and the Easter Rising the 'Sinn Féin rebellion' to achieve a 'Sinn Féin republic', Griffith and his friends suddenly found themselves in the curious position of having been catapulted into the forefront of active militant nationalism. They were popularly credited with a strength and power which they had never commanded, and with ideas and aims which they not only had never held but had actually gone to considerable pains to repudiate.

The Revived IRB

Ever since the English dynamite campaign of the 1880s the IRB had experienced a long and slow decline. Despite a brief revival of interest in republicanism during the Wolfe Tone centenary celebrations in 1898, no new blood had been recruited into the organisation, and by the turn of the century its members had become a sluggish and pathetic group of ageing 'armchair republicans', many of whom were habitual drunkards. In all the years of its existence the IRB had achieved absolutely nothing; the Irish republic to which its members had sworn allegiance was still no more than a shadowy phantom, and no one seemed to have any constructive plans for bringing it into existence.

The early years of the twentieth century, however, witnessed the start of an internal revolution during which the old lethargic leadership was gradually replaced by a group of activists. The people responsible for this were (with one important exception) all young men, and most of them were from Ulster. The first of these was Denis McCullough, the son of a Belfast publican, who was sworn into the IRB by his father in 1901. In 1904 McCullough in turn swore in his friend and fellow-Belfastman, Bulmer Hobson. The two young men agreed that the organisation needed a thorough overhauling. They devoted their considerable energies to purging the inactive older members, (McCullough even going so far as to get rid of his own father) and replacing them with carefully selected young enthusiasts, such as Dr Pat McCartan of Co. Tyrone, P. S. O'Hegarty of Dublin and Major John MacBride of Westport, Co. Mayo.

The most important of the new recruits was Seán Mac Diarmada of Co. Leitrim, who joined in 1906 and who proved to be a dedicated worker and organiser with an infinite capacity for intrigue and internal power-politics — qualities which by 1916 had enabled him to become the guiding brain behind the extreme revolutionary element of the IRB. In the meantime, against great opposition from the cautious older members, Mac Diarmada in 1910 succeeded in launching a newspaper, *Irish Freedom,* in which militantly republican views were openly expressed. Hobson and O'Hegarty, both accomplished journalists, were the principal contributors to this paper.

The prestige of the group of IRB activists soared in 1907, when one of the 'old men' of the Fenian movement returned from America and wholeheartedly threw in his lot with them. Tom Clarke had served fifteen years in jail for dynamiting activities, but, unlike his contemporaries, his fiery fanaticism and his eagerness for action were as strong as ever. His link with the Fenian past, his contacts with Irish-American Fenians and his inspiring enthusiasm were great advantages to the revitalised IRB. Clarke struck up a particularly strong friendship with Mac Diarmada and eagerly fell in with all the latter's ideas and schemes; this partnership was to have momentous consequences in later years when the two men between them effectively exercised complete control over the IRB and the Irish Volunteers.

Gradually the influence of the militant new generation permeated the entire IRB and within a few years had penetrated its highest ranks. Whenever a vacancy occurred on the Supreme Council, the progressives saw to it that it was filled by one of themselves. By 1915 the three most important posts on the Supreme Council, comprising the Directory or Standing Executive which ran the general affairs of the IRB were occupied by McCullough, Clarke and Mac Diarmada. The revived IRB, numbering no more than 2,000 members but infused with a vital new spirit, stood poised and alert, ready to seize any new opportunity that might present itself, whether in the shape of a new organisation or a fresh turn of events, and exploit it to their own advantage.

The Connolly-Larkin Labour Movement

Working-class Dublin

Visitors to Dublin at the end of the nineteenth century remarked on the extent of its slums and the poverty and misery of the working classes. It was inevitable that some effort should be made to introduce social reform into Ireland. All over Europe the proletariat was beginning to assert its rights, and even in faraway Russia, Lenin was soon to make his voice heard, demanding justice for the workers. The industrial revolutions in Germany, France and America had created a situation where the workers were being exploited and were seeking redress through their trade unions. Ireland, too, needed trade unions and labour leaders.

The working-class formed the great majority of the population of Dublin. In 1901 out of the 40,000 male labour force, over 7,000 were 'carriers' or carters, 23,000 were labourers, and the rest – only 25 per cent – were employed in skilled labour. There was a demand for skilled labour in the building trade, in tailoring, cabinet-making, etc., but most of the other jobs available called for no particular skill or qualification. Unemployment varied from year to year and season to season, but it averaged about 20 per cent. As there were always more workers than work available, and as most unskilled labour in Dublin was employed on a casual rather than a permanent basis, the workers were in no position to bargain with their employers: anyone with a reputation for trouble-making soon found himself black-listed and unable to obtain work.

Wages were very low. The average earnings per family in 1900 came to 22s per week. The head of the family earned about 15s while the other members contributed 7s. Food and rent accounted for 78 per cent of the family's income, leaving very little for fuel, clothing and the other necessities of life. Few were able to save, and many were forced to rely on the pawn shop in time of emergency. No provision was made for holidays, doctor's bills, furniture, old age, school fees, or any of the comforts of life. Seán O'Casey's description of his early life in Dublin provides ample evidence of the reality of poverty among the working class.

The average death rate for the whole of Ireland in the decade 1901-10 was 17.3 persons per thousand of the population. In Dublin it was 24.8 for the same period, while in Belfast it was 20.2. The two main causes for the high death rate were infant mortality and tuberculosis. Deaths from tuberculosis in Ireland were 50 per cent higher than in England or Scotland. Dublin was famous for its 'slum-jungle' in which some 87,000 people, or 30 per cent of the city's 300,000, lived. A public enquiry found that 26,000 families lived in 5,000 tenements, while over 20,000 families lived in one room, and another 5,000 had only two rooms. The living conditions of these slum-dwellers approached the sub-human. Many of the houses were without adequate light, heat, water or sanitation.

What with low wages, unemployment, poor housing and almost widespread poverty and sickness, the time was ripe for a social revolution in Dublin. Trade unionism did exist in nineteenth-century Ireland, but the unions were offshoots of the English amalgamated unions. Eventually an Irish Trades Congress was established in 1894, and by 1900 its membership stood at 60,000; but it was a cautious and conservative body geared mainly to the interests of skilled workers and half its constituent associations had their headquarters in Britain. Such an arrangement had obvious advantages. The Irish groups could benefit from the capital and power behind the parent English trade union. But the English trade union leaders took little or no interest in Irish problems, and there was a continual demand for an independent and wholly-controlled Irish trade union organisation. The two men who gave a lead in this matter were James Connolly and James Larkin.

James Connolly

James Connolly (1868-1916) was born in Edinburgh, of Irish parents. His father was a carter and the family lived in the slum area of Cowgate. They lived in extreme poverty. Connolly said years later: 'I remember reading my first book by the light of the fire embers; we had no other light. My first pencils were charcoal sticks. My first job, at the age of eleven, was as a printer's devil.' When he was fourteen Connolly joined the

British army. His regiment was sent to Cork in 1882, and it was on this occasion that he got his first sight of Ireland. He spent seven years as a soldier, and remained in Ireland all the time. It is important to remember this military stage of Connolly's career, as it ties in with his later involvement in the Irish Citizen Army, and his taking command of the forces in the GPO during the Rising. Throughout his youth and the period of his military service Connolly continued his process of self-education, avidly reading all the socialist and nationalist literature he could lay his hands on. He was particularly attracted to the ideas of John Mitchel, whose *Jail Journal* became his bible.

In 1889 Connolly left the army to get married and returned to Edinburgh, where he worked as a carter for a number of years. During these years he came under the influence of John Leslie, a Scottish socialist, who taught him history, public-speaking, and converted him to the teachings of Karl Marx. In 1896, being out of a job, Connolly accepted the position of organiser of the Dublin Socialist Society, a post which he held for eight years, on a salary (not always forthcoming) of £1 a week. He lived in the slum area of Charlemont Street, and had ample opportunity for studying the reality of Dublin working-class life.

All this time he dreamed of establishing an Irish socialist republic, and in 1896, he founded the Irish Socialist Republican Party (ISRP). He proposed an ambitious programme: nationalisation of railways and canals, state banks, graduated income tax, pensions for widows, orphans, and the aged, a forty-eight hour working week, children's allowances, free education up to and including university level, universal suffrage. He believed that political action would be necessary to bring about these reforms, and failing that, then the forces of labour would one day have to fight. Connolly took as his motto the words of Camille Desmoulins, the French Revolution leader, 'The great appear great because we are on our knees; let us rise.' In his manifesto on behalf of the new party Connolly outlined the connection between socialism and nationalism which lay at the heart of all his thinking:

> The struggle for Irish freedom has two aspects: it is national and it is social. The national ideal can never be realised until Ireland stands forth before the world as a nation, free and independent. It is social and economic because no matter what the form of government may be, as long as one class owns as private property the land and instruments of labour from which mankind derive their substance, that class will always have it in their power to plunder and enslave the remainder of their fellow-creatures.

Connolly also established a newspaper, the *Workers' Republic*, in 1898 in order to publicise his teachings and to report the activities of the ISRP.

In fact there was very little to report. By 1903 Connolly had achieved international renown as a major social thinker, but his efforts had yielded no tangible results in Ireland, and both his party and his paper were languishing. Somewhat disappointed with his lack of success, Connolly emigrated to America, where he acted as one of the chief organisers for the Industrial Workers of the World. While in America he came to realise that the social problems of Ireland were the same as those of other countries. He received much encouragement from Daniel de Leon, the leader of the American Socialist Labour Party. Connolly's time in America proved a very enriching experience. He lectured and wrote widely on the problems of national and international socialism. Yet his heart was in Ireland, and so, when in 1910, he was offered a job as chief organiser of the Belfast branch of the newly-formed Irish Transport and General Workers' Union, he accepted it.

He found ample opportunity for his socialist acumen in the Belfast setting. During the dockers' strike of 1911, he was instrumental in obtaining favourable terms for the men. He likewise threw himself into a campaign to improve the working conditions of women in the linen mills. Here again, he met with singular success. He proved himself a man of action and often repeated the phrase: 'We must have less theory and more action.' In 1911 Connolly also launched a second newspaper, the *Irish Worker*, which proved a much greater success than his earlier venture and which soon had a circulation of over 90,000. (Arthur Griffith's weekly journal, *Sinn Féin*, never sold more than 5,000 copies a week at this time.)

Although based in Belfast, Connolly was called upon to help in trade disputes all over Ireland. Thus he came to Dublin during the 1913 lockout and found himself in the midst of an industrial war. It was in this context that he helped to found the Irish Citizen Army (see below). By the end of 1913, therefore, Connolly was involved in a movement that was partly political, partly social and partly military. He believed that 'the cause of labour is the cause of Ireland and that the cause of Ireland is the cause of labour; they cannot be dissevered'. The outbreak of the First World War had a shattering effect upon Connolly, especially as the European socialist parties threw themselves into the fray on the side of the capitalists and the imperialists. He continued with his routine work as an ITGWU organiser, trying to build up the union as a solid and solvent body. But his experiences of the lockout and the catastrophe of the European war were turning his thoughts steadily in the direction of an armed revolutionary uprising, and this was to be his main preoccupation for the rest of his life.

James Larkin

James Larkin (1876-1947), the founder of the ITGWU, was born in Liverpool of Irish parents. His father died of tuberculosis when Jim was only a young boy. The young Larkin had to begin earning his living before he was twelve. After a short time spent at sea, he returned to Liverpool and worked as a docker. Physically he was a powerful man with a big voice, and he soon became known by the name of 'Big Jim', which stuck to him all his life. He gradually improved his position and became a foreman. All this time he was interested in social problems. He was well aware of the injustices and inequalities inflicted upon the working classes. A gifted speaker with a flair for oratory, he often addressed groups of dockers and told them that they should join together to better their position. He claimed to preach 'the divine gospel of discontent' and certainly he had the power to stir men to action.

In 1907 he was invited by the British-based National Union of Dock-Labourers to go to Belfast to organise the dockers of that city. He persuaded not only the dockers, but also a section of the police force to go on strike, maintaining that they were underpaid. As James Sexton, the general secretary of the union said at the time: 'Jim Larkin crashed upon the public with a devastating roar of a volcano exploding without even a preliminary wisp of smoke.'

Larkin then moved on to Dublin in 1908 and immediately set about organising a series of strikes which led to higher wages for dockers, carters and labourers. However, by this time his union superiors in Liverpool were taking a poor view of Larkin's 'sympathetic strike' policy. They objected to having to hand over large sums of money by way of compensation to the strikers, and Larkin soon found himself suspended from his job. His immediate response was to establish a union of his own, the Irish Transport and General Workers' Union, in December 1908. Its general aim was to obtain higher wages and better working conditions for unskilled labourers. Larkin gave the union a motto: 'Each for all and all for each'. The ITGWU was an immediate success, and by 1913 it had over 10,000 members. A further development at this time in which both Larkin and Connolly were involved was the creation between 1912 and 1914 of an Irish Labour Party, which was closely identified with the Irish TUC.

The ITGWU went from strength to strength and seemed well on the way to achieving Larkin's 'syndicalist' ideal, i.e., the absorption of many small unions into 'one big union' which would by concerted action, sympathetic strikes and general strike smash the power of capitalism and pave the way for ownership of the work by the worker. Between January and August 1913 there were no fewer than thirty strikes in Dublin, most of them accompanied by a good deal of disorder. It was no wonder that Dublin businessmen became alarmed. They had already begun to close their ranks against the onslaught of the workers by forming an Employers' Federation in 1911; this organisation consisted of about 400 of Dublin's chief employers, the most active of them being William Martin Murphy, the chairman of the Dublin United Tramway Company, who also controlled the *Irish Independent* and the city's largest department store. It was Murphy who now gave the employers a lead by persuading the Employers' Federation to declare war on the ITGWU. As a result of this decision, the following document was handed to tens of thousands of Dublin workers:

I hereby undertake to carry out all instructions given me by or on behalf of my employers, and further, I agree to immediately resign my membership of the Irish Transport and General Workers' Union, and I further undertake that I will not join or in any way support the Union.

The 1913 lockout

Larkin's reaction to this move by Murphy was to call for a general strike. He issued an order to all his members: 'Strike declared. Stop at once. By order of the Union. Signed: J. Larkin'. The strike began on Tuesday 26 August 1913, when 700 tramway-men walked off their trams, leaving them wherever they happened to be. It was Horse Show week, and Dublin was full of visitors. Murphy and his fellow-employers promptly retaliated by locking out all their ITGWU workers. Soon 25,000 men were out of work. Larkin told his followers: 'This is not a strike, it is a lockout of the men who have been tyrannically treated by a most unscrupulous scoundrel. We will demonstrate in O'Connell Street. It is our street as well as William Martin Murphy's. We are fighting for bread and butter. By the living God, if they want war, they can have it.'

The O'Connell Street meeting was held on Sunday 31 August 1913 and led to bitter street fighting. The Dublin Metropolitan Police attacked the crowd who were listening to Larkin's speech. Two people were killed and several hundred injured, and Larkin himself was arrested.

The lockout lasted for five tense months, during which the working people of Dublin and their families suffered untold hardships, especially during the severe winter of 1913-14. Food kitchens were set up by the Countess Markievicz and other philanthropic people, while financial support for the strikes came from abroad, as well as several foodships dispatched to Dublin by sympathisers in England and America.

By the beginning of 1914 the victory had gone to the employers. The workers were literally starved into submission, and they returned to work relinquishing their membership of the ITGWU if their employers insisted on it. Larkin, his hopes frustrated, left the country for America later in the year. Yet in the long run, the lockout had some positive results for the workers. The ITGWU, though gravely depleted, was not destroyed as Murphy and his colleagues had intended. Trade unionism at last gained a kind of grudging acknowledgement from employers, who never again attempted to adopt such extreme measures or treat their workers so harshly. The succeeding years were marked by a slow but sure improvement in working conditions and rates of pay. Furthermore, the solidarity of their protest and the sufferings they endured together gave the workers an awareness of their common identity and instilled a new spirit of belligerence into the heart of the Dublin poor. This new mood manifested itself in a tiny organisation which came into existence as a direct result of the lockout — the Irish Citizen Army.

The Irish Citizen Army

This 200-member force was founded on 23 November 1913 with the support of Larkin and Connolly. It had a twofold purpose: (1) to enable the strikers to protect themselves in clashes with the police over blackleg or imported labour or at public demonstrations like that on 31 August; (2) to keep them fit and give a sense of unity, cohesion and purpose during their idleness.

When the men went back to work there seemed no reason to keep the army in existence, but thanks to the efforts of its hard-working secretary, Seán O'Casey (better known as a playwright), it was revived and kept in training. This reorganisation had the full approval of Connolly, who saw the little army as the nucleus of a great insurrectionary movement which would by force of arms secure the national independence of Ireland and the rights and liberties of her workers.

The Irish Volunteers

If the Irish Citizen Army was founded to cope with the threat of civil liberties in the city of Dublin, the Irish Volunteers were launched to create an Irish army on Irish soil, to defend the democratic rights of the people of Ireland. On 1 November 1913 an article appeared in *An Claidheamh Soluis,* the Gaelic League journal, entitled 'The North Began'. It was written by Eóin Mac Néill, Professor of Early Irish History at UCD, who, while commenting on the progress of the Ulster Volunteers, proposed that the other counties of Ireland should follow the example of the North. Mac Néill's suggestion aroused considerable interest — particularly within the IRB, whose leaders saw it as their long-awaited opportunity to set up a popular military force which might one day be used to fight for an Irish republic.

An organising Provisional Committee was therefore formed, half of whose members were IRB men, and a public meeting was arranged at the Rotunda, Dublin, for 25 November 1913. At this meeting the Irish Volunteers were formally inaugurated with the enrolment of over 3,000 men. Many of the rank and file were GAA members, while the Gaelic League provided several of the officers, one of whom was Éamon de Valera. Mac Néill himself was chosen as the Volunteers' president and chief-of-staff; Bulmer Hobson was secretary; The O'Rahilly and Sir Roger Casement managed the force's finances; and Colonel Maurice Moore was appointed inspector-general.

Perhaps the most enthusiastic Volunteer was Pádraic Pearse, who at this time also became a member of the IRB. Pearse was, like many other Europeans at this time, a confirmed and outspoken militarist. He wanted to see every Irishman ready to defend his rights — whatever his idea of his rights might be. He praised the Ulster Volunteers for taking the initiative and, before the corresponding southern body was created, even urged Ulstermen to join the UVF.

> I am glad, then, [wrote Pearse], that the North has begun. I am glad that the Orangemen have armed, for it is a goodly thing to see arms in Irish hands. I would like to see the AOH armed. I would like to see the Transport Workers armed. I would like to see any and every body of Irish citizens armed. We must accustom ourselves to the thought of arms, to the sight of arms, to the use of arms.

Pearse's militarism was taken to extreme lengths with his idea that an authentic national regeneration might be brought about by a baptism in blood:

> We may make mistakes in the beginning and shoot the wrong people; but bloodshed is a cleansing and sanctifying thing and a nation which regards it as the final horror has lost its manhood. There are many things more horrible than bloodshed; and slavery is one of them.

Few Irish Volunteers in 1913-14 agreed with Pearse about this last point, but his wholehearted efforts to build up an efficient people's army in accordance with his militarist principles ensured that he quickly became the most active and influential of the Volunteer leaders; and it is not surprising that when the remnant of the force eventually became involved in military action the man chosen to command it was Pearse.

Pearse and the other members of the Volunteers' Provisional Committee intended that the force should be non-sectarian, national, democratic and voluntary. Its motto was 'Defence not defiance', and its purposes were outlined as follows:

> The object proposed for the Irish Volunteers is to secure and maintain the rights and liberties common to all the people of Ireland. Their duties will be defensive and protective, and they will not contemplate either aggression or domination. Their ranks are open to all able-bodied Irishmen without distinction of creed, politics or social grade.

The Irish Volunteers were *not* formed to fight the Ulster Volunteers, nor to fight for Home Rule; that was the business of the British government, which was taking the responsibility of enacting Home Rule and which would, therefore, have the duty of imposing it in Ireland.

By the summer of 1914 the number of recruits had reached about 100,000 and was still rising. But in spite of all Pearse's talk about guns and shooting, they still had to drill with hurley-sticks. The story of the Irish Volunteers' acquisition of arms in July 1914 and their subsequent activities is told in the next chapter.

Women's and Boys' Organisations

Inghinidhe na hÉireann

The first decade of the twentieth century saw the rise of the women's suffragette movement in England, France and elsewhere in Europe. Irishwomen were also caught up in this same spirit. Maud Gonne, an Englishwoman living in Ireland, was very prominent in feminist circles. In 1899 she was one of the founders of a nationalist organisation called *Inghinidhe na hÉireann* (Daughters of Ireland). Another member was the Countess Markievicz. The association ran classes in the Irish language and many other cultural activities. The Inghinidhe also campaigned to discourage Irishmen from enlisting in the British army. In 1908 Maude Gonne founded a monthly magazine called *Bean na hÉireann,* which served as an instrument of propaganda for the movement.

Cumann na mBan

With the foundation of the Irish Volunteers in 1913, a women's auxiliary force, Cumann na mBan, was also organised. The main activities of its members were directed towards military affairs, such as signalling, first-aid and drill. Among the most active members of Cumann na mBan were Agnes O'Farrelly, Mary MacSwiney and the Countess Markievicz. The organisation gradually absorbed Inghinidhe na hÉireann. When its members adopted a uniform in 1915, it took on the appearance of a regular army.

Na Fianna Eireann

In 1909 Bulmer Hobson and the Countess Markievicz founded Fianna Eireann, or Irish Boy Scouts, as a nationalist youth movement. The original idea (adapted from that of a previous boys' organisation of the same name founded by Hobson in Belfast in 1902) was to form clubs, where classes in the Irish language and Irish history could be held, as well as sporting activities. But it was also hoped to use the clubs for political purposes and eventually to teach the boys drill and military discipline. Bulmer Hobson also intended using the Fianna as a means of recruiting suitable members into the IRB. According to the *Fianna Handbook* of 1914, the 'objects of the organisation were to re-establish the Independence of Ireland; the means to be adopted were the training of the youth of Ireland, mentally and physically, by teaching, scouting, military exercises, Irish history and the Irish language'. Several of the future leaders in the struggle for Irish independence, such as Con Colbert and Liam Mellows, had been members of the Fianna. The organisation took part in the landing of arms at Howth in July 1914.

Talking Points

Chapter 5: Developing Nationalism, 1880-1914

1 Discuss the evolution of the 'Irish-Ireland' movement, with special reference to the writings of D. P. Moran. How did this new nationalism differ from that of Daniel O'Connell and Thomas Davis?

2 What contribution did the Gaelic Athletic Association make to the social and political life of Ireland between 1884-1914?

3 Show how the Gaelic League played a significant role in the struggle for Irish independence. Contrast the careers of Douglas Hyde and P. H. Pearse, and the divergent views they had of the Gaelic League.

4 Explain how the Sinn Féin movement came into existence. Assess critically the career of Arthur Griffith up to 1916.

5 Write a social survey of living conditions among the working classes in Dublin and Belfast during the years 1890 and 1914. Show how the work of either James Connolly or James Larkin helped to improve these conditions.

6 Compare the origins and organisation of the Irish Citizen Army and the Irish Volunteers.

Chapter 6

THE EASTER RISING AND THE NEW SINN FEIN, 1914-18

During the First World War Ireland witnessed two extraordinary developments which were so totally unexpected that few observers in 1914 could have believed them possible, but which were of such momentous consequence that they set Irish history on an entirely new course. Firstly, a small section of the Volunteer body declared war on the British Empire in the name of an Irish Republic and complete separation from Great Britain. By actually asserting their claim to national sovereignty in an armed insurrection which took a terrible toll in terms of loss of life and damage to property, the rebel Volunteers forced their fellow-countrymen to sit up and take notice of their ideas.

Secondly, and even more astonishingly, within less than two years of the Easter Rising, majority political opinion in Ireland underwent a profound and dramatic change. It swung sharply away from the old Irish Parliamentary Party and from the Home Rule settlement which it had succeeded in winning for Ireland after a forty-year struggle. The popular nationalist aspiration for a limited measure of self-government now suddenly gave way to a far more radical demand — the fully autonomous Irish Republic for which the 'men of 1916' had given their lives. One aspect of this change of front was that in the public mind the new and defiant mood of separatism became associated with the name of Sinn Féin, the tiny group which had advocated nothing more startling than a dual monarchy as the constitutional solution to the Irish question. In 1916 most Irishmen regarded Arthur Griffith and his followers as a handful of ineffectual cranks; by 1918 Sinn Féin had been swept to the forefront of the Irish political scene and the men who were to shape the destinies of the Irish Republic were eagerly flocking to it and adapting it to their own purposes.

This chapter provides an outline of the events which lay behind these sensational changes. It traces, firstly, the stages by which moderate, essentially defensive Irish Volunteers were transformed into a revolutionary republican fighting force, and secondly, the stages by which moderate, essentially conservative Irish nationalists were transformed into ardent extremists; in short, it shows how Home Rulers became 'Sinn Féiners'.

The Easter Rising: Essential Features

In attempting to analyse the causes of the Easter Rising it is important to realise that the events which preceded it between 1914 and 1916 took place on three different planes: open, secret, and ultra-secret. The 'open' pre-history of the Rising is mainly concerned with the progress of the Volunteer movement and with the international situation during the European war. The secret plane was dominated by the strong IRB element within the Volunteers, with its avowed aim of using force of arms at some undetermined future time to establish an Irish Republic, whose head of state would be the IRB President and whose governing body would be the IRB Supreme Council.

But within the IRB organisation there was a small group or cabal, consisting originally of only two men (Seán Mac Diarmada and Tom Clarke), who chose to operate on an ultra-secret level. They were prepared to bypass the rules of the IRB constitution; they frequently made decisions of the utmost importance without consulting their IRB colleagues and superiors (including the President): and they revealed their plans only to their most trusted comrades, whom, if necessary, they swore into the IRB on their own responsibility. In this way the membership of the little inner circle eventually increased to seven (the signatories of the Easter Proclamation). It was they who decided that a rising would take place, not at some vague future date, but at Easter 1916, and took firm steps to implement their decision. They chose to keep their secrets to themselves partly for fear of being betrayed by informers or loose talk, partly for fear of being overruled by the more cautious and less determined members of the Supreme Council.

The most important member of the ultra-secret cabal of revolutionary activists was Seán Mac Diarmada, ably assisted and encouraged by his devoted right-hand man, Tom Clarke. Mac Diarmada was a master of behind-the-scenes organisation and control. It was in his fertile and ingenious brain that the plans that made the Rising possible were concocted; and it was he also who devised the elaborate network of command, all the strings of which were held in his own hands, which was essential if the decisions of the conspiratorial junta were to be presented as orders to the Volunteer rank and file. The ideology which inspired the revolutionary inner circle was supplied and expounded by a comparative newcomer, Pádraic Pearse (whose career and ideas are discussed separately below).

The Easter Rising was thus an 'artificial' phenomenon, deliberately contrived by a minority within a minority. It was not a spontaneous reaction to intolerable conditions. Indeed, the country as a whole had seldom been so peaceful and contented as at the beginning of 1916. The war had brought economic prosperity to Ireland, and thousands of Irishmen eagerly availed of the opportunity to earn high wages in the British armed forces and at the same time to demonstrate their natural allegiance to Home Rule and the British Empire. An idea of where most Irishmen's ultimate loyalties lay in 1916 can be gauged from the fact that approximately 200,000 Irishmen fought for the British Empire in the European war, 60,000 of them giving their lives for it, while the breakaway group of Irish Volunteers led by Eóin Mac Néill numbered a mere 16,000, only one-tenth of whom actually engaged in the insurrection in Dublin.

It was nothing new for rebellion to be plotted by small groups of individuals. Ireland had already experienced three such risings in 1803, 1848 and 1867, but they were all abortive affairs which never got off the ground, achieving no tangible results and making little impact upon public opinion. The unique and extraordinary feature of the 1916 Rising was that the conspiratorial schemes were translated into large-scale action with effects that were all too evident. Hundreds of people were killed in the fighting and the centre of Dublin was left a devastated ruin. To ordinary Irishmen the Rising came like a bolt from the blue. The horrifying reality of the carnage and the grim series of secret trials and executions which followed it struck them with the force of a stunning shock, leaving them strangely disturbed and utterly bewildered. Even the names of the executed leaders were unfamiliar to them, and the motives which had led them to take their suicidal action seemed incomprehensible. By the summer of 1916 thousands of awe-struck, wondering Irishmen were asking themselves: What sort of men were these?

Whatever hidden forces were at work in the background, the rebellion itself was carried out by the Irish Volunteers. The process by which the Volunteers were converted into an effective military force which could be exploited by extreme republican elements is crucial to an understanding of the Easter Rising. Any examination of the causes of the Rising must therefore begin by concentrating on the 'open' plane of events and by tracing the changing fortunes of the Volunteer movement.

The Volunteers, May – October 1914

Redmond's takeover

By early 1914 the Irish Volunteers had grown into a formidable force of over 100,000 men. As summer approached and the Home Rule Bill entered the final stage of its passage through parliament the Volunteers began to receive a good deal of attention from an anxious John Redmond and his colleagues in the Irish Party. Redmond was expecting to become the first Prime Minister of Ireland in the very near future, and if his government was to have any real authority, it was clear that it could not tolerate the existence of a large private army in the country.

Redmond, therefore, determined to bring the Volunteers under his own control pending the introduction of Home Rule. In June 1914 he demanded that twenty-five of his own nominees should be appointed to the Provisional Committee of the Volunteers. None of the Volunteer leaders welcomed this proposition, but they realised that if they rejected it, the movement would split in two. The group who were at that very moment involved in smuggling arms were anxious to avoid any division, and after a long and angry debate they outvoted the hardliners on the Provisional Committee and agreed to accept Redmond's proposal. The unity of the Volunteers was thus preserved – though only for another three months.

The Howth Gun-running

The Volunteers had encouraged all their members to purchase rifles, but in practice few were able to do so, and even if they could, there was no ammunition available. In order to meet this problem it was decided to raise a sum of money and buy a supply of arms and ammunition from Germany. The project was given an additional impetus at the end of April 1914, when news of the Larne gun-running became known (see page 84).

The principal organisers of the enterprise were Bulmer Hobson, The O'Rahilly and Sir Roger Casement, while Mac Néill was also aware of all the details. The actual purchase and smuggling of the arms was carried out by Darrell Figgis and Erskine Childers, assisted by a group of Anglo-Irish liberals, who believed that an armed Volunteer force would both strengthen the Home Rule position and provide an effective native territorial army in the event of an international war and the threat of a foreign invasion. The entire operation was conducted in the strictest secrecy, the scheme being revealed to no one except those actually involved in it.

The 1,500 rifles and 45,000 rounds of ammunition were brought from Hamburg and the bulk of them were transferred to Childers's yacht, the *Asgard,* which arrived in Howth in broad daylight on Sunday 26 July 1914. About 800 Volunteers and some of the Fianna were involved in unloading the arms and getting them safely away. Although eighty soldiers of the King's Own Scottish Borderers tried to stop the Volunteers at Clontarf, the gun-runners succeeded in getting away with the loss of only nineteen rifles. Later that day, as the British troops were marching along Bachelor's Walk on their way back to their barracks, they were jeered at and insulted by the Dublin crowd. Owing to a misunderstanding of orders, the soldiers opened fire and also used their bayonets. Three people were killed and thirty-eight wounded.

The Howth gun-running was of tremendous propaganda value to the Volunteers. As a result of the publicity given to the affair, money poured in from America and elsewhere at the rate of about £1,000 a month. It also helped to boost recruiting, so that by September 1914 the Volunteers numbered 180,000. The tragic sequel in Bachelor's Walk aroused much bitter anti-British feeling, especially since the crown forces had made no attempt to prevent the much more serious gun-running in Larne three months earlier. The funerals of the victims were made the occasion for a massive nationalist demonstration.

The Volunteer split

The First World War broke out on 4 August 1914, a few weeks before the Home Rule Bill was due to be enacted. Asquith's government now became completely engrossed in a full-scale war and decided to shelve the contentious subject of Home Rule until the war was over. The government now looked on Ireland as a potential source of much-needed recruits, and Lord Kitchener, the commander-in-chief of the British Army, cast greedy eyes at the two ready-made Volunteer forces in Ireland. He told Redmond: 'Get me 5,000 men and I will say, thank you; get me 10,000 and I will take off my hat to you.'

Redmond, though bitterly disappointed at having been thwarted of his life-long objective at the last minute, gave his wholehearted support to the war effort, asking Asquith to entrust the defence of Ireland to the Volunteers, north and south. His action was dictated partly by his deep and genuine loyalty to the British Empire and his belief that Britain's cause in the war was also Ireland's cause, and partly by the hope that when the war was over a grateful government would grant Home Rule to Ireland on the best possible terms. (However, Carson and the Ulster Unionists were also adopting a similar line, though with precisely the opposite objective in view.) Initially Redmond did not ask a single Volunteer to serve abroad. Then, in a speech delivered at Woodenbridge Co. Wicklow, on 20 September 1914, he suddenly reversed his policy and urged the Volunteers to enlist in the Irish regiments of the British army and be prepared to go 'wherever the firing-line extends'.

Redmond's speech unleashed a storm of protest and split the Volunteer movement in two. The larger of the two groups, numbering 170,000, remained loyal to Redmond and was reconstituted as the National Volunteers. Several thousand of them followed Redmond's advice and departed for the battle-fields of Flanders. The National Volunteers played no further part in the story of the Rising, except that some of the Dublin units were involved in helping to defeat their former comrades in Easter Week 1916.

The other section of the Volunteers consisted of the more extreme nationalists, numbering only 11,000. They retained their original name and comprised the group henceforth known as the Irish Volunteers. Although they formed a distinct minority, they included nearly all the leading members of the original Provisional Committee and the majority of those who had been most enthusiastic and active in building up the original body. They immediately set about tightening their military organisation, replacing the old Provisional Committee with a General Council. The real power, however, was held by a small, streamlined nine-member Central Executive, the chief posts in which were held by Eóin Mac Néill (Chief of Staff), The O'Rahilly (Director of Arms), Bulmer Hobson (Quartermaster-General), Pádraic Pearse (Director of Organisation), Joseph Plunkett (Director of Military Operations), Thomas MacDonagh (Director of Organisation), Eamonn Ceannt (Director of Communications from 1915). Except for Mac Néill and O'Rahilly, all were members of the IRB or were shortly to be admitted into the organisation through the influence of Mac Diarmada and Clarke. Except for Hobson, all these IRB members of the Central Executive were 'new men' inspired by the ideals of the 'Irish

Ireland' philosophy. They can even be regarded as a new breed of Irish nationalist whose principal characteristics were utter dedication, extreme militancy, and a determination to engineer an armed insurrection at whatever cost to themselves, before the European war was over. The man most responsible for formulating these ideals and principles and disseminating them among his comrades was Pádraic Pearse. Because of this, Pearse was in 1916 nominated by his fellow-conspirators both as their commander-in-chief and as the president of the provisional government of the Irish Republic.

Padraic Pearse

Pádraic Henry Pearse was born in Dublin in 1879. His father was an English stone-mason, while his mother came from Co. Meath. Educated by the Christian Brothers, Westland Row, he took an early interest in the Irish language, retaining his enthusiasm for it throughout his life. He joined the Gaelic League (eventually editing its journal, *An Claidheamh Soluis*, between 1903 and 1909) and when only seventeen founded his own New Ireland Literary Society to promote the study of Irish poetry. In 1901 he graduated in arts and law at the Royal University.

His interests soon extended to the area of education. During a tour of Belgium he was very impressed by that country's successful educational system, and especially by the fact that most of the people there were bilingual. Out of his Belgian experience grew the ideas he developed in *The Murder Machine* (1912), a book which indicted the whole Irish educational system. He advocated teaching Irish in all the schools and produced aids to teaching the language. In 1908 he founded St Enda's College (Scoil Eanna) at Cullenswood House, Rathmines, Dublin, and announced the purpose and scope of the school as 'the providing of an elementary and secondary education of a high type for Irish-speaking boys, and for boys not Irish-speaking, whom it is desired to educate on bilingual lines'. In 1910 St Enda's moved to The Hermitage, Rathfarnham, and became a boarding school.

But Pearse lacked experience in the practical side of running a school, so that he was soon in financial difficulties. His family and friends came to his rescue, and he also received financial and moral support from the IRB whose leaders took a special interest in St Enda's, and the kind of Irish patriot-enthusiast which Pearse was turning out there. Early in 1914 Pearse went on a lecture tour of the United States to collect funds for his school. While in America he met many of the Irish-American Fenians, and it is interesting to note that he made a particularly strong impression on John Devoy, as he had already done on Tom Clarke in Ireland. Neither of these tough-minded old Fenians had much time for romantic and idealistic visionaries of Pearse's type, but there was some curiously compelling quality in the young man's personality that won them over; they seem to have recognised that Pearse would one day attempt to turn his dream into reality.

Pearse's nationalism had a strong spiritual basis. He was a poet and dreamer who steeped himself in the literature and art of ancient Ireland, believing that a real regeneration of Ireland's nationhood must be accompanied by a cultural reawakening in which the restoration of the Irish language could be a vital factor. He declared that 'Ireland would die when the Irish language died', and one of his biographers has written 'Pearse no more questioned that the language of the Irish nation should be Irish than he would have questioned the existence of God.'

The depth and intensity of Pearse's passionately-held convictions do not mean that he was always a political extremist or a republican. In fact the evolution of his political thought was very slow. In 1907 he supported the Irish Council Bill (see page 58), thus showing himself to be even more moderate than Redmond, who rejected it contemptuously. Thereafter he supported the campaign for Home Rule until as late as 1913. But in that year his political opinions underwent a radical change, which seems to have been triggered off by the formation of the Ulster Volunteers. This event turned Pearse's mind towards militarism (see page 109) and led him to develop his belief in the value of bloodshed as an agent of national regeneration: 'The old heart of the earth needed to be warmed by the red wine of the battlefields.' He turned away from the Irish Party and from Home Rule, which, he said, would make Ireland 'smug, contented and loyal'. He distrusted British politicians and threatened that 'If they trick us again, I will lead an insurrection myself.' In rejecting constitutionalism and parliamentary politics, he looked back to the older tradition of Tone, Emmet and Mitchel, whom he saw as the real fighters for Irish freedom. By the time the Irish Volunteers were founded in November 1913 Pearse had become an enthusiastic convert to advanced physical-force nationalism and republicanism. By the end of the year he was a leading member of the Volunteers' Provisional Committee and had also joined the IRB.

Few of the IRB leaders liked Pearse, whom they regarded as being too eager for promotion to high positions in the Volunteer and republican organisations. Seán Mac Diarmada was particularly suspicious of Pearse's apparent ambitions, and he reacted sharply when Pearse was proposed for the IRB presidency in 1915: 'Oh, for the love of God, don't be stupid, don't be foolish. We could never control that bloody fellow.' As usual Mac Diarmada had his way. In fairness to Mac Diarmada, it should be remembered that he had put in years of unacknowledged toil in perfecting the machinery of the IRB, and he was naturally resentful of any newcomer who expected to jump on to the IRB bandwagon on the strength of a few fiery speeches. However, by this time Pearse was beginning to make his mark both as a worker and as principal exponent of the ideology of the new militant republicanism.

The most remarkable idea put forward by Pearse was the concept of a blood-sacrifice for the cause of Irish nationality — a sacrifice not of other people, but of oneself. He believed that the spirit of the Irish nation could be successfully restored by the willing deaths of devoted patriots. Pearse drew the inspiration for this theory from the examples of Christ and Cuchulainn, both of whom had suffered death for the salvation of their people. Pearse took these two figures as his personal heroes and tried to model his life on theirs. His guiding thought was also expressed in Cuchulainn's saying which he had painted around a fresco in St Enda's: 'I care not though I were to live but one day or one night, if only my fame and deeds live after me.' Such ideas and examples introduced a messianic motif into Pearse's interpretation of Irish nationalism; and his play *The Singer*, written in 1915, clearly shows that he saw himself as cast in the role of the Irish messiah. This play and his poems 'Renunciation', 'The Mother' and 'The Fool' also present evidence that he was personally prepared to sacrifice his life for the redemption of his fellow-countrymen. The peculiar intensity of Pearse's nationalism raised it to the level of a religious faith, surpassing everyday reason and common sense and far removed from the political manoeuvrings of the Irish Party or the IRB Supreme Council. This is reflected in his poetry, much of which is highly charged with a strange apocalyptic fervour:

> I have turned my face
> To this road before me,
> To the deed that I see
> And the death I shall die.
> ('Renunciation')
> O wise men, riddle me this: what if the dream come true?
> What if the dream come true? and if millions unborn shall dwell
> In the house that I shaped in my heart, the noble house of my thought?
> Lord, I have staked my soul, I have staked the lives of my kin
> On the truth of Thy dreadful word. Do not remember my failures,
> But remember this my faith.
> ('The Fool')

Pearse's most remarkable achievement was his success in spreading his gospel of self-sacrifice among his fellow-conspirators, including such hard-headed realists as James Connolly and Seán Mac Diarmada. Their acceptance of Pearse's ideology was of crucial importance at the very final stage of the preparation for the Easter Rising. Without it, their plans would have fizzled out like a damp squib; but under its inspiration, the Rising became imbued with a supernatural and almost mythical quality.

Planning the Rising: The IRB, 1914-15

According to the old belief that 'England's difficulty is Ireland's opportunity', Britain's involvement in the First World War seemed to provide the revolutionaries with the chance for which they had been waiting. Within a month of the outbreak of hostilities the IRB Supreme Council had decided to embark on an insurrection before the end of the war, the Clan na Gael leaders had established contact with Count von Bernstorff, the German ambassador to America, in order to arrange for German assistance, and the republican IRB extremists on the Volunteer Central Executive (Pearse, Plunkett and MacDonagh) were actually discussing detailed plans for an immediate rising. This last move was promptly overruled by the more cautious Supreme Council, which refused to countenance dangerous and unauthorised initiatives taken by hot-headed splinter groups. The Supreme Council's action had the effect of driving the extremists underground: it put them on their guard against the Supreme Council, so that in future they revealed all their most important plans only to those in whom they had absolute trust.

The Supreme Council empowered Clarke and Mac Diarmada to put out feelers regarding the proposed insurrection among a number of non-IRB nationalists such as James Connolly and Arthur Griffith. The resulting meeting was held on 9 September 1914 at the Gaelic League headquarters, and among those attending were Pearse, Plunkett, MacDonagh and Ceannt. Having approved in principle the decision to stage a rising, the meeting decided to speed up recruitment to the Volunteers, the Irish Citizen Army, Fianna Éireann (Hobson's 'teenage army') and Cumann na mBan. They also agreed to assist German forces landing in Ireland, provided the Germans gave their military support to an Irish insurrection. Finally, they resolved to resist any attempt to impose conscription on Ireland or to disarm the Volunteers.

The split in the Volunteer movement which occurred shortly after this meeting came as a severe setback which made it necessary to postpone the plans for a rising. However, throughout the year 1915 Mac Diarmada and Clarke worked hard to build up the depleted Irish Volunteers, being careful to insert as many trusted IRB men as possible into key positions within the organisation. They instituted lecture courses for the Volunteers on military tactics, street warfare, guerrilla fighting, etc. They also established a communications network with the Clan na Gael leaders, Devoy and Cohalan, and with the German government. Sir Roger Casement was sent to Germany to negotiate for a supply of armaments and military assistance, and Joseph Plunkett, after meeting Casement in Germany in March 1915, went to America in the following autumn to liaise with Clan na Gael and the German ambassador and to handle the business from that end.

Most important of all, Mac Diarmada and Clarke got themselves appointed to two of the three most powerful posts on the IRB Supreme Council, and they later contrived that the third post should be given to Denis McCullough, an absentee Ulster partner who had no idea of their clandestine plotting (see below). Mac Diarmada and Clarke between them, therefore, now had effective control of the IRB and, through the IRB, of

Mac Néill's Irish Volunteers. All that remained to be done was to decide on a date for the rising and to draft a detailed military plan of operations. Mac Diarmada and Clarke decided to set up a special secret committee for this purpose, and in May 1915 they managed to persuade the Supreme Council to give them full authority to do this. It is unlikely that the Supreme Council realised the full implications of their decision.

Planning the Rising: The Military Council, 1915-16

The formation of the Military Council in May 1915 marks the stage at which the Supreme Council finally ceased to count as the principal architect of the Easter Rising. From this point onwards all the running was made by the Military Council, while the Supreme Council, confused and misinformed about what was going on, lumbered blindly in the wake of the little group of activists.

The Military Council originally consisted of Pearse, Plunkett and Ceannt. They were joined in September 1915 by Mac Diarmada and Clarke, who gave their approval to the detailed military scheme which the others had drawn up. It seems that they originally intended the rising to take place in the autumn of 1915 (Pearse's famous oration at the grave of O'Donovan Rossa in August was certainly intended to foster an atmosphere of imminent insurrection), but their failure to obtain aid from Germany at this time brought about a further postponement. They continued their activities under the veil of absolute secrecy and never reported back to their superiors in the IRB, who seem to have forgotten about the Military Council's existence. Towards the end of 1915 the five conspirators had fixed on Easter 1916 as the firm date for the insurrection, and at about the same time they covered their tracks still further by engineering the appointment of Denis McCullough as President of the IRB: McCullough had no idea of the existence of the ultra-secret cabal and was totally unaware that the military planning of the insurrection had reached such an advanced stage. Indeed, at the beginning of 1916 the Supreme Council, after much argument, went no further than reaffirming their earlier decision to organise a rising before the war was over. By a curious irony, they even set up a new committee to make the necessary arrangements, never dreaming that the IRB representatives they appointed to it were members of the already existing Military Council! The IRB Supreme Council thus seemed to be in full control of the situation, but in reality it had played right into the hands of Sean Mac Diarmada, who proceeded to use the authority vested in him by the IRB to bring his revolutionary plans to fruition.

Early in 1916 the Military Council co-opted its two final members, James Connolly and Thomas MacDonagh. Connolly had proved something of a nuisance to the Military Council, for he had adopted an openly militant stance and seemed likely to lead an insurrection of his own with the aid of his miniature Citizen Army. This, of course, would have ruined the carefully laid plans for a major rising at Easter, and the Military Council were forced to take the drastic step of kidnapping Connolly, taking him fully into their confidence and swearing him into the IRB. Connolly, thereafter, abandoned his independent line and threw in his lot with the Military Council. With the addition of Connolly and MacDonagh, the Military Council consisted of the seven men who were to sign the Easter Proclamation.

Government Miscalculation, February – April 1916

By February 1916 the arrangements made by Plunkett and Devoy for the importation of a consignment of 20,000 rifles and ten machine-guns from Germany were well under way. The weapons were scheduled to arrive in Tralee Bay immediately before the rising was due to begin on Easter Sunday. The German government believed that an insurrection in Ireland would force Britain to withdraw troops from the western front and thus give the German offensive in France, planned for the late spring, a better chance of succeeding. However, British intelligence agents were aware of these negotiations, and although rumours of an impending insurrection leaked out, the government authorities made the fatal mistake of believing that Casement was the ringleader of the whole affair and concentrated their attention on the secret telegrams passing between America and Germany.

Meanwhile the leading officials in Dublin Castle, Augustine Birrell, the Chief Secretary, and Sir Matthew Nathan, the Under-Secretary, also had advance warning that something was in the air, but they were unwilling to take any firm action to deal with it and even closed their eyes to a good deal of pro-German sentiment in magazines. This was partly because they did not wish to jeopardise the generally peaceful conditions then prevailing in Ireland, and partly because they were lulled into a false sense of security by the activities of the Volunteers themselves. During the spring of 1916 the IRB leaders in the Volunteers organised a series of parades, route marches, practice military manoeuvres, etc., all of which were conducted in the public eye and ended with the peaceful dispersal of the participants. These mock operations were completely successful in their aim: the Castle authorities refused to believe that the Volunteers were potentially dangerous and found it impossible to take any threat of a rising seriously. Although Nathan was fully informed about the increased recruitment to the Volunteers in late 1915 and early 1916, a mere fortnight before the Rising he was writing: 'Though the Irish Volunteer element has been active of late, especially in Dublin, I do not believe that its leaders mean insurrection or that the Volunteers have sufficient arms if the leaders do mean it.'

Eoin Mac Néill and the Irish Volunteers, February – April 1916

If it was relatively easy for the Military Council to pull the wool over the eyes of the Castle authorities, the deception of the non-IRB members of the Irish Volunteers was a much more delicate matter. Few of the rank and file of the Volunteers and the Citizen Army realised how close they were to being involved in an insurrection and attached no particular significance to Pearse's notice in the *Irish Volunteer* of the 8 April instructing all Volunteers to assemble for routine 'manoeuvres during the Easter holidays'. But Pearse and his friends found themselves faced with a much more serious problem when it came to dealing with the 'front' leadership of the Volunteers – men like Eóin Mac Néill and The O'Rahilly who saw the Volunteers not as a revolutionary army but as a pressure group whose existence would be sufficient to induce the British government to concede a generous measure of Home Rule when the war was over.

Mac Néill, who as president of the Irish Volunteers and chief-of-staff of the military directory had in theory the power to regulate all commands issued to the force, got an inkling of what was afoot when he discovered that certain orders received by some of his officers had come not from his own staff office but from an unknown source. Gravely alarmed by the rumours of an insurrection that were in the air, in February 1916 he decided to make his position absolutely clear to his followers. The Irish Volunteers, he said, would be justified in using force only to resist attempts to arrest or disarm them or to introduce conscription in Ireland. Furthermore, an insurrection would be justified only if it had the support of an overwhelming majority of the population and if it had a reasonable chance of success (these two qualifications were based on orthodox Catholic theology). Since the Volunteers numbered a mere 16,000 out of the total population, and since Ireland was experiencing an unprecedented economic wartime boom and many Irish families were deriving considerable benefits from service allowances etc., the two conditions did not apply. Mac Néill's statement therefore firmly ruled out the possibility of a rising, and he was somewhat pacified by assurances given to him by Pearse, Plunkett and MacDonagh that this had never been their intention.

Mac Néill had failed to reckon with three weaknesses in his argument. (1) By admitting that the Volunteers were entitled to resist disarmament etc., he laid himself open to exploitation by the desperate men among his followers, who might either provoke the government into taking such drastic action or who might circulate lying rumours that it was impending; (2) Mac Néill himself was essentially of unmilitary disposition, and he was blind to the tension and urge for action among men who had guns and only awaited further supplies to begin the shooting, regardless of whether they had popular support or not; (3) In basing his standpoint on reason and common sense, Mac Néill was totally outside the scope of Pearse's ideal of blood-sacrifice. He never realised that a handful of his followers were beginning to reject contemptuously the idea of a rising which had a 'good hope of success' and were deliberately preparing instead to follow a path that would lead inevitably to disaster and death.

In spite of all Mac Néill's objections and obstruction, the members of the Military Council were confident that their secret chain of command was preserved intact throughout the Volunteer organisation and that their trusted local commandants could be relied on to lead their units into rebellion on Easter Sunday. They pressed on with their preparations, and as the deadline approached they received the encouraging news that the vital cargo of German arms had been dispatched from Lübeck for the Kerry coast on 9 April.

The Plans Go Wrong, 20-23 April 1916

During the week preceding the Rising two setbacks occurred which were so serious that they seemed to wreck all the carefully laid plans of the Military Council: (1) The German arms never reached their destination; (2) Mac Néill, having discovered that he had been grossly deceived and that an insurrection was imminent, did everything in his power to prevent it.

(1) Owing to a misunderstanding, there was confusion about the time that the *Aud,* the steamer carrying the German guns, was to arrive outside Tralee Bay. The *Aud,* in fact, arrived on Thursday 20 April, and her captain, Karl Spindler, was dismayed to find no pilot boat to meet him and guide him to the harbour where the cargo could be unloaded. Having waited all night, the *Aud* was intercepted by British warships on Good Friday 21 April and forced to sail to Queenstown (Cobh); at the entrance to the harbour Spindler scuttled his ship and the precious cargo of guns went to the bottom of the sea.

Equally disastrous was the landing of Sir Roger Casement, who was put ashore at Banna Strand, Co. Kerry, on 21 April and was almost immediately taken into custody. Casement had left Germany bitterly disappointed at his failure to secure German military intervention in Ireland. He was convinced that no insurrection could succeed without a German landing, and in view of his later trial and execution for treason, it is a tragic irony that he came to Ireland determined to stop a rising which he believed was doomed to failure. Casement's arrest, however, together with the news of the loss of the *Aud,* had the effect of convincing the government authorities that the situation had been defused and that there was no longer any danger of a rebellion. They believed Casement to be the chief figure in the plot; like Mac Néill, they knew nothing of the Military Council's secret arrangements, while the concept of a blood-sacrifice simply did not enter into their calculations.

(2) The Military Council were anxious that Mac Néill should place no further obstacles to impede the progress of the events which they had set

in motion. On Wednesday 19 April he was shown a mysterious item known as the 'Castle Document'; this purported to be a copy of a government instruction for the supression of the Volunteers and the arrest of leading members, but it was almost certainly a forgery concocted by Mac Diarmada and Plunkett. On the same day Mac Néill learned of the Military Council's existence and of the proposed rising, and realised that for over two years he had been nothing more than a tool in the hands of unscrupulous men. He was profoundly shocked, but the threat implied in the Castle Document, the revelation that a large consignment of arms would shortly be arriving in the country, and the realisation that he would only create dangerous confusion by issuing orders conflicting with those that had already gone out, forced his hand. Believing that the Volunteers had a legitimate right to resist disarmament, and that the possession of the German guns would give their resistance a reasonable chance of success, he issued a warning to the Volunteers on Good Friday 21 April: 'Government action for the suppression of the Volunteers is now inevitable and may begin at any moment; preparations are going on for that purpose. We are compelled to be on our guard until our safety is assured.'

On the same day the Military Council received the news of the *Aud's* capture, but they did not inform Mac Néill. On the following day (Saturday 22 April), however, he discovered not only that the *Aud* had been sunk but that the Castle Document was a forgery. He now realised the full extent to which he had been deceived, and in the certain knowledge that the planned rising would be suicidal, he issued his famous countermanding order:

Volunteers completely deceived. All orders for
special action are hereby cancelled, and on no
account will action be taken.

Mac Néill also inserted in the *Sunday Independent* an order prohibiting all Volunteer movements for Easter Sunday 23 April, thus making it impossible for any rising to take place on that day.

But Mac Néill had once again failed to comprehend the determination of men who were committed to the ideal of blood-sacrifice, which by now was clearly the only reason for having a rising at all (though they were probably also aware that the proof which the government now had of a connection between the Volunteers and the German government would lead to the arrest of the leaders). On Easter Sunday the Military Council met and decided that the rising would take place on the following day. They were resigned to the fact that it would be a purely Dublin affair, as it was now impossible to bring in the country as a whole. Their secret orders to the IRB officers of the Volunteers were confirmed, and as many men as possible were mobilised. Even in Dublin it was impossible to get everyone out at such short notice, and when the total force of insurgents assembled at Liberty Hall towards noon on Easter Monday 24 April 1916, they numbered no more than 1,600.

The Easter Rising, 24-29 April 1916

The insurgents had no difficulty in carrying out the initial part of their plan. They quickly occupied the General Post Office in Sackville Street (now O'Connell Street), which they established as their headquarters, and six other prominent buildings in the city. But the leaders lacked military experience, and the changed circumstances in which the Rising began meant that far fewer men were involved than had been expected, so that the original plan had to be modified. The ensuing confusion and uncertainty revealed that the leaders had no workable alternative strategy; they simply dug themselves in and waited for something to happen. The failure of the Citizen Army to capture Dublin Castle (and Sir Matthew Nathan, who was in his office there) showed the weakness of their intelligence system, for the Castle was virtually unguarded and could easily have been taken by a small detachment.

Shortly after midday on Easter Monday 24 April, Pearse, in his capacity as president of the provisional government, formally proclaimed the Irish Republic by reading the following document to a small group of puzzled citizens who had gathered outside the GPO:

POBLACHT NA hEIREANN

THE PROVISIONAL GOVERNMENT
OF THE
IRISH REPUBLIC
TO THE PEOPLE OF IRELAND

IRISHMEN AND IRISHWOMEN: In the name of God and of the dead generations from which she receives her old tradition of nationhood, Ireland, through us, summons her children to her flag and strikes for her freedom.

Having organised and trained her manhood through her secret revolutionary organisation, the Irish Republican Brotherhood, and through her open military organisations, the Irish Volunteers and the Irish Citizen Army, having patiently perfected her discipline, having resolutely waited for the right moment to reveal itself, she now seizes that moment, and supported by her exiled children in America and by gallant allies in Europe, but relying the first on her own strength, she strikes in full confidence of victory.

We declare the right of the people of Ireland to the ownership of Ireland, and to the unfettered control of Irish destinies, to be sovereign and indefeasible. The long usurpation of that right by a foreign people and government has not extinguished the right, nor can it ever be extinguished except by the destruction of the Irish people. In every generation the Irish people have asserted their right to national freedom and sovereignty: six times during the past three hundred years they have asserted it in arms. Standing on that fundamental right and again asserting it in arms in the face of the world, we hereby proclaim the Irish Republic as a Sovereign Independent State, and we pledge our lives and the lives of our comrades-in-arms to the cause of its freedom, of its welfare, and of its exaltation among the nations.

The Irish Republic is entitled to, and hereby claims, the allegiance of every Irishman and Irishwoman. The Republic guarantees religious and civil liberty, equal rights and equal opportunities to all its citizens, and declares its resolve to pursue the happiness and prosperity of the whole nation and of all its parts, cherishing all the children of the nation equally and oblivious of the differences carefully fostered by an alien Government, which have divided a minority from the majority in the past.

Until our arms have brought the opportune moment for the establishment of a permanent National Government, representative of the whole people of Ireland and elected by the suffrages of all her men and women, the Provisional Government, hereby constituted, will administer the civil and military affairs of the Republic in trust for the people.

We place the cause of the Irish Republic under the protection of the Most High God, Whose blessing we invoke upon our arms, and we pray that no one who serves that cause will dishonour it by cowardice, inhumanity, or rapine. In this supreme hour the Irish nation must, by its valour and discipline, and by the readiness of its children to sacrifice themselves for the common good, prove itself worthy of the august destiny to which it is called.

Signed on Behalf of the Provisional Government.

THOMAS J. CLARKE.
SEAN Mac DIARMADA, THOMAS MacDONAGH,
P. H. PEARSE, EAMONN CEANNT,
JAMES CONNOLLY. JOSEPH PLUNKETT.

The Proclamation contained a number of important points. (1) It firmly based the legitimacy of the new state on the historic rights of Irish nationality. It thus established the Rising not as a mere revolutionary coup but as the logical outcome of the long process of Ireland's emergence into full nationhood. (2) It specifically identified the constitution of the new state as a republican one. While there is some doubt as to whether this arrangement was regarded as a permanent one by the signatories, there was no doubt at all in the minds of their successors. The Republic proclaimed in 1916 was ratified by the First Dáil in 1919, and the Proclamation is the seminal document of the modern twenty-six-county state. (3) In mentioning the assistance received from Germany, the Proclamation laid all the participants in the Rising open to the charge of treason and to ruthless retaliatory measures on the part of the government. (4) The Proclamation contained the germ of a programme of social reform, based on the principle of equality of all Irish citizens. This clearly reflects the ideals of Connolly.

The military history of the Rising is soon told. The essentially defensive posture taken by the Volunteers enabled the British military command to adopt a vigorous and aggressive plan. It was an easy matter to bring in massive reinforcements and heavy artillery; the only effective resistance the incoming troops encountered was from a small outlying contingent of de Valera's Boland's Mills garrison stationed at Mount Street Bridge. By Thursday there were over 12,000 British soldiers in Dublin, a gunboat, the *Helga*, had sailed up the Liffey and was bombarding the GPO with heavy shell-fire, and the newly arrived commanding officer, Lieutenant-General Sir John Maxwell, was clearly in control of the situation. By Friday the GPO was on fire and had become untenable, and in the afternoon of the following day (29 April) Pearse decided to surrender unconditionally.

Aftermath of the Rising, April – May 1916

The total casualties of the Easter Rising amounted to about 450 killed and 2,600 wounded. The majority of these were civilians (approximately 300 killed and 2,000 wounded). Accurate figures are available only for British troops and the police (132 killed and 397 wounded). The centre of Dublin city was in ruins, and the total damage to property was in the region of £2½ million. Over 3,500 persons were arrested; half of these were soon released, but the remainder, 1,840 persons, were sent to England for internment.

The ordinary people of Dublin had first found the affair exciting. Many of the occupants of the slum areas took advantage of the general disruption of normal life to break into shops and pubs and loot the contents. The poor and underprivileged had little interest in politics, or whether they were to be subjects of the United Kingdom or the Irish Republic; their own desperate needs were reflected in the type of goods they stole from the shops: clothes and shoes, food and drink, sweets and toys. But as ordinary life became paralysed, communications interrupted, food scarce and as civilian casualties mounted property was destroyed and martial law proclaimed, the reality of the situation dawned on them, and by the end of Easter Week they came to view the Rising as a tragedy. The cessation of hostilities found Irishmen reeling from the shock of the Rising as they counted the cost and asked themselves why such a terrible thing had happened. As the *Freeman's Journal* said, when it resumed circulation on 5 May, 'The stunning horror of the past ten days in Dublin makes it all but impossible for any patriotic Irishman who has been witness of the tragedy enacted in our midst to think collectedly or write calmly of the event.'

The initial reaction of bewilderment gave way to one of outrage reflected in the middle-class *Irish Independent's* call for 'condign punishment to be meted out to the rebels'. Bishop Mangan of Kerry denounced the Volunteers as 'evil-minded men affected by Socialistic and Revolutionary doctrines'. In such an atmosphere of public hostility towards the insurgents, the British government had a splendid opportunity to discredit extreme nationalism in general. But the country was now under martial law, and the man who made the decision about how to deal with the ringleaders was General Maxwell. He looked upon the Rising from the purely military angle, regarding it as a treacherous stab in the back during Britain's time of crisis, and he had no forebodings of any political repercussions.

Irish political leaders tried to warn the government of the dangers which would result if the situation were mishandled. Redmond, while voicing his 'detestation and horror' at what he considered to be a German-inspired plot against Home Rule, advised the government to show mercy to those involved, and his plea was echoed in much stronger language by his deputy, John Dillon, who prophesied that the government were 'letting loose a river of blood' by executing their prisoners. Even non-political figures like George Bernard Shaw advised against the risk of manufacturing martyrs.

But these sensible counsels did not prevail. Maxwell initiated a series of 170 secret courts martial, as a result of which ninety persons were condemned to death. All but fifteen of these had the sentences commuted to penal servitude for life (these included Éamon de Valera who escaped the death penalty because there was some confusion over his nationality, it being wrongly thought that he was an American citizen; the Countess Markievicz, who was spared because she was a woman; Thomas Ashe; and W. T. Cosgrave). The fifteen death sentences were carried out, two or three at a time, over the ten nerve-racking days (3-12 May). All the seven signatories of the Proclamation were shot, as well as the following men: Edward Daly, William Pearse, Michael O'Hanrahan, John MacBride, Michael Mallin, Con Colbert, Seán Heuston and Thomas Kent (in Cork). Casement was executed in London in August, thus bringing to a total of sixteen the number of those who paid with their lives for the part they played in the Easter Rising.

Maxwell's action was justifiable from a purely military standpoint, but if it is viewed in the light of its psychological impact on Irish public opinion, it was a colossal blunder. Particularly distressing aspects of the executions were that Colbert and Heuston were little more than boys; that Plunkett was a dying man; that Connolly was so disabled by the wounds he had received during the fighting that he had to be tied in a chair before he was shot; that English public opinion was turned against Casement by means of an unsavoury smear campaign against aspects of his private life which had nothing to do with the charge for which he was on trial; that the harmless Willie Pearse, who was only an ordinary Volunteer private, was executed for no other reason than that he was Pádraic's brother.

Change in Irish Public Opinion, 1916

The executions caused a wave of horror and revulsion to pass over Ireland. Ordinary people were appalled at the barbarity and severity of the revenge exacted by the military authorities. It was remembered that the insurgents, however mistaken their aims, had fought bravely as soldiers for Ireland, and it was widely felt that they deserved a better fate. On the other hand, stories soon began to emerge about a number of atrocities commited by the British troops in Dublin during the Rising. The feelings of many Irishmen were expressed in a letter written by Bishop O'Dwyer of Limerick to Maxwell on 17 May:

> You took good care that no plea for mercy should interpose on behalf of the poor young fellows who surrendered to you in Dublin. The first information we got of their fate was the announcement that they had been shot in cold blood. Personally, I regard your action with horror, and I believe that it has outraged the conscience of the country. Then the deporting of hundreds and even thousands of poor fellows without a trial of any kind seems to me an abuse of power as fatuous as it is arbitrary, and altogether your regime has been one of the worst and blackest chapters in the history of the misgovernment of the country.

In focusing attention on the inadequacy of British rule in Ireland, the final statement in O'Dwyer's letter provided an effective answer to those Englishmen who had for generations been questioning whether the Irish were fit for self-government. Now the boot was on the other foot: in the aftermath of the executions and internments Irishmen were asking whether the men who could perform or condone such acts were fit to govern Ireland.

By early June 1916 Irish majority public opinion had swung round in favour of the Easter rebels. The great sympathy felt towards the dead leaders was reflected in the large attendances at commemorative masses, which were made occasions for large-scale displays of extreme nationalist and anti-English feeling. Pictures of the leaders of the Rising were sold in shops, and considerable interest was being shown in the poetry of Pearse, Plunkett and MacDonagh. Thus within the space of a single month 'evil-minded men' had been transformed first into 'poor young fellows' and then into the idols of a national cult. In the words of the poet W. B. Yeats,

> All changed, changed utterly;
> A terrible beauty is born.

The Easter Rising ultimately became buried in mythology. From the military viewpoint it was a disaster, but the blood-sacrifice of Pearse and his comrades eventually had the effects for which they had scarcely dared to hope. The Rising was thus not an end in itself, but rather a beginning; a point of departure. When moderate nationalists realised that the dead leaders had willingly given their lives for the benefit of their fellow-Irishmen, they were prepared to forgive them for being so presumptuous as to embark on a violent and unpopular course of action in the name of the Irish people. They began to ask themselves whether the ideals of the Easter martyrs could possibly form the inspiration for a new and more satisfactory solution to the question of Irish self-government. But it remained to be seen exactly how the powerful emotional fervour stirred up by the Easter Rising would be translated into political terms.

Sinn Féin Transformed, 1916-17

Arthur Griffith's little Sinn Féin organisation was opposed to the use of physical force, had never advocated an Irish Republic and was not involved in the Easter Rising. Nevertheless, it was commonly believed that Sinn Féin had, somehow or other, been responsible for the Rising, and this view received greater currency when Griffith was included among those sent for internment in England. The following eighteen months were to witness a process by which the name 'Sinn Féin' was taken over and given a new meaning by the forces of resurgent nationalism, and in which the original movement's relatively moderate policies were swamped by the ideals of the 'men of 1916'.

There was little organised resistance to British rule in Ireland in the months immediately following the Rising, though the general sense of resentment was kept alive by the continuance of martial law until November 1916. However, the IRB, though considerably reduced in numbers by the wholesale deporatation of its members, managed to remain active and helped to set up the Irish National Aid Association and the Irish Volunteers' Dependants' Fund. These organisations created a link between those who had been involved in the Rising and the general public and also served as a focus of support in England and America. They provided a nucleus around which gathered those forces which later emerged as 'Sinn Féin'.

In December 1916 the new British Prime Minister, David Lloyd George, decided to make a goodwill gesture towards Ireland and ordered the release of all the internees except for the convicted ringleaders. The majority of the prisoners had originally cared little about the philosophy of advanced nationalism or republicanism, but during their internment they had completed their political education and returned to Ireland as confirmed 'Sinn Féiners'. They also returned as national heroes, and it was obvious that from among them would be supplied the much-needed leadership which would harness and direct the energies of the new militant nationalism. Among the released prisoners who were to play important roles in shaping Ireland's future were Arthur Griffith himself and two relatively unknown young men, Michael Collins and Cathal Brugha.

Griffith at once began to publicise his theories, concentrating on those aspects which would be most acceptable in the changed circumstances. But throughout the spring and early summer of 1917 there was no real attempt to organise the new 'Sinn Féin' on a central or national basis. Instead the initiative was taken at local level. Sinn Féin clubs began to spring up in the parliamentary constituencies, and by the time the first Sinn Féin *árd-fheis* was held in October 1917 their number had reached 1,200, claiming a membership of 250,000. And it was in the constituencies that the new popular nationalism won its first tangible victories.

The Volunteers Re-formed, 1917

In the early months of 1917 Collins, Brugha and Thomas Ashe began building up the Volunteer force. The changed climate of opinion gave a tremendous impetus to recruiting, and within little more than a year membership had risen to 100,000, giving the force a strength similar to that of the original Volunteers in early 1914 before the Redmondite split. But the re-formed Volunteer body was different in one important respect from the pre-1916 movement. Whereas the earlier Volunteers had been uncertain as to their exact relationship with the political movement — or even as to which political movement they should identify with — and as to the exact circumstances in which their weapons should be used for political purposes, their successors in 1917 were left in no doubt. Sinn Féin and the Irish Volunteers formed two wings, political and military, of a single national movement whose clear objective was the achievement of an independent Irish Republic. When Sinn Féin effectively provided the functional government of an Irish Republic in 1919, the Volunteers became the army of the Republic, otherwise known as the IRA, whose military power was to be used to defend the new state against the enemy forces of occupation.

By-Elections, 1917: North Roscommon, etc.

Parliamentary elections are the acid test of any supposed change in public opinion. In November 1916 a candidate standing on a 'Sinn Féin' ticket contested a by-election in West Cork. He was defeated, but his attempt was significant, since for the first time since 1874 (except for the North Leitrim by-election of 1908, see page 100) nationalist electors had been presented with an alternative to Home Rule. In the first eight months of 1917 this choice was given to four other constituencies, and in each case the Sinn Féin candidate was victorious.

The first of these by-elections was in North Roscommon in February 1917. The militant nationalists decided to put forward Count Plunkett, the father of the executed Joseph Plunkett, as their candidate. Although Plunkett chose to stand as an independent, he espoused all the new Sinn Féin principles and his campaign was assisted by the IRB and other groups of advanced nationalists. On being elected he refused to take his seat at Westminster and thus became the first Irish abstentionist MP.

Another victorious by-election candidate was Joseph McGuinness in

South Longford in May. He was in jail at the time of the election and won the seat on the appeal 'Put him in to get him out'. But the most important of the series of by-elections was that in East Clare in July, for it first brought into prominence the outstanding political leader of the modern Irish state.

The Rise of de Valera, 1917

In the summer of 1917 the government extended its amnesty to the remaining detainees. Among the last of these to return to Ireland in June was Éamon de Valera, the senior surviving commandant of the Easter Rising. Although he was almost completely unknown to the Irish public, his past record was sufficient to secure his nomination to the next parliamentary vacancy that occurred, East Clare in July 1917. His election by a large majority was a foregone conclusion. De Valera, like Count Plunkett, won his seat solely on the strength of his connection with the Rising; but unlike the Count, he soon revealed himself as an astute and capable politician whose keen and subtle mind was well adapted to dealing with the problems posed by the transformed political situation in Ireland.

One of the greatest of these problems was the need to weld together into a harmonious and concerted force the various nationalist elements that were flocking beneath the Sinn Féin banner: moderate separatists and extreme republicans, old-style Sinn Féin traditionalists and activists imbued with the principles of 1916. During his election campaign he therefore gave a somewhat guarded welcome to the idea of a permanent republican settlement:

> We want an Irish republic because if Ireland had her freedom, it is, I believe, the most likely form of government. But if the Irish people wanted to have another form of government, so long as it was an Irish government, I would not put in a word against it.

If Arthur Griffith was the man who formulated the philosophy of Sinn Féin, de Valera was the man who showed how it could be put into practice.

The Sinn Féin Árd-Fheis and the Volunteer Convention, October 1917

Until the late summer of 1917 Sinn Féin was little more than a loosely organised collection of local clubs scattered throughout the country. Moves were then begun to bring them under some sort of central co-ordinating control and to hammer out a comprehensive set of policy objectives acceptable to all.

The *árd-fheis* was held on 25 October 1917. Thanks to the ingenuity of de Valera, a formula of Sinn Féin's basic principles had been devised which would reconcile the republican and non-republican sections of the movement:

> Sinn Féin aims at securing the international recognition of Ireland as an independent Irish Republic.
> Having achieved that status, the Irish people may by referendum freely choose their own form of government.

Providing Sinn Féin with a national organisation meant that officers had to be chosen. De Valera was unanimously elected President (both Griffith and Plunkett standing down in order to avoid a vote), and Collins and Brugha were among those appointed to the national executive. Although de Valera's carefully worded formula had reconciled the pre-1916 Sinn Féiners to post-rising developments, it is clear that the organisation had been taken over by the new generation of advanced nationalists.

On the following day (26 October) the annual Volunteer convention was held. De Valera was elected President; and Brugha as Chief of Staff and Collins as Director of Organisation became members of a reconstituted executive. There was thus considerable overlapping in the membership of the two wings of the national movement: de Valera, Collins and Brugha were by no means the only personnel who served on both bodies.

As in the pre-Rising period, there was a secret IRB presence in both organisations: this was substantial in the case of the Volunteers, but much less strong in Sinn Féin. However, this was offset by a new and powerful anti-IRB element: Brugha, for example, was vigorously opposed to the IRB, which he claimed had outlived its usefulness and ought to be replaced by open popular resistance to British rule; de Valera also had been, at best, a reluctant member of the secret society, and he refused to rejoin it after 1916. On the other hand, Collins, who was rapidly emerging as the most gifted organising genius of the national movement, was a dedicated IRB man; in addition to his work for the two open organisations, he also functioned at this time in the important post of IRB executive secretary.

The Irish Convention, 1917-18

Meanwhile the government was making its last serious attempt to find out what Irishmen wanted. The United States government had issued a declaration in favour of self-determination for all nations, and after America's entry into the First World War in April 1917 President Woodrow Wilson urged Lloyd George to produce an equitable solution to the Irish question. Lloyd George, therefore, summoned a large convention of representative Irishmen of all shades of political opinion to make recommendations about some form of self-government on which they would all agree. The Irish Convention gathered under the chairmanship of Sir Horace Plunkett and was in session from July 1917 until April 1918.

The Irish Convention was doomed from the start. It was boycotted by

Sinn Féin and organised labour, so that it was not as representative of the full spectrum of political opinion as had been hoped. The Ulster Unionists proved just as inflexible as they had done in 1914, with the result that the only constructive discussion was between the Irish Parliamentary Party and the Southern Unionists and was limited to the Home Rule context. The only proposal that emerged from their deliberations was a modified form of Home Rule, and even this compromise did not have anything like the full support of the two groups involved. The Convention was a total failure and broke up amid disagreement and recrimination.

The only people to benefit from the Irish Convention were (1) Lloyd George, who shifted the onus of failure to settle the Irish question onto the Irish themselves, who had by their quarrelling destroyed the opportunity presented to them, (2) the Ulster Unionists whose intransigent attitude indicated clearly that the partition of Ireland was now inevitable, and (3) Sinn Féin, who profited by the general discredit which the Irish Party's dealings had brought upon itself. The more the Irish Party declined in popularity, the stronger Sinn Féin became.

The death of John Redmond, which occurred as the Convention drew to a close in March 1918, passed almost unnoticed. For thirty-seven years he had worked unceasingly to win Home Rule for Ireland. He had been on the very verge of success, but a mere two years later his entire life's work lay in ruins.

The Conscription Crisis, 1916-18

Militant nationalist activity after 1916 was not limited solely to the campaign for political independence. It was also channelled into a vigorous and active campaign against the introduction of conscription in Ireland. The anti-conscription movement united all shades of nationalist opinion — including even the Home Rulers — so that, apart from the north-east, the whole country presented a solid and unified front against the British government. Indeed, since conscription would directly affect the lives of virtually everyone in Ireland, the resistance to it was of greater urgency and immediacy to most people than the winning of an independent republic. People who cared nothing at all about politics cared a great deal about being drafted into the army against their will, and they therefore rallied to Sinn Féin.

Conscription had been introduced in England in 1915, and in the remaining three years of the war there was a rising clamour for it to be extended to Ireland. The steadfastness of Irish resistance and the intensity of the government authorities' reaction were largely responsible for the worsening political situation in Ireland during 1917. Meetings were banned, individuals prosecuted for making seditious speeches, and a general policy of harassment was pursued by the government. One of those arrested was Thomas Ashe, the president of the IRB, who died in prison as a result of being forcibly fed while on hunger strike in September 1917. But the government's tough line only served to drive more people into the ranks of Sinn Féin, which took all the credit for leading the anti-conscription campaign. By the spring of 1918 a massive German offensive on the western front brought the conscription crisis to a head. In April parliament passed a Military Service Act which empowered the government to extend conscription to Ireland, and the Irish Party, now led by John Dillon, withdrew in a body from Westminster and for once made common cause with the Sinn Féiners. A short-lived alliance was formed between the forces of constitutional and revolutionary nationalism which resulted in the anti-conscription Mansion House Conference. The conference accepted a pledge drafted by de Valera:

> Denying the right of the British government to enforce compulsory service in this country, we pledge ourselves solemnly to one another to resist conscription by the most effective means at our disposal.

Since the Irish Party had at this late stage embraced the abstentionist principle of Sinn Féin, and since the latter was clearly the dominant partner in the alliance, the Irish Party's morale was damaged and it was confronted with the choice of either being swallowed up by Sinn Féin or dissolving the alliance and facing the possibility of perishing in isolation. It chose the latter course.

The 'German Plot', May 1918

In May 1918 a desperate government decided to take a firm line with the anti-conscription agitation and sent Field-Marshal Lord French to Ireland as the new Lord Lieutenant with extensive powers of coercion. French was a tough-minded military man, of much the same stamp as General Maxwell, and it was widely believed that he had come to Ireland to enforce conscription.

A week after his arrival French swooped down on the anti-conscriptionists. On the night of 17 May the leaders of Sinn Féin, the Volunteers, the Gaelic League and several other nationalist organisations were arrested. Collins and Brugha were the only prominent nationalists to evade the net. Two months later all the leading nationalist organisations were suppressed. The excuse given by the authorities for these actions was the almost entirely fabricated story that Irish nationalists were involved in a treasonable 'German plot' to overthrow British rule with German aid.

The arrests caused a great upsurge of support for Sinn Féin. In June Griffith, in jail since his arrest in May, was victorious in a by-election in East Cavan. Membership of the Sinn Féin clubs and Volunteer companies increased rapidly, although both organisations had been driven underground and forced to conduct their activities in secret. The key figure in adapting the anti-conscription and republican forces to the new situation was

Michael Collins, whose ruthless efficiency and skill as an undercover organiser of resistance became almost legendary. Assisted by a small group of devoted fellow-workers, Collins avoided arrest and began to lay down the organisational framework of what was later to become an alternative Irish government.

The General Election, December 1918

The First World War ended with the surrender of Germany on 11 November 1918, and immediately a general election was called. It was the first general election for exactly eight years — an unusually long interval — which meant that a great many of the younger electors were voting for the first time. Furthermore, the Representation of the People Act (1918) brought about a massive franchise reform, increasing the Irish electorate from just over 700,000 in 1910 to almost 2 million in 1918. Among those who now got the vote for the first time were men over twenty-one living in their parents' homes and women over thirty. All this meant that the issue of the election would be very largely decided by women and young men — two sections of society who are particularly inclined to adopt a militant stance.

For the first time the Irish electorate as a whole was given a choice between two forms of nationalism, and many seats in nationalist areas were now contested for the first time since the Parnell split. Although Sinn Féin was now an illegal organisation 'on the run', its 1,500 local clubs conducted a vigorous election campaign. The Sinn Féin republican programme was based on four main points: abstention from Westminster; complete separatism and freedom from British rule, to be secured by all means available; full autonomy for Ireland, including an independent Irish parliament; and international recognition, to be obtained through the participation of the Irish Republic in the post-war Peace Conference of Allied sovereign powers. In comparison with this, the best that the Irish Party could offer was what they called 'Dominion Home Rule', a somewhat stronger measure of self-government than that which had been enacted in 1914.

The election result changed the course of Irish political history. At the time of the dissolution of parliament the Irish seats were distributed as follows: Nationalists (i.e. Home Rulers) 78; Sinn Féin 7; Unionists 18. After the election a totally new picture emerged: Nationalists 6; Sinn Féin 73; Unionists 26. In terms of parliamentary power, the Home Rulers and Sinn Féiners had reversed their positions. In political terms Sinn Féin had achieved a landslide victory; yet in numerical terms this victory was not a walkover, since a significant minority of 237,000 people voted for Home Rule against the 485,000 who voted for Sinn Féin. Nevertheless Sinn Féin had clearly emerged as the largest and most representative political force in Ireland, and following its election achievement its right to speak for the majority of the Irish people would have to be acknowledged by the British government. But would it be acknowledged? After all, Sinn Féin had been officially proclaimed an illegal organisation, and exactly half the victorious Sinn Féin MPs were in British jails.

Talking Points

Chapter 6: The Easter Rising and the New Sinn Féin 1914-18

　1 Outline the IRB involvement in the planning of the Easter Rising, with special reference to the work of Seán Mac Diarmada and Tom Clarke.

　2 Write a brief history of the Irish Volunteers from 1913-16. How did Eóin Mac Néill become compromised by his position as commander-in-chief of the Volunteers in 1916?

　3 In what way was Pádraic Pearse a key figure in bringing about the Easter Rising? Give a short biographical sketch of his life and work.

　4 Explain and contrast Dublin Castle's complaisant attitude towards the preparations for the Rising and the British government's vigorous reaction to the events of Easter Week 1916.

　5 Write in diary form an account of the main events in Dublin from Monday to Saturday of Easter Week 1916.

　6 Comment on Yeats' line 'All changed, changed utterly', with reference to the aftermath of the Rising. Compare the fortunes of the Irish Parliamentary Party with those of Sinn Féin during the period from May 1916 to December 1918.

Chapter 7
THE WAR OF INDEPENDENCE, 1919-21

The Founding of Dáil Éireann, 1919
The first session of Dáil Éireann (Assembly of Ireland) was held in the Mansion House, Dublin on 21 January 1919. Invitations had been sent to *all* the Irish MPs elected in 1918, but Unionists and the surviving Home Rulers refused to participate, and the attendance was therefore limited to the Sinn Féin members. Since many of these were in prison or absent for other reasons, no more than twenty-seven were present.

The session lasted for only two hours, and most of its proceedings were in Irish. Cathal Brugha acted as provisional President of the assembly. At this meeting was read and approved a provisional constitution, a declaration of independence, a 'Message to the Free Nations of the World', and a socio-economic policy document known as the Democratic Programme. The Dáil formally ratified the republic which had been proclaimed in 1916 and selected delegates to the post-war Peace Conference at Paris, at which it was hoped that the Irish Republic would secure recognition from the other European powers.

The adoption of the provisional constitution marks the beginning of the present twenty-six county state. The Dáil's main concern was the setting up of the necessary machinery for running an independent Irish government. It adopted the same kind of parliamentary procedure and the same kind of civil service as existed in England.

The Dáil regarded itself as a constituent assembly, i.e. a body possessing the power to frame a constitution and whose members had the duty and responsibility of carrying on the government. They approached their task with enthusiasm, but suffered from lack of experience in parliamentary procedure. They were over-optimistic and even utopian in their Democratic Programme, which was of little lasting value, though it evidently helped to advertise the Dáil's views to the world. It would appear that the members of the Dáil had their sights set on the approaching Peace Conference at Versailles near Paris. They hoped that the Irish government (i.e. Dáil Éireann) would be invited to send a representative to Versailles. They hoped too that President Wilson of the USA would champion their cause, but he proved unwilling to endanger his country's good relations with Britain. In spite of considerable pressure exerted on him by the Dáil and various Irish-American groups, Wilson refused to urge international recognition of the new Irish government.

The British government reacted to the establishment of the rival administration in Dublin with extreme caution. It had no wish to run the risk of further outbreaks of trouble in Ireland, as well as criticism at home and from the foreign powers at the Peace Conference. The Dáil also was resolved to avoid an appeal to unnecessary physical force: the alternative Irish government was to be implemented not by means of a second rising, but by moral force and passive resistance.

In early 1919 England was suffering from a serious influenza epidemic, and Lloyd George feared that further Irish 'martyrs' might be created if any of the Sinn Féin internees died in jail. He ordered their release in March (many of them, including de Valera, had already escaped). Fifty-two members were therefore free to attend the second session of the Dáil when it met on 1 April. At this meeting de Valera was elected President (Príomh-Aire), and he nominated his cabinet as follows: Griffith (Home Affairs and Deputy President); Collins (Finance); Brugha (Defence); Cosgrave (Local Government); Plunkett (Foreign Affairs); Markievicz (Labour); Mac Néill (Industries); Robert Barton (Agriculture).

Two months later the President departed on a mission to the United States, during which he succeeded in gaining considerable financial and moral support for the Dáil government from the American public, but failed to win official recognition of the Irish Republic and diplomatic intervention on its behalf from the American government. De Valera intended his visit to be a fairly short one, but he did not return to Ireland until the end of 1920.

The Dáil Government, 1919-21

The Dáil's first concern was that its government should function as smoothly as possible throughout the country. From the very start of its existence it had to face a number of serious problems: the lack of experience of the new administrators; the continuing presence of a long-established rival regime with which, sooner or later, the Dáil was bound to come into conflict; the difficulty of establishing control over the Volunteers in order to convert them into a loyal national army; and the total lack of funds.

This last problem was tackled with characteristic energy by the Minister for Finance, Michael Collins. He managed to raise a Dáil Loan of £358,000 which was later augmented by about £1,000,000 collected by de Valera in America. This money supplied the financial basis of the Dáil government and the struggle for Irish independence. Barton in the Department of Agriculture founded a Land Bank which assisted the process of land purchase by advancing loans to farmers. In order to counter the illegal activities of agrarian radicals in the west and south a land commission was established with powers to regulate land redistribution on a basis acceptable to the Dáil, and special land courts were set up to settle disputed cases.

A completely new judicial system was also devised, originating in 'arbitration courts' which were set up as a result of local initiative in various parts of the west in 1919. These courts were examples of self-government by local communities: they had no legal status, their 'magistrates' were respected local figures rather than trained lawyers, and the parties to disputes had to be trusted voluntarily to accept their decisions. They worked so well that in 1920 Griffith regularised the system and extended it over the entire area controlled by the Dáil. By the time of the truce in 1921 over 900 Parish Courts and 70 District Courts were in operation, as well as a Supreme Court in Dublin. Sessions of the Dáil courts were often held side by side with those of the official Dublin Castle courts, and litigants had to decide which of the two it would be more expedient to patronise. The authority of the Dáil courts was upheld and their decisions enforced by a body of Republican Police, whose presence in a locality served as a counterweight to the RIC.

No such drastic innovations were necessary for bringing local government under the control of the Dáil. Apart from north-east Ulster, the entire existing system of county councils and urban and rural district councils was simply taken over by Sinn Féin in the local government elections of 1920. Cosgrave and Kevin O'Higgins, his deputy in the Department of Local Government, asked the Sinn Féin-dominated councils to sever their connections with the British government and give their allegiance to the Dáil, and despite the considerable financial losses which they suffered as a result of the withdrawal of their government grants, all of them did so.

One group of people who were pleasantly surprised by the early achievements of the Dáil government were the Southern Unionists. While refusing to relinquish their loyalty to the crown, they readily admitted the Dáil's success in maintaining civil order firmly and fairly at local level and protecting the existing rights of property. If the Dáil was a revolutionary body, it was so only in a purely *political* sense; it initiated no radical social, economic or sectarian policies, and the Southern Unionists were unmolested by the civil government.

IRA Attacks, 1919

The early months of the Dáil's existence were overshadowed by two grave questions, both relating to the use of physical force. (1) How should the Dáil react if confronted with the threat of forcible repression by the Dublin Castle authorities? (2) Could the civil government (the Dáil) establish full control over the republican military forces (the Volunteers)? The Volunteers, after all, were the senior body and possessed their own organisational framework and command, which was only connected with that of the Dáil in that they shared the same President. Dáil members hoped that the Irish Republic could be maintained without recourse to a military offensive, but many Volunteers believed that further fighting would be necessary to complete the revolution and 'get the English out of Ireland'. Many of the Volunteer companies in the provinces were made up of young activists who were virtually independent of central control. During 1918 these men carried out a number of raids on police barracks and private houses. Their aim was to capture arms and ammunition, which were in very short supply. Eventually the inevitable happened: on 21 January 1919—the very day of the Dáil's first session—a party of Volunteers including Sean Treacy, Dan Breen and Seamus Robinson, ambushed a cartload of gelignite at Soloheadbeg, Co. Tipperary, and shot dead the two constables who were escorting it. These fatal casualties are generally reckoned to mark the start of the War of Independence.

Further attacks and more deaths occurred in the spring and summer of 1919. The Dáil administration had no more love for the RIC than had the Volunteers, but it was uneasy over the accelerating campaign of violence, which was being carried out on the orders of local commandants and without the sanction of the Dáil. Cathal Brugha, as Minister for Defence, was particularly anxious that the confused and ill-defined relationship between the Volunteers and the Dáil should be regularised and that the former should be formally constituted and recognised as the military arm of the latter. The situation was further complicated by the fact that Collins was highly regarded throughout the Volunteers and, as their Adjutant-General and Director of Organisation and Intelligence, was unquestionably more influential than Brugha, who was technically his superior. The two men disliked and distrusted one another, and this animosity was worsened by the fact that Collins was at the head of the IRB, which maintained a secret presence within the Volunteers. Brugha detested the IRB, believing that its ultimate allegiance was to its own Supreme Council rather than to the elected government of the country. However, in August 1919 Brugha managed to extract an oath of allegiance from all individual Volunteers, and the force thereby became the national army of the Republic, otherwise known as the IRA. But in spite of the oath, it appears that the IRA continued to operate to a large extent independently of the civil government.

The first phase of the war lasted until the spring of 1920 and consisted largely of IRA attacks on RIC barracks, police huts and patrols. The RIC bore the brunt of the IRA's campaign partly because they were the most conspicuous representative of British rule throughout the country, and partly because they possessed the supplies of arms and ammunition which the IRA so badly needed. The deep popular resentment which their fellow-Irishmen had displayed towards the police since 1916 had helped to demoralise the force. Intimidation and conflicting loyalties caused frequent resignations, and it was almost impossible to find new recruits. As the attacks intensified, the RIC gradually withdrew from their more isolated barracks and posts (which were then systematically destroyed by the IRA), leaving Sinn Féin as undisputed masters over large areas of the countryside.

Collins was determined that the activities of the IRA should not be betrayed by government spies and informers. He master-minded an ingenious counter-espionage network which penetrated even the government headquarters in Dublin Castle. He also set up a small 'squad' of special agents under his personal direction who, towards the end of 1919, ruthlessly eliminated all the leading detectives of the notorious G Division of the Dublin Metropolitan Police and a number of other persons considered to be dangerous. At about the same time the IRA, emboldened by their recent successes against the police, began to carry out attacks on the British soldiers stationed in Ireland, and in December they almost succeeded in a daring attempt to assassinate the Viceroy, Lord French.

The British government clearly had to take some kind of firm action if it was to regain control of the situation. It had held its hand throughout most of 1919, partly for fear of adverse public reaction to repressive policies, partly because it was anxious to preserve the impression that the conflict was not a war but a civil disorder created by a subversive criminal or 'murder gang' which should be dealt with by the appropriate civil authorities, i.e. the police. The Dáil was proclaimed an illegal body in September 1919 and met very seldom thereafter. Most of its work now fell onto the shoulders of the individual ministers acting on their own initiative as they hurried from one hiding-place to another. Collins became the most wanted man in Ireland, a reward of £10,000 being offered for his capture. He never used disguise, but walked or rode his bicycle through the streets of Dublin, knowing that the Castle authorities had no reliable description of him.

By the beginning of 1920 Lloyd George realised that he could not revive his government's flagging authority in Ireland by hunting down individual Sinn Féiners. He decided to apply a policy of compromise—a mixture of conciliation and coercion. Conciliation would take the form of the implementation of Home Rule for Ireland. Coercion was to be provided by an enlarged police body; and since Irishmen could not be induced to join the RIC, Lloyd George resolved to fill the depleted ranks of the force with Englishmen.

The Government of Ireland Act, 1920

Lloyd George's Home Rule scheme had been planned during 1919 and became law as the Government of Ireland Act in late 1920. The act granted a limited measure of self-government, very similar to that proposed in the 1912 bill. However, it also contained two important innovations: (1) It effected the partition of the country by providing for two Home Rule parliaments, one in Belfast to govern the six north-eastern counties, and one in Dublin to govern the remaining twenty-six counties. All elected representatives were to take an oath of allegiance to the crown, and if a majority of members in either of the parliaments failed to do so, that parliament was to be dissolved and direct rule instituted in that part of Ireland. (2) Since the British government regarded partition as a strictly temporary measure, necessitated by the existing political climate, it made some provision for the eventual reunification of the country by creating a Council of Ireland. This all-Ireland body was intended as a forum for discussion of matters of common interest to North and South, and it was hoped that its powers would be gradually increased with the consent of the two parliaments until it and they could be replaced by a single legislative assembly for the whole country.

No one in Ireland welcomed the Government of Ireland Act. To the Sinn Féiners, it was simply irrelevant to the post-1916 situation: it took no account at all of the radical transformation of majority political opinion in the country. The Ulster Unionists remained as firmly opposed as ever to any weakening of the Union and the link with Westminster. However, the act had at least removed them from the jurisdiction of the Dublin parliament, and they therefore gave it a grudging acceptance. But they were determined that it should be the permanent, not just a temporary, solution to the Irish question; they refused to consider the eventual reunification of the country and resolved to have nothing to do with the Council of Ireland. Their opposition to the republican government in the South (which claimed jurisdiction over the whole island) was strengthened by the activities of the republican army in the six counties. Unionists regarded the IRA in the North as dangerous traitors in their midst and responded with a vicious backlash. In 1920 Belfast experienced its worst-ever sectarian rioting, during which large numbers of Catholics were killed, injured or driven from their homes. British conciliation had clearly not brought about Irish reconciliation.

The Black and Tans, 1920

Meanwhile the first of the new English police recruits had arrived in Ireland in March 1920. They were not the type of men who would have been accepted by any police force in normal circumstances. They were young men who had served in the war and had been unable to find work after their demobilisation. In the post-war economic depression which had struck Britain, unemployment was at a very high level, and few employers were prepared to offer steady jobs to untrained men whose wartime experiences had given them a taste for adventure and had inured them to violence and brutality. Such men eagerly grasped the opportunity to return to the only kind of life they knew or cared about—at the very attractive wages of ten shillings a day. On their arrival in Ireland it was found that there were not enough of the dark police uniforms to go round, and the missing items of clothing were supplied from khaki army uniforms. Their parti-coloured outfits inspired the nickname 'Black and Tans' and also served to symbolise their anomalous position: they were technically policemen, but they acted as a military combat force.

A second armed force, known as the Auxiliaries, was created in August

1920 to supplement the Black and Tans. The Auxiliaries were ex-officers and tended to be slightly older, tougher, and more responsible than the Black and Tans. They formed an elite commando-style force; they were paid £1 a day and were allowed considerable freedom of action.

As well as sending the police reinforcements to Ireland, Lloyd George made a number of changes at a higher administrative level which he hoped would make the Dublin Castle government more effective throughout the country. He appointed a new Chief Secretary, Sir Hamar Greenwood, who adopted the policy of allowing the forces of law and order a free hand in their struggle against terrorism. The command of the regular military forces in Ireland was given to General Sir Neville Macready, who was known to favour direct military rule, while another general, H. H. Tudor, was put in charge of the police.

In the second half of 1920 there were about 30,000 regular soldiers in Ireland, as well as 11,000 police (including the Black and Tans and Auxiliaries). The soldiers remained to some extent outside the struggle, partly because the IRA was reluctant to pit its strength against experienced professional soldiers, and partly because Lloyd George did not want the army to play an active role in maintaining the peace, since to do so would be to concede full belligerent status to the IRA and thus, in a sense, to recognise the existence of the Irish Republic. Armed and active IRA members numbered little more than 3,000 at any one time. It remained to be seen whether the reinforced RIC was now of sufficient strength to counter the activities of these men and restore British rule in those areas where it was fast breaking down.

Guerrilla Warfare, 1920

The Black and Tans quickly found that fighting the IRA was a very different matter to fighting the Germans. The First World War had been conducted according to the international rules of war. The opposing armies were clearly recognisable to one another; they were ranged in trenches which faced each other across a clearly defined no man's land; they advanced or retreated across definite tracts of territory and measured their progress by the amount of land they could defend behind their front line. But in the kind of guerrilla warfare that now prevailed in Ireland there were no rules; there was no front line—or rather the front line was everywhere; the enemy was invisible—but he was everywhere. The IRA wore no uniform (since this would have immediately invited the attention of the numerically superior British forces), and an apparently innocent group of by-standers could suddenly be transformed into a detachment of armed men who could strafe an RIC patrol with gunfire and then slip away quickly and quietly to mingle with the local population.

In conditions like these the Black and Tans' nerves were strained to breaking-point. Their pent-up tensions sometimes exploded in deeds of inhuman savagery. They had to regard every ordinary member of the public with deepest suspicion, and it was quite possible for a harmless man to be shot dead merely because he had his hands in his pockets. In turn, ordinary people throughout the country felt that they were being terrorised by the Black and Tans. Whereas the independently operating Volunteers of 1918-19 had been regarded by many people as something of a nuisance, by the end of 1920 they were seen as the only defenders of public safety against the British forces. Considered as soldiers, the heavy-handed Black and Tans achieved a certain degree of success against their opponents. Considered as policemen, their record was appalling: they had no knowledge of local terrain, no understanding of the rural Irish character: instead of preserving the peace, they inflamed the conflict; and they succeeded only in utterly alienating the general public.

The truth was that in guerrilla warfare no one could win. The British forces were immensely superior in numbers and equipment, but the IRA had extensive local knowledge, the support of the majority of the people, and the advantage of surprise tactics. The conflict seemed destined to become stalemated into a pattern of terror and counter-terror. The British commander-in-chief, Macready, was convinced that if martial law was introduced throughout Ireland, he would be able to use his increased military powers to crush the rebels decisively, but Lloyd George was unwilling to sanction this move because it would lay his government open to censure from sections of the British public and from world opinion in general. However, he did agree to give Macready certain special powers, and eventually, in December 1920 and January 1921, he allowed the most disordered part of the country (the entire province of Munster and two southern counties of Leinster) to be placed under martial law.

Macready's special powers in the final months of 1920 enabled him to authorise the Black and Tans to arrest and intern anyone suspected of belonging to Sinn Féin. In areas where crown courts had been superseded by Dáil courts he was instructed to set up special military tribunals to try cases of political crime. The Black and Tans roared through the countryside in their powerful Crossley tenders (military lorries) making sudden swoops on towns and villages by day and night, bursting into houses and carrying off suspects for interrogation. The populace at large was by now openly hostile towards the Black and Tans, and the IRA, confident of widespread local support, began to carry out a number of well-planned ambushes, such as that at Kilmichael, Co. Cork, in November when two lorry-loads of Auxiliaries were wiped out by an IRA column led by Tom Barry. In retaliation to this type of attack, the Black and Tans virtually declared war on the entire population. They became more and more uncontrollable, carrying out indiscriminate arrests, burning houses, wrecking property (particularly the co-operative creameries which had been the most successful recent venture in agricultural development) and looting public houses.

The crescendo of terror reached its highest pitch as 1920 drew to a close. This ominous new feature of the struggle found its outlet in a policy of reprisal and counter-reprisal. For every IRA attack on the crown forces, revenge would be taken on anyone believed to support Sinn Féin; for example, a portion of the town of Balbriggan, some twenty miles north of Dublin, was systematically destroyed after the murder of an RIC inspector in September. At first such reprisals were often carried out by off-duty soldiers and Black and Tans who had formed themselves into an unofficial 'Anti-Sinn Féin Gang', but they later seem to have acted with the knowledge and approval of their officers, and by the beginning of 1921 a number of reprisals were actually being officially authorised by top military command. But the IRA retaliated in a like manner, stepping up their campaign against the police and also wreaking their vengeance on loyalists and informers, and even Macready was obliged to admit that the IRA had the upper hand in this type of activity. The outcome of the policy of reprisal was a vicious circle of violence which seemed to grow worse every day.

A few incidents during this reign of terror deserve special mention. (1) In October 1920 Terence MacSwiney, the Sinn Féin Lord Mayor of Cork, died in Brixton Prison after a hunger-strike of seventy-four days. His death aroused massive popular emotion, similar to that which had followed the execution of the leaders of the Easter Rising. (2) In November Kevin Barry, an eighteen-year-old student, was hanged for his part in an attack on a party of British soldiers in Dublin. He had been sentenced by a military tribunal, and it was widely felt that his execution was a legalised reprisal. (3) On 21 November ('Bloody Sunday') Collins's 'squad', in a ruthless and carefully planned operation, shot dead eleven top British intelligence agents in their Dublin hotels. The Black and Tans took their revenge the same afternoon when they fired indiscriminately into a crowd watching a football match in Croke Park, killing twelve people and wounding sixty. The two IRA officers who had planned the morning raid with Collins were taken to Dublin Castle, where they were shot in mysterious circumstances. (4) On the night of 11 December, a band of drunken Black and Tans and Auxiliaries, enraged by the ambush of a party of Auxiliaries not far from Cork, ran amok through the city. They started fires which burned down a large part of the city centre and caused £3,000,000 worth of damage. Sir Hamar Greenwood made matters worse by foolishly pretending that Cork had been burned by its own citizens—a claim which not even the Auxiliaries bothered to support.

Flying Columns, 1921

The ambushes successfully carried out by local units of the IRA in the final months of 1920 boosted their morale and suggested their principal tactics during the final phase of the War of Independence. Small, streamlined, heavily armed bodies of men moved rapidly through the countryside, making sudden surprise raids on detachments of the crown forces or anyone who supported them. They then melted swiftly away into the surrounding countryside before British reinforcements arrived in full strength. The members of these IRA flying columns never returned to their own homes, but lived off the land, receiving food and shelter from friendly farmers and the rural population. In this way they managed to evade detection and arrest. Some of the support they received from local communities was no doubt inspired by fear or intimidation, but the traditional resentment of British authority enforced by arms, combined with the recent excesses of the Black and Tans, ensured that popular sympathy for the IRA was largely genuine and that aid was willingly given.

The flying columns operated mainly in the southern and western counties, most of the bitterest fighting taking place in the martial law area, i.e. south of a line roughly drawn from Galway to Wexford. Most of the column commanders came from farming backgrounds and had no formal military training, but many of them, such as Tom Barry, Sean Treacy, Ernie O'Malley, Michael Kilroy and Liam Lynch, revealed a natural genius in the strategy and tactics of guerrilla warfare, including the all-important technique of the hit-and-run attack. The conditions under which they operated meant that they had very little contact with the Dáil authorities, who, whether they liked it or not, had to allow each independent guerrilla unit to direct its own campaign. Collins, at least, was content to allow the flying columns a free hand: efficient and resourceful himself, he admired the same qualities in others. In any case, Collins's time was fully taken up in this period: in addition to the three IRA posts which he held and the important counter-espionage operations he was directing against Dublin Castle, he was still a leading figure in the IRB and Minister for Finance in the Dáil government (having taken overall responsibility for the government in the interval between Griffith's arrest in November 1920 and the return of de Valera from America at the end of the year) and was always ready to take on the work of less capable colleagues.

One type of action perpetrated by the IRA would certainly never have received official sanction. As fighting had intensified and law and order had increasingly broken down, many of the Anglo-Irish landowners, fearful for their safety, had closed up their houses and departed with their families to England. In the spring and summer of 1921 several of the empty 'big houses' were burned by the IRA. Their immediate motive was strategic, for the houses could easily have been converted into defensible garrisons by the crown forces, a manoeuvre which would have put the guerrillas at a severe disadvantage. But the column men were probably also moved by historical class resentments against the ascendancy, as well as by a more practical economic consideration. For if the absconding landowners had no homes to return to, they might be persuaded to remain permanently out of the country, and it was hoped that their estates would then be available for redistribution among small farmers under the aegis of a sympathetic republican government.

By 1921 republican Ireland was virtually a nation on the run. The Dáil, its local courts and the republican councils and other local government bodies had long been driven underground. They continued to meet and transact business as far as possible, though they operated under extremely difficult conditions. The First Dáil had only six sessions in the whole of 1920 and 1921. On the other hand, the British government agencies found themselves boycotted over much of the country, gaining reluctant recognition only when backed up by an overwhelming show of force. The IRA made their work practically impossible in May 1921 by burning the Custom House in Dublin, which was the seat of the Irish local government offices and the repository of most of the important government records. Thus by the summer of 1921 neither of the rival regimes was able to operate with real efficiency. Over most of the south the only 'law' was gun law, and the type of 'order' that was enforced in any particular neighbourhood depended on whether the nearest military presence was an IRA flying column or a lorry-load of Black and Tans.

The General Election, May 1921

In the midst of this chaos and confusion Lloyd George called a general election in Ireland for May 1921. It was to be the first general election held in the newly-created statelets of Northern Ireland and Southern Ireland. Under the Government of Ireland Act, the Southern House of Commons was to contain 128 members, and the Northern House of Commons 52.

Sinn Féin maintained that Ireland was a sovereign and independent state and was therefore under no obligation to accept a British-sponsored election as valid. However, the party relaxed its principles on this point and decided to accept the election as a challenge. Actual voting in the South took place only in the Dublin University constituency, where four Unionists were elected. The other 124 seats in the twenty-six-county area were taken by Sinn Féiners, who were all returned unopposed. The failure of any other candidates to stand was clearly due both to intimidation and to genuine widespread support for the Sinn Féin cause, but it is impossible to judge in what proportion these two motives were mingled. Instead of acting in accordance with the Government of Ireland Act and attending the new Dublin Home Rule parliament, the Sinn Féin MPs established themselves as TDs of the Second Dáil.

The Second Dáil was a larger body than the 69-man First Dáil. The average age of its members was somewhat lower, and they tended to be more militantly republican. Many of the new provincial members were IRA officers, and there was an increased proportion of members whose only claim to fame was that they were widows or other relatives of those who had 'died for Ireland' in the Easter Rising or the War of Independence. Such people were often inclined to become emotional and to let their hearts rather than their heads dictate their choice of words and ideas. Sinn Féin refused to take the oath of allegiance to the crown and boycotted the Home Rule parliament, so that when that assembly met on 28 June the House of Commons was attended only by the four Unionists. Under the terms of the Government of Ireland Act, direct rule would have to be inaugurated in Southern Ireland within a fortnight, and Lloyd George was faced with the prospect of extending martial law over the twenty-six counties and drafting in massive military reinforcements.

In Northern Ireland the election followed a completely different pattern. The seats were contested, though against a background of violence and rioting, with the following result: Unionists 40; Sinn Féin 6; Nationalists (i.e. the successors of the old Irish Party) 6. In contrast to the stormy election, the first meeting of the Northern parliament went off exactly as planned on 22 June and Sir James Craig was elected the first Prime Minister of Northern Ireland, having succeeded Carson as Unionist leader on the latter's retirement from politics earlier in the year. The birth of Northern Ireland had been attended by bloodshed and strife, but it seemed that, in the North at least, the new constitutional arrangement was going to work.

Towards a Truce, 1921

From late 1920 onwards British public opinion was becoming increasingly uneasy about what was going on in Ireland, and the government was subjected to a growing volume of criticism from liberal and left-wing quarters. A British Labour Party commission travelled through Ireland, and as a result of its investigations it uncovered grim stories of Black and Tan atrocities and also publicised the true version of the burning of Cork. Such revelations shocked English moderates. Moreover, the war was costing the British taxpayer £20,000,000 a year.

Lloyd George was gradually forced to admit to himself that he was fighting not a massive crime wave but a popular organised movement for national liberation operating by means of a guerrilla army. Once he had conceded this point, only two courses of action were open to him: he must either inflict a total military defeat on the guerrilla forces, or he must treat with the enemy. The former course would involve pouring huge army reinforcements into Ireland and undertaking the complete conquest of the country. This, Lloyd George knew, would never be tolerated by the British public or by the governments in America and other foreign countries, who were, to Britain's great embarrassment, focusing a good deal of attention on the situation in Ireland. Lloyd George was well aware that the influential President Wilson, despite his loathing for Irish-American nationalists and his persistent refusal to recognise the Irish Republic, was anxious that the

British government should effect a speedy and just settlement of the Irish question. Thus the second alternative was the only practicable one.

In Ireland too there was a growing desire for peace. The nationalist majority, loyal as they were to the Sinn Féin cause, were experiencing intense war-weariness by early 1921; they were desperately eager for all the tension, violence and anarchy to cease and normal life to be resumed. Southern Unionists wanted a settlement on any terms, so long as it brought peace. Northern Unionists, their position safeguarded by partition, were no longer likely to stand in the way of an arrangement made between Britain and the twenty-six counties; instead they were prepared to encourage such a solution in the hope that it would lead to a cessation of IRA hostilities in the six counties. Indeed, in May 1921 Craig took the extraordinary step of travelling to Dublin and meeting de Valera at a secret rendezvous; the fact that the meeting resulted in total disagreement was perhaps less important than the fact that it was held at all. Finally, the IRA, having fought for two years against heavy odds had suffered severe losses of men and equipment and were in a very shaky condition. Collins later admitted that at the time of the truce they could not have held out for another three weeks.

Lloyd George's earliest attempts to promote a peace initiative failed because he was unwilling to recognise the IRA's belligerent status and insisted that they must surrender unconditionally before discussions could begin. Naturally they refused to do this. But as the situation continued to deteriorate he became increasingly conscious of the unreality of his attitude and was eventually prepared to abandon his earlier demands. He also totally rejected the idea of negotiating with Collins, whom at this stage he believed to be nothing more than a murderous gangster. However de Valera, after his return from America at the very end of 1920, was acceptable to the British government as an accredited politican who could talk the language of diplomacy and who was generally held to be one of the more moderate members of Sinn Féin.

The immediate impetus which pushed the two sides together to work out a peace formula was provided by the political circumstances which were clearly going to prevail in the twenty-six counties after the May general election. Thus Sinn Féin's refusal to accept the Home Rule assembly and the Government of Ireland Act meant that, in accordance with the act, direct rule would have to be imposed; this in turn would necessitate an extension of martial law, a vastly increased military presence and a vigorous increase in coercion and reprisals—in short, total war. During June Lloyd George's cabinet did, in fact, prepare contingency plans for the introduction of direct rule—and all that went with it—on the 12 July, but they were extremely reluctant to accept the responsibility for the dire consequences that would undoubtedly follow in Ireland or to face the prospect of outraged public opinion at home and abroad. A ceasefire, followed by a political rather than a military solution of the Irish question was obviously a far more attractive alternative, and Lloyd George and his colleagues therefore dropped their earlier objection to negotiating on equal terms with rebels.

The British government's principal official agent in establishing contact with the Dáil government was Alfred Cope, the Assistant Under-Secretary at Dublin Castle. An important unofficial agent was Jan Smuts, the Boer general who had served in the war between Britain and the Boer republic. Smuts helped to draft the speech made by George V when he opened the Northern Ireland parliament on 22 June. In a moving appeal for peace the king said:

> I speak from a full heart when I pray that my coming to Ireland today may prove to be the first step towards an end of strife amongst her peoples, whatever their race or creed. In that hope I appeal to all Irishmen to pause, to stretch out the hand of forbearance and conciliation, to forgive and forget and to join in making for the land which they love a new era of peace, contentment and goodwill.

Smuts also visted Dublin on 5 July and placed his peace proposals before de Valera.

De Valera had by this time been recognised by Lloyd George as 'the chosen leader of the great majority in Southern Ireland' and was therefore prepared to respond favourably to the king's gesture of goodwill and the overtures made by Cope and Smuts. He was supported by both the debilitated IRA and by the ordinary civilian population, Unionist and Nationalist alike, who were tired of the increasing round of violence, destruction, murder and reprisal. On 8 July, therefore, de Valera met General Macready at the Mansion House, Dublin, to discuss the terms of a ceasefire or truce, which was intended to be followed after further talks by a permanent settlement by treaty which would (in Lloyd George's words) 'end the ruinous conflict of centuries'. The truce came into effect on the 11 July 1921–just one day before the deadline for direct rule.

The truce was a moral victory for Sinn Féin, since de Valera had relinquished none of his political principles and had won the right for his government to negotiate directly with the British government. It was a solid and material victory for Irish and British public opinion, since it restored peace between the two nations. It was a valuable practical advantage for the British government, since it extricated it neatly from the awkward and dangerous political situation in which it was trapped.

Talking Points

Chapter 7: The War of Independence, 1919-21.

1 Describe the scene in the Mansion House during the first session of Dáil Éireann, on 21 January 1919. Give an analysis of its proceedings. What do you think of the 'Democratic Programme' which it proposed?

2 Outline the main problems facing the Dáil government during the years 1919-21. How would you assess its overall achievement?

3 How do you explain the outbreak of the War of Independence? Was such a war inevitable? Why, and to what extent, did Dáil Éireann endorse the 'men of the gun'?

4 What were the main points in Lloyd George's Government of Ireland Act 1920? What new dimensions did it introduce into the Irish political scene? How did it affect the people in the six counties of Northern Ireland?

5 Outline the main military features of the War of Independence. Mention some of the major events which occurred during the so-called reign of terror in the period October-December 1920.

6 What were the main reasons which led the British government to propose a ceasefire? What were the main conclusions to be drawn from the results of the Irish general election of May 1921? Did anyone really win the War of Independence?

Chapter 8

THE TREATY AND THE CIVIL WAR, 1921-23

Negotiation by Heads of Government, July-September 1921

Two days after the truce had been agreed de Valera met Lloyd George in London for the first of a series of private conferences. Their preliminary aim was to discover whether it was possible to devise a form of government for Ireland which would be acceptable to majority opinion in both Ireland and Britain. De Valera made it clear that he regarded himself and the Dáil as speaking for the majority in the whole of Ireland, and he therefore insisted that no representative of the Northern Ireland government should be present at any stage of the negotiations.

Lloyd George's position was a rather difficult one. Although eager to reach a settlement which would rid him once and for all of the troublesome problem of Ireland, his freedom of movement was considerably hampered by the fact that he was the Liberal Prime Minister of a Coalition government which was dominated by Conservative/Unionist elements. Lloyd George also knew that parliament would never tolerate any move to take Ireland outside the British Empire or Commonwealth, since it might be taken as a general precedent for the secession of India and other overseas possessions. It was also widely felt that Britain had a certain responsibility for ruling Ireland which could not simply be shaken off overnight. The recent Government of Ireland Act was seen as confirming this commitment.

These pressures determined Lloyd George's basic bargaining position: (1) that Ireland must remain within the Empire; (2) that Northern Ireland must not be disestablished against the will of the Unionist majority. These were his fundamental principles in all his negotiations with the Irish representatives. He never budged from them, and in the end he had his way, for they formed the basis of the Anglo-Irish Treaty.

De Valera's position was at first sight much stronger. As undisputed head of a united, single-party government, and as undisputed spokesman for almost the entire twenty-six-county population, he appeared to be very well placed for presenting his demand for Irish independence. However, this apparently simple objective was to create grave difficulties for the Irish leaders. 'Independence' was an idea capable of widely differing interpretations. Lloyd George's requirements were practical and easily understandable, and as the talks proceeded it became clear that their purpose was to define 'independence' in such a way as would suit him.

The protracted Anglo-Irish talks of 1921 were also conducted with one eye continually on their possible breakdown, and each side tried to manipulate the proceedings in such a way that the circumstances of any breakdown would place the blame for a resumption of hostilities squarely on the other side.

Lloyd George's initial proposals were outlined in a document delivered to de Valera on 20 July. He offered Ireland the status of a Commonwealth dominion, with the right to 'exercise all those powers and privileges upon which the autonomy of the self-governing dominions is based'. The offer was subject to certain conditions, all of which were to Britain's advantage: continued naval and air access to Ireland, the prohibition of protective trade tariffs between the two countries, and an Irish contribution to the British war debt; furthermore, the Dublin government would be obliged to recognise the inviolability of Northern Ireland. De Valera professed himself 'greatly disappointed' by these proposals, but agreed to submit them to the Dáil, which thereupon rejected them decisively.

The Second Dáil was clearly adopting a more militant attitude than its predecessor, and after making it plain to Lloyd George that it was in no mood to tolerate his plan for Ireland's future within the Empire, it went on to demonstrate its hardening republicanism during its August sessions. De Valera's title was changed from 'President of Dáil Éireann' to 'President of the Irish Republic', and all TDs were required to take an oath of allegiance to 'the Irish Republic and the Government of the Irish Republic which is Dáil Éireann'. De Valera also nominated a small, high-powered cabinet consisting of only seven ministers: himself, Griffith (Foreign Affairs), Collins (Finance), Austin Stack (Home Affairs), Brugha (Defence), Cosgrave (Local Government) and Barton (Economic Affairs). Both Stack and Brugha were known to be republican extremists. In spite of these changes, neither the British government nor the Dáil wanted to be responsible for a resumption of war, and letters continued to pass between the two leaders throughout August and September.

De Valera wrestled with the problem of how to reconcile the Dáil's desire for a fully autonomous and united Ireland with the British government's insistence on Ireland's remaining within the Empire. It seemed an impossible task, but in September he produced a characteristically ingenious solution:

> A certain treaty of free association with the British Commonwealth group, as with a partial league of nations, we would be ready to contemplate, and as a government to negotiate and take responsibility for, had we an assurance that the entry of the nation as a whole into such association would secure for it the allegiance of the present dissenting minority, to meet whose sentiment alone this step would be contemplated.

This statement contains the germ of the idea of *external association*, which was to be the subject of several further draft proposals put forward by de

Valera in the ensuing months. The essence of external association was that while Ireland would not actually be a part of the British Empire, it would be closely linked with it by means of a special alliance. Although such an arrangement was to be used successfully within the British Commonwealth in the period after the Second World War, in 1921 it was an entirely new concept which few politicians, British or Irish, found easy to understand, and both the British government and the Ulster Unionists were highly suspicious of it. Nevertheless, it seemed to indicate to Lloyd George that the Irish were moving towards a compromise and an acceptance of some form of connection with Britain. He therefore carried the negotiations on to a further stage on 29 September by suggesting to de Valera 'a conference in London on 11 October where we can meet your delegates as spokesmen of the people whom you represent with a view to ascertaining how the association of Ireland with the community of nations known as the British Empire may best be reconciled with Irish national aspirations'. This seemed reasonable enough, and the Dáil cabinet agreed to accept the invitation. But in doing so it might be said that they were automatically acknowledging that the prospect of an autonomous republic was ruled out.

Negotiation by Delegations, October-December 1921

There was some difficulty in selecting the Irish delegation. Brugha and Stack refused outright to take part, Collins was extremely unwilling, and de Valera resolved that he himself would not be a member. The team which was eventually nominated consisted of three cabinet ministers, Griffith, Collins and Barton, and two legal experts, Eamonn Duggan and George Gavan Duffy. Griffith, Collins and Duggan were the more 'moderate' members of the delegation, while Barton and Duffy favoured a more 'separatist' line; Erskine Childers, secretary to the delegation, was also a strong 'separatist', but as he did not have a voice in the proceedings, and as Griffith and Collins were the most important delegates, the hardline republican element in the Dáil was virtually unrepresented. The choice of Childers as secretary was perhaps unfortunate, as Griffith had taken an unreasoning dislike to him.

The delegation was further weakened by de Valera's decision not to participate. It was, after all, an acknowledged fact that he was the most skilful politician in the Dáil government, and also the best fitted to expound the difficult concept of external association. There were several reasons for his refusal to attend: (1) Since his election as President of the Irish Republic he found himself faced with a dilemma: as well as head of government, he was now also head of state. He believed that the latter position precluded his participation in discussions relating to the constitutional future of the sovereign state over which he presided. He believed that he was as out of place on the Irish delegation as George V would have been on the British one. (2) The British public had a preconceived image of de Valera as a notorious extremist. If the negotiations were to break down under de Valera, public opinion would immediately place the blame on him. But if they were to break down under a known moderate like Griffith, there was much less chance of this happening. (3) By remaining in Dublin, de Valera would have a chance to win hardliners like Brugha and Stack over to the idea of external association. (4) During his earlier discussions with Lloyd George, de Valera undoubtedly realised that he was dealing with a cunning and even unscrupulous statesman who possessed an almost uncanny ability to confuse. It was thus vitally necessary to have a second line of defence and an opportunity for cool reflection far removed from the influence of the 'Welsh wizard'. By instructing the delegates to refer all decisions back to himself in Dublin for final ratification, de Valera believed that he had effectively made the delegation foolproof against Lloyd George. Time was to show that he had dangerously underestimated the Welshman's capacity for cajolery.

On 7 October the Dáil cabinet issued its instructions to the delegates. They contained a fateful ambiguity. The delegates were accredited as 'envoys plenipotentiary' with full power 'to negotiate and conclude with the representatives of His Britannic Majesty George V a Treaty or Treaties of association and accommodation between Ireland and the Community of Nations known as the British Commonwealth'. Yet it was also made clear that the delegates were not to have the ultimate power of decision; their terms of reference were as follows: 'It is understood, however, that before decisions are finally reached on the main questions, that a dispatch notifying the intention of making these decisions will be sent to the members of the cabinet in Dublin and that a reply will be awaited by the plenipotentiaries before the final decision is made. It is also understood that the complete text of the draft treaty about to be signed will be similarly submitted to Dublin and a reply awaited.' The fundamental contradiction, resulting partly from de Valera's fears of Lloyd George's persuasive personality and partly from the fact that Ireland was totally inexperienced in sophisticated diplomatic procedures, was eventually to be exploited by Lloyd George.

The delegates' instructions contained no detailed directions as to what terms they should seek, nor even a ruling as to the basic bargaining position on which the Irish case should rest. This was presumably considered to be a matter for cabinet decision. Nevertheless, the omission of even a broad directive on this matter made the task of Griffith and his colleagues all the more difficult. However, they were given a valuable piece of advice on tactics: if the talks looked like breaking down, the Irish delegation should do all it could to turn the discussion to the Ulster question, for it was widely known that the Dáil government had the sympathy of a large section of the British public on the subject of Irish unification, and a 'break on Ulster' would put Lloyd George in a very awkward position.

On arriving in London the Irish delegates found themselves confronted by a formidable team of British negotiators. Unlike the Irish, who were negotiators by necessity, the British delegates were negotiators by profession. In addition to the Prime Minister, the British team consisted of Winston Churchill, the Secretary of State for War; Austen Chamberlain and Lord Birkenhead, prominent Conservatives; Sir Laming Worthington-Evans, a career politician; Sir Hamar Greenwood, the former Chief Secretary for Ireland; and Sir Gordon Hewart, the Attorney-General. Faced with a professionalism which they themselves lacked, unsettled by the unfamiliar and even hostile surroundings in which the negotiations were conducted, and conscious of the grave responsibility which rested upon them, the Irish delegates were already under a very severe strain before the talks started; and in the following weeks all of them were to suffer increasingly from a sense of mental oppression and great emotional stress.

Between 11 and 24 October the two sides met in a series of seven plenary sessions with all the delegates present. The main issues that emerged in these discussions were (1) the constitutional status of Ireland and the nature of its link with Britain, (2) the problem of partition, and the circumstances in which unification might be implemented, (3) British security and defence requirements in Ireland. This last point was speedily settled by the provision of British naval bases in Ireland, as eventually outlined in the Treaty. Only Childers seems to have realised that the arrangement forfeited Ireland's sovereign independence; none of the plenipotentiaries appear to have shared his misgivings.

The remaining two points proved much more difficult to deal with and occupied almost all the time during the remaining negotiations. An additional complication was created by underlying tactical influences. The Irish delegation insisted on a recognition of the essential unity of their country before any question of its status could be settled. They wanted to keep the Ulster question at the forefront of the negotiations, since if the talks broke down on this subject, public opinion would be largely on their side. The British, on the other hand, knew that only a breakdown on the 'imperial' issue would be to their advantage: ordinary English people would never countenance a resumption of war over Northern Ireland, but they would react sharply to any threat to the Empire. Lloyd George therefore did everything he could to steer the discussions away from the Ulster question and onto the more promising ground of Ireland's constitutional status.

By a series of particularly crafty moves the British Prime Minister eventually succeeded in removing Ulster altogether as a problem for immediate solution. He first of all tackled Griffith separately in November and explained that he was faced with a revolt of the Conservative elements in the British coalition government over the proposed coercion of Ulster. If successful, this would bring about his resignation and the replacement of the coalition by an unfriendly administration led by the ultra-Unionist Bonar Law. But if Griffith would only agree to waive his demand for immediate Irish reunification, Lloyd George promised to set up a Boundary

Commission which would redraw the border in such a way as to make the northern statelet non-viable as an economic entity, and he also pledged himself to exert what pressure he could on Craig and the Ulster Unionists to accept a Dublin government. Griffith agreed to this proposal, and at the final session before the Treaty was signed Lloyd George produced Griffith's signed statement to this effect. By that time Lloyd George had also managed to persuade Collins to change the demand for 'essential unity' to acceptance of the Boundary Commission, persuading him that unity would very quickly be achieved by natural economic forces. Once again the Ulster question had been shelved, not solved, and the chance for the Irish delegation to 'break on Ulster' had vanished.

The central issue of the conferences was then Ireland's constitutional status, the nature of its connection with Britain and the Empire, and the role of the crown. On 24 October Griffith introduced a new version of the external association proposal:

> On the one hand Ireland will consent to adhere for all purposes of common agreed concern to the League of Sovereign States associated and known as the British Commonwealth of Nations. On the other hand Ireland calls upon Great Britain to renounce all claims and authority over Ireland and Irish affairs.

This formula, which implied that the crown would not stand at the head of the new Irish state, failed to satisfy Lloyd George, who continued to insist that nothing short of dominion status would be acceptable. But on this point the Irish remained adamant, de Valera warning his envoys from Dublin: 'If war is the alternative [to Irish allegiance to the crown], we can only face it.'

By now Lloyd George was beginning to gauge his opponents' weaknesses and to realise that the Irish delegation was not quite unanimous in its views. He split the conference up into subcommittees, which gave him a better chance to exert his powers of persuasion on the three 'moderate' delegates, especially Griffith, who was clearly feeling the effect of the intense pressures under which he was forced to work. But although the subcommittee system enabled spectacular progress to be made on all the less contentious minor matters, by the end of November the best the British could offer on the question of status was a modified oath of allegiance, and the best the Irish could propose as an alternative was a further formula for external association:

> Ireland shall agree to be associated with the British Commonwealth for purposes of common concern such as defence, peace and war; and she shall recognise the British Crown as head of the association; and that, as a token of that recognition, she shall vote an annual sum to the King's Civil List.

But 'recognition' of the crown fell very far short of the 'allegiance' which Lloyd George demanded, and he angrily sent the delegates back to Dublin to submit his final proposals to the Dáil cabinet.

On 3 December the Dáil cabinet met to discuss the latest British proposals. There was much heated argument as to whether Lloyd George was likely to stand firm on dominion status and his opposition to external association and as to whether the British concessions were worth accepting. The debate had to be cut short by the delegates' hurried departure for London, and they took with them only general instructions given at the last minute by De Valera: to reject the oath of allegiance drawn up by Lloyd George, and 'to state that [the proposed treaty] is now a matter for the Dáil, and to try to put the blame on Ulster'. De Valera drafted a new form of the oath to be placed before Lloyd George:

> I ... do solemnly swear true faith and allegiance to the constitution of the Irish Free State, to the Treaty of Association and to recognise the King of Great Britain as head of the Associated States [of the Empire].

In exasperation Lloyd George pointed out that this oath merely restated the principle of external association, which had already been discussed and rejected by the British team. The two sides now appeared to have reached an insuperable deadlock. But Lloyd George still held the trump card of Ulster. At the final session of the conference on 5 December he succeeded in making it impossible for the Irish representatives to 'put the blame on Ulster'. He then proceeded to bring the full force of his personality to bear on the hard-pressed Irishmen. His mingled threats and inducements culminated in a melodramatic but carefully contrived ultimatum. The following vivid account of the final hours of the fateful conference is compiled from the recollections of witnesses, notably Lloyd George's secretary, Tom Jones:

> The ultimate choice remained: status within the Empire or nothing. Lloyd George refused even to consider Griffith's plea to refer this to the Dáil. The messengers, he said, must sail to Belfast that night [in time to deliver the terms of whatever agreement was signed concerning Ulster to the Northern Ireland parliament before its meeting on the following day] and the destroyer was already waiting at Holyhead. If the answer was no, it was war. The Irish had to sign and disregard whatever their Sinn Féin mandate said, or, if they believed the Prime Minister, face the accumulated might of the British forces. The British could concede no more and debate no further. The Irish delegates must settle now; they must sign the agreement for a treaty or else quit, and both sides would be free to resume whatever warfare they could wage against each other.
>
> Griffith undertook, whatever the reply, to sign the Treaty himself. But this was not enough for the Prime Minister, who wanted the same assurances from Collins and Barton: 'Every delegate must sign the document and undertake to recommend it, or there can be no agreement. We as a body have hazarded our political futures; you must do likewise and take the same risks.' Finally, in a famous gesture, he held up two letters. 'I have to communicate with Sir James Craig tonight.

Here are alternative letters which I have prepared, one enclosing Articles of Agreement reached by His Majesty's Government and yourselves, and the other saying that the Sinn Féin representatives refuse to come within the Empire. If I send this letter, it is war, and war within three days. Which letter am I to send? Whichever letter you choose travels by special train to Holyhead, and by destroyer to Belfast. The train is waiting with steam up at Euston. [The courier] is ready. If he is to reach Sir James Craig in time, we must know your answer by 10 p.m. tonight. You have till then but no longer to decide whether you will give peace or war to your country.'

The Irish withdrew to consider this ultimatum in private. Their final wrangle, a tragedy for the Republicans, brought gloomy apprehension to all, as first Collins, then Duggan and finally—after desperate heart-searching—Barton and Duffy declared that they would follow Griffith and sign. Strangely, no one, not even Childers, invoked the cabinet mandate they had had the day before, and no one thought to use the telephone to Dublin.

Thus was the resistance of the Irish delegation worn down until they succumbed to the pressures to sign an agreement which, their instincts told them, would provoke severe criticism at home. Within a few hours of signing the Treaty Collins expressed his own forebodings: 'Will anyone be satisfied at the bargain? ... I tell you—early this morning I signed my death warrant.' But the five signatories were united in their belief that (1) the British had been pushed as far as they would go, and no further concessions could be wrung from them, and (2) in signing they had saved Ireland from the ravages of a war so devastating as to make the troubles of 1920 and 1921 seem mild by comparison.

Was Lloyd George bluffing? Certainly his insistence on an immediate decision by the plenipotentiaries, together with all his talk about special trains and destroyers and the necessity for conveying the news to Craig by the following morning, was pure bluff. It was undoubtedly important that Craig should know the outcome of the talks as soon as possible, but there was no reason why a final decision could not have been postponed for a further few days to enable the Irish delegates to consult de Valera. Lloyd George deliberately created an atmosphere of urgency which instilled a sense of panic into his exhausted opponents and made them susceptible to his demands. As to whether he was serious in his threat of 'war within three days', it is impossible to be certain. He believed he had engineered the negotiations to such a point that, if they had been broken off owing to the Irish delegates' refusal to accept dominion status, English public opinion would have endorsed a resumption of full-scale hostilities. However, there is some evidence to suggest that he had overestimated the amount of support he might have expected for such a move. Finally, there is also some slight evidence which indicates that Lloyd George's blustering tactics during the last conference served to cover up deficiencies in his own team: some members of the British delegation (notably Churchill and Birkenhead, both strong-willed and capable politicians) were almost as shattered by the gruelling debate as the Irish and were overwhelmed with a sense of failure. Had the Irish delegates realised this, it is just possible that, by standing firmly by their original demands and resisting Lloyd George's harassments, they might have thrown the British into considerable disarray. But even if this had occurred, it is impossible to suppose that any further major concession would have resulted, or that any modification of Lloyd George's basic precept—that Ireland should remain within the British Empire—would have been forthcoming.

The Anglo-Irish Treaty, December 1921

The document entitled 'Articles of Agreement for a Treaty between Great Britain and Ireland' was signed at 2.10 a.m. on 6 December 1921. There were eighteen articles in all, the most important of which are outlined below.

Status: Articles 1-4 defined the constitutional status of the twenty-six-county area, its relationship with Great Britain, including the role of the crown, and the oath of allegiance to be taken by members of the parliament or Dáil.

(1) Ireland shall have the same constitutional status in the community of nations known as the British Empire as the Dominion of Canada, the Commonwealth of Australia, the Dominion of New Zealand, and the Union of South Africa, with a parliament having powers to make laws for the peace and good government of Ireland and an executive responsible to that parliament, and shall be styled and known as the Irish Free State.

(2) Subject to the provisions hereinafter set out the position of the Irish Free State in relation to the imperial parliament and government and otherwise shall be that of the Dominion of Canada, and the law, practice and constitutional usage governing the relationship of the crown or the representative of the crown and of the imperial parliament to the Dominion of Canada shall govern their relationship to the Irish Free State.

(3) The representative of the crown in Ireland shall be appointed in like manner as the governor-general of Canada, and in accordance with the practice observed in the making of such appointments.

(4) The oath to be taken by members of the parliament of the Irish Free State shall be in the following form: I . . . do solemnly swear true faith and allegiance to the constitution of the Irish Free State as by law established and that I will be faithful to H.M. King George V, his heirs and successors by law in virtue of the common citizenship of Ireland with Great Britain and her adherence to and membership of the group of nations forming the British Commonwealth of Nations.

Defence: Article 7 catered for Britain's defence requirements. Britain was to retain full harbour facilities in the ports of Queenstown (Cobh), Berehaven and Lough Swilly. In wartime Britain was to receive any other facilities in Ireland which were felt necessary for national defence. A further article made Britain responsible for Ireland's coastal defence for the next five years.

Northern Ireland: Articles 11-15 dealt with the relationship between the two parts of Ireland. They effectively maintained the status quo created by the 1920 act. Article 11 permitted Northern Ireland to opt out of the Free State's jurisdiction if its parliament expressed such a desire within one month of the Treaty's ratification. Article 12 stated that if the Northern Ireland parliament did so choose to opt out (as, of course, it would), 'the powers of the parliament and government of the Irish Free State shall no longer extend to Northern Ireland, and the provisions of the Government of Ireland Act, 1920 (including those relating to the Council of Ireland) shall, so far as they relate to Northern Ireland, continue to be of full force and effect'. Furthermore, a Boundary Commission should be set up to 'determine in accordance with the wishes of the inhabitants, so far as may be compatible with economic and geographic conditions the boundaries between Northern Ireland and the rest of Ireland'. Article 13 empowered the Free State parliament to elect representatives to the Council of Ireland. (Articles 14 and 15, which dealt with the circumstances which would be created if the Northern parliament chose to enter the Free State, may be discounted as a dead letter.)

Machinery of transition: Since the Second Dáil was not recognised as a valid parliament by the British government, it was necessary to establish an Irish body to which the British authorities could transfer administrative power. The parliament of Southern Ireland (i.e. the Dáil deputies plus the four Dublin University ex-Unionists) was acceptable to the British government, since it had been brought into being under the auspices of the British-sponsored Government of Ireland Act, and under Articles 17 and 18 of the Treaty it was therefore given the responsibility for establishing a provisional government which would liaise with the British government and receive the transferred administrative powers.

The Treaty Debate, December 1921-January 1922

The Irish delegation returned home to find a sharp division of opinion on the settlement they had secured. For the purposes of analysing reaction to the Treaty it is necessary to divide the Irish population into three categories: the general public, the politicians, and the IRA. The general public would, of course, if necessary, have a chance to express their decision on the Treaty in a general election. The politicians were shortly to give their verdict on it in the Dáil. The IRA did not play a significant role in the initial stage of the Treaty debate—but in the conditions of anarchy into which the country was sliding after January 1922 the only real power was that which was enforced by the gun, and the standpoint of the armed men of the IRA came to be of crucial importance.

The immediate response of the majority of ordinary people to the Treaty was one of intense relief. For them, the Treaty had brought peace and the opportunity to resume normal life without the constant threat of terror which had overshadowed the country for the previous two years. They were also aware of the practical advantages that had been won: the Black and Tans and Auxiliaries would be sent home, the RIC disbanded, and almost all the visible trappings of British rule dismantled. Irishmen would govern their own country, and the British had agreed to recognise such a government. Most people therefore welcomed the Treaty. However, approval was not unanimous. There was a by no means inconsiderable minority which believed that the Irish representatives had sold their country into the Empire. Some of these critics argued that the Irish representatives should have held out for nothing short of an autonomous republic, no matter what the cost.

But in December 1921 the main interest centred on what the politicians thought of the Treaty. On 8 December the Dáil cabinet met to discuss the Treaty and found itself split down the middle. De Valera angrily upbraided the delegates for disobeying their clearly understood instructions to sign nothing without consulting him, and he was supported by the hardliners Brugha and Stack. Cosgrave supported Griffith, Collins and Barton in voting for the Treaty's acceptance. The cabinet thus had no agreed policy to recommend to the Dáil when it met on 14 December. De Valera issued a 'Proclamation to the Irish People' which stated: 'The terms of this agreement are in violent conflict with the wishes of the majority of this nation as expressed freely in successive elections during the past three years. I feel it my duty to inform you that I cannot recommend acceptance of this Treaty either to Dáil Éireann or to the country.'

The Dáil debate, which began on 14 December, lasted for twelve sessions, some of which were held in secret, and ended on 10 January 1922, with the Christmas recess intervening. Every deputy spoke, but apart from the masterly contributions of the leading politicians, particularly Griffith, Collins, de Valera, Childers and Kevin O'Higgins, the speeches were tedious, repetitive and often irrelevant. The ghosts of dead heroes were summoned to influence the Dáil's decision, Mrs Pearse informing the deputies that her sons would never have supported such a treaty. It is interesting to note that Northern Ireland was scarcely mentioned during the debate. The Dáil deputies, like Griffith and Collins, were obviously convinced by Lloyd George's assurances about the effects of the forthcoming Boundary Commission and believed that the speedy reunification of the country and the final settlement of the Ulster question was a foregone conclusion. The main point at issue in the debate was Ireland's relationship to the Empire, in particular the oath of allegiance to the crown. The main arguments for and against the Treaty can be briefly summarised as follows.

The case for the Treaty: The Treaty might not be an ideal document, containing everything that Ireland wanted: like all treaties, it was essentially a compromise, and in agreeing to participate in negotiations the Dáil government had automatically accepted that a compromise was inevitable. The British had clearly indicated that they would never accept either a republic or external association. Instead of complaining about what had not been achieved, the bargain should be assessed by examining its positive benefits. Prominent among these was the fact that a ruinous war, which had threatened to drag on for ever and whose principal sufferers were the Irish people, had been ended. The menace of an even more terrible war had been averted at the last minute. The plenipotentiaries had exceeded their orders, at the insistence of Lloyd George, by not referring the final decision back to Dublin, but since the issue was the extraordinary and supremely urgent one of immediate war or peace, they were justified in acting on their own initiative. (They might have added that if the Dáil really wanted total war, it had only to tear up the Treaty: by opting for peace the delegates had at least given the Dáil the opportunity to choose.) Other gains were the ending of the presence of the occupying British forces, and the recognition by Britain of the right of Irishmen to control their own affairs with their own parliament, their own financial, legal and economic institutions, their own police force and their own army. Summing up the practical advantages of the Treaty, Kevin O'Higgins declared: 'It represents such a broad measure of liberty for the Irish people and it acknowledges such a large proportion of its rights [that] you are not entitled to reject it without being able to show them you have a reasonable prospect of achieving more.'

Dominion status had its advantages. No longer would Great Britain be able to adopt a high-handed attitude towards its diminutive neighbour. Any attempt at undue interference in Ireland would be an affront to all the other British Dominions and would rock the Empire. Irish freedom was guaranteed rather than lessened by membership of this powerful group of nations. The continued association with Britain also meant that a link was preserved between the two parts of Ireland: this would help to smooth the process of reunification. Furthermore, as O'Higgins pointed out, Dominion status itself was undergoing a process of change: 'I believe the evolution of this group must be towards a condition, not merely of individual freedom but also of equality of status.' The idea that the Treaty was not a static settlement but a stepping-stone to further developments was taken even further by Griffith and, more forcefully, by Collins, who claimed that the agreement 'gives us freedom, not the ultimate freedom that all nations aspire and develop to, but the freedom to achieve it'.

The members of the delegation were adamant that they had secured the best terms possible in the circumstances. Lloyd George, who had absolutely refused to consider Dominion status for Ireland in 1919, had now been forced to consent to it, and in a form far more favourable to Ireland than had been envisaged even in his offer in the summer of 1921. This was a remarkable achievement, and the Irish delegates were convinced that the British could not have been pushed an inch further. They had to face a good deal of disbelief on the point, but they stoutly maintained that their own presence at the negotiations had placed them in a far better position than their home-based critics for judging the state of mind of the British. Finally, Griffith dismissed the suggestion that the Dáil delegates had broken the republican oath of allegiance they had taken in August: 'We took an oath to the Irish Republic, but, as President de Valera himself said, he understood that oath to bind him to do the best he could for Ireland. So do we. We have done the best we could for Ireland.'

The case against the Treaty: Opposition to the Treaty came from two different groups. Firstly, there were the 'anti-imperialists', who gathered around de Valera. They resented Ireland's inclusion within the Empire and wanted to replace it with the external association arrangement. Secondly, there were the diehards or 'doctrinaire republicans', who declared that they would be satisfied only by an isolated Irish republic. Although there were fundamental differences in these two viewpoints, the doctrinaire republicans were largely content to allow de Valera to lead the campaign against the Treaty in the Dáil. However, when hostilities broke out in 1922 these positions were reversed (see below).

The anti-imperialists pointed out that the delegates had been guilty of insubordination. They had contravened the clearly understood orders, given on repeated occasions and endorsed by the government, not to sign any agreement which placed Ireland within the Empire, and to refer back to Dublin before a final decision was made. The oath of allegiance to the king was based on a principle which was repugnant to Irish nationality. The Treaty, de Valera claimed, 'is absolutely inconsistent with our position; it gives away Irish independence, it brings us into the British Empire; it acknowledges the head of the British Empire not merely as the head of an association but as the direct monarch of Ireland, as the source of executive authority in Ireland'. He was backed up by Childers, who stated bluntly: 'It places Ireland definitely and irrevocably under the British crown.' Any agreement based upon such a premise was a disgraceful compromise, and any Irishman who accepted it would be dishonouring himself and his country.

The main argument for the Treaty was that it had brought peace, but as well as being a shameful peace, it would not be an enduring peace. History had shown that, for as long as there was a direct constitutional connection between Ireland and Great Britain, there would be enmity and antagonism between them. Britain would never resist the urge to exploit the link with her weaker neighbour to her own advantage. The Canadian analogy outlined in the Treaty was a fallacy: whereas the dominion of Canada was a huge country thousands of miles away, Ireland was geographically dominated by Great Britain, and without the assurance of complete independence she would be politically dominated too. The Treaty was thus perpetuating the state of affairs that had been responsible for 'centuries of conflict between the two nations'.

The delegates had clearly allowed themselves to be fooled and outwitted by Lloyd George. They should have realised that he was employing a considerable measure of bluff, and instead of surrendering abjectly to his hectoring tactics they should have stood firmly by their original demands 'The sad part of it', said de Valera, 'is that a grand treaty could at this moment be made.' He produced his own hastily prepared draft of an alternative 'Proposed Treaty of Association between Ireland and the British Commonwealth', generally known as Document No. 2. Based to some extent on the original Treaty, it was more remarkable for its omissions than its contents. It was essentially a restatement of the principle of external association, omitting the oath of allegiance (and, incidentally, all mention of Northern Ireland). Its most important clauses were:

That the legislative, executive and judicial authority of Ireland shall be derived solely from the people of Ireland [i.e. not, as under the Treaty, from the crown].

That, for purposes of common concern [e.g. defence, peace and war, political treaties], Ireland shall be associated with the States of the British Commonwealth.

That when acting as an associate, the rights, status and privileges of Ireland shall be in no respect less than those enjoyed by any of the component states of the British Commonwealth.

That, for the purposes of the Association, Ireland shall recognise His Britannic Majesty as head of the Association.

The doctrinaire republicans supported de Valera's arguments against the Treaty, though they did not agree with his proposed alternative solution. In taking their stand solely upon principle, they proved even more intractable than the anti-imperialists. Not only were they resolutely opposed to Ireland's remaining within the Empire, but they refused to consider any constitutional status for Ireland except that of a fully autonomous republic. Such a republic already existed; it had been declared in 1916, ratified in 1919, and every member of the Dáil had sworn allegiance to it in 1921. This republic was claimed by its supporters to be inviolable. Not only was it treason to attempt to disestablish it, but it was beyond the competence of anyone—even a majority in the Dáil—to do so. The republic was not to be made the object of barter and compromise with the British. Instead of betraying their solemn oath, the Irish delegates should have given Lloyd George the simple choice of recognising the Irish Republic or rejecting it. If he rejected it, the threatened war, however terrible, was preferable to dishonour. Many republican deputies declared their willingness to 'go another round with England'. The republicans' point of view was stated in its full simplicity, and with all its ominous implication, by Austin Stack: 'I stand for what is Ireland's right, full independence and nothing short of it. If I, as I hope I will, try to continue to fight for Ireland's liberty, even if this rotten document be accepted, I will fight minus the oath of allegiance and to wipe out the oath of allegiance if I can do it.'

The hardline republicans were not interested in the practical benefits that had been conferred by the Treaty settlement. They were concerned solely with principles and ideology, and their uncompromising stance made them impervious to other arguments. The fervour with which they denounced the Treaty was given a strong emotional slant by an appeal to the cult of the dead patriots.

The Dáil's decision: If a vote had been taken at the time of the Dáil's adjournment for Christmas on 22 December, it is almost certain that the Treaty would have been rejected by a very slender majority. But the interval helped to counteract the emotional tensions raised and gave the deputies an opportunity for cooler reflection. It also enabled them to sound out public opinion in the constituencies, which was on the whole in favour of accepting the Treaty. Whatever influence the IRB still possessed was wielded by its President, Michael Collins, and was thrown behind the Treaty, and the Catholic bishops and the press both spoke out strongly in its favour. As a result of these popular pressures, a small but numerically significant handful of anti-Treaty deputies had changed sides by the time the Dáil reconvened on 3 January 1922.

The final week of the Treaty debate witnessed many painful scenes in the Dáil. Smouldering personal resentments exploded into heated and unseemly exchanges, and the old antagonism between Brugha and Collins burst out in a volley of vituperative insults on either side. When the vote on the Treaty was taken on 7 January, 64 votes were cast for it, and 57 against. Semantic to the last, De Valera insisted that while the Dáil might 'approve' the Treaty, it was beyond its powers as a republican assembly to 'ratify' it.

Following the unimpressive victory of the pro-Treaty party, de Valera resigned the presidency on 9 January, and on the following day Griffith was elected in his place and nominated a new cabinet. It was decided to keep the Republic in being as a temporary measure, and the new Minister for Defence, General Richard Mulcahy, assured the Dáil that the army would remain the army of the Irish Republic. De Valera and the anti-Treatyites withdrew permanently from the Dáil. His final statements in the Dáil were a conditional pledge of loyalty to the new government and a conditional promise not to disturb the peace. He assured the Dáil that Griffith, as 'President of the Irish Republic, will receive from me personally, and I hope from every citizen, *while he is acting in that capacity,* the fullest respect which his office entitles him to. We are not going to interfere with you', he told Griffith and his colleagues, *'except* when we find that you are going to do something that will definitely injure the Irish nation.'

Drifting into War, January-June 1922

The pro-Treaty politicians were now faced with the complicated business of organising the transfer of power from the British authorities. For this purpose it was necessary to convene the Southern Ireland parliament in order to establish a provisional government in accordance with Articles 17 and 18 of the Treaty. The parliament duly met on 14 January and set up the provisional government, of which Collins was chosen as chairman. In addition to Collins, several other members of the provisional government, such as Cosgrave, O'Higgins and Duggan, were also members of the Dáil ministry. So for most of the year 1922 the twenty-six-county area was in the curious position of possessing two co-operating caretaker administrations: the Dáil government of the Irish Republic under President Griffith, and the British-approved provisional government under Collins. De Valera and the anti-Treaty politicians refused to associate themselves with either body; they withdrew into the political wilderness and exerted little real influence on events during the first half of 1922.

Collins and his associates in the provisional government had to cope with a number of tricky problems: (1) how to find the money to finance the new state and, above all, to provide jobs for the 130,000 unemployed in the country, (2) how to organise an Irish civil service and take over the various public services from the British, (3) how to enforce law and order on a dissident minority and at the same time maintain general goodwill towards the government, (4) how to control the army.

(1) The provisional government received £500,000 from the House of Commons to get things started, but it was so preoccupied with combating the state of anarchy into which the country was sliding that little immediate progress was made in dealing with the severe economic depression which Ireland was suffering in the aftermath of the First World War and the War of Independence. Organised labour was beginning to air its grievances and was obviously going to play a significant role in the life of the new state. (2) Dublin Castle was handed over to Collins by the Lord Lieutenant on 16 January 1922, and at the same time the evacuation of British troops began. The disbandment of the RIC and their replacement by a force of unarmed Civil Guards was also put in train. In contrast to the economic difficulties which beset the new government, it was soon apparent that the process of taking over the country's administrative machinery was going to be a very straightforward matter. All the institutions of a perfect readymade system of government at all levels were already in existence. There was remarkably little need for change. (3) The 'law and order' question was to be a major headache for the provisional government; indeed, it may be said to have dogged the entire career of Collins's colleague and successor, W. T. Cosgrave. Confronted with the presence of a group of dissidents who refused to recognise the authority of the government or the legitimacy of the state it was going to establish, the provisional government had to walk the tightrope between two policies: enforcing strong coercive measures against its opponents (which would risk the alienation of the government's more liberal supporters) or allowing them freedom

of action (which would be an admission of the government's own weakness and lack of authority). Furthermore, there was an ingrained suspicion and distrust of all forms of political authority in Ireland, and this had been greatly accentuated by the events of the past six years. The first native Irish administration could not expect this kind of feeling to vanish overnight; criticisms which had formerly been directed at the British would now be levelled against the Irish authorities. If the provisional government wanted to overcome the old tradition of hostility and turn erstwhile rebels into loyal conformists, it would have to work hard to do it. (4) Mulcahy had promised the Dáil that the IRA would remain loyal to the Dáil government pending its reconstitution as the national army of the Free State. But what did the IRA itself think about this? The IRA had sworn an oath of allegiance to the Irish Republic and its governmental assembly, the Dáil. But now that oath was clearly inconsistent, for the Dáil had voted to take a course of action that many argued would lead to the disestablishment of the Republic. The IRA, stemming as it did from the old Volunteer movement, was in existence before either the Dáil or the Republic, and it had developed a proud tradition of independent action, which had been reinforced by the military circumstances of the War of Independence. As a result, the IRA was never completely under the control of the civil authorities, and it was accustomed to regard itself as much more than the military tool of the political leaders. With the departure of the British troops, the IRA became the only armed force in the twenty-six counties, and its members therefore possessed the power to make or break the government. If they favoured the Treaty, all would be well for the provisional government, since the Treaty was its *raison d'être*. If they opposed the Treaty, the provisional government would collapse. If they split on the issue, there was a serious danger of civil war. The IRA thus played a crucial role in the events of the first half of 1922.

The IRA did indeed split on the Treaty, but in a different proportion to the Dáil deputies or the civilian population. Possibly as many as three-quarters of its members were opposed to the settlement. Through the influence of Collins and the IRB, the majority of headquarters staff stood by the Treaty, though some were against it. In addition, many of the brigade commandants in the provinces, particularly in Munster, e.g. Tom Barry, Liam Lynch and Ernie O'Malley, were among the most implacable foes of the Treaty. A large number of the rank and file were still trigger-happy after the hectic days of the War of Independence and were not looking forward to finding civilian jobs and settling down to ordinary everyday life. Far from dreading the resumption of war, these veteran guerilla fighters relished the exhilarating prospect of further excitement and adventure.

Shortly after the Dáil voted on the Treaty a move was initiated by its opponents in the army to release them from their allegiance to the government. Their point of view was stated concisely by Liam Lynch: 'we have declared for an Irish Republic and will not live under any other law.' Although the convention they had planned to ratify their position was forbidden by Mulcahy, it nevertheless took place on 26 March. This assembly repudiated the authority of the Dáil, swore undying allegiance to the Republic, and set up their own executive government, a junta of officers responsible only to itself. On being asked whether this meant that Ireland was to have a military dictatorship, Rory O'Connor, who had played a leading part in the convention's proceedings, replied with a soldier's bluntness: 'You can take it that way if you like.' The IRA had thus split into two opposing factions: the troops loyal to the government, generally to be known as the 'national army', and those hostile to it, generally known as 'irregulars'. Together with their civilian supporters, the two groups were termed respectively 'Free Staters' and 'Republicans'.

Events, though of a somewhat less momentous nature, were also taking place on the political front. On 21 February, the Sinn Féin *árd-fheis* was held and was attended by de Valera and his followers as well as by the pro-Treaty Dáil deputies. Both sides were determined to preserve the unity of the party and to prevent the possibility of an outbreak of violence. Griffith and de Valera therefore agreed that the forthcoming general election should be postponed until a draft constitution could be prepared for submission to the electorate. Optimists were still hoping at this stage that the constitution could be framed in such a way as to be acceptable to both de Valera and Lloyd George. In the weeks following the *árd-fheis* de Valera toured the country in an attempt to rally support for his views. He had by now conceded that the anti-Treatyites were in a numerical minority, but like the Unionist Bonar Law, de Valera too based his case on the claim that 'there are things stronger than parliamentary majorities'. For de Valera sovereignty was more important than the democratically expressed will of the majority. In his speeches in the spring of 1922 he warned the country of the strength with which this feeling was shared by the irregulars and prophesied the dire consequences which might result: 'They [the irregulars] would have to wade through Irish blood, through the blood of the soldiers of the Irish government and through, perhaps, the blood of some of the members of the government in order to get Irish freedom.' Many of de Valera's opponents saw such statements not as warnings but as threats.

But by this time the threat of violence had already begun to materialise without any prompting or encouragement from political figures. The barracks and military posts which had been vacated by the British were taken over systematically by local IRA units. Some of these units supported the Treaty, others opposed it. Anti-Treaty soldiers raided arms depots to augment their own stocks of weapons. The earliest of these raids was carried out on 26 February by a party led by Ernie O'Malley against the RIC barracks at Clonmel, Co. Tipperary. Although no one realised it at the time, this incident was, in effect, the first engagement of the Civil War. It set a pattern that recurred with increasing frequency during the following weeks. Within a few days of it, Limerick was the scene of a clash between the opposing IRA factions as they struggled inconclusively to gain a foothold in the barracks. In fact Limerick in March 1922 presented a strange picture, with three different army groups in different sections of the barracks: the British, who had not yet been completely evacuated, the pro-Treaty IRA and the anti-Treaty IRA. As such confrontations multiplied, affecting Kilkenny and a number of other military strongpoints, the threat of full-scale conflict in the twenty-six counties loomed ever larger.

The situation in the six counties of Northern Ireland was also giving cause for concern. The Treaty's provision for a Boundary Commission and the continued activities of the IRA in the province angered the Unionists, who saw them as a menace to the security of the state. There was considerable sectarian strife in the spring of 1922, with the police and the newly established B Specials taking the part of the Protestants, and the IRA, regardless of their stand on the Treaty, coming to the aid of the Catholics. Two agreements between Collins and Craig in January and March (ending the trade boycott of Northern goods in the South in return for protection of the Northern Catholic population) failed to stop the violence, and Craig found it necessary to impose a stringent Special Powers Act to deal with subversion. The appointment of the notorious hardline Unionist Sir Henry Wilson as military adviser to the Northern government also indicated its determination to smash the IRA. Indeed, the situation of the Northern nationalists was so desperate that for a time it seemed that it would serve to heal the breach in the Southern IRA; if this had happened, the war which was threatening to engulf the country would have taken a completely different form: instead of a civil war in the twenty-six counties, it would have been a war between North and South, triggered off by a concerted IRA attack across the border. Even while the Civil War was actually in progress, Collins was, unknown to his colleagues in the provisional government, supplying arms to the anti-Treaty IRA brigades in Northern Ireland.

Although the sporadic incidents of fighting between the rival sections of the army showed no sign of lessening, it was by no means inevitable that they would accelerate into a disastrous situation of total war. Collins worked hard to preserve some sort of unanimity between the factions. As chairman of the provisional government, he was naturally concerned to maintain peace in the country, but he was also inspired by a more personal motive. Unlike his civilian colleagues in the provisional government and the Dáil ministers, Collins was at heart a soldier, with a strong understanding of the military mind and a strong sense of comradeship with his fellow-soldiers, whatever their views on the Treaty. Whereas the attitude of politicians like Griffith, Cosgrave and O'Higgins was that the army should be brought firmly under the control of the civil authorities and insubordination punished, Collins viewed the problem of the military split with greater insight and sympathy. He believed that the irrevocable falling-out of old comrades was the ultimate tragedy, and he did everything in his power to prevent such a disaster.

The belligerent behaviour of the irregulars made Collins's efforts to act as peacemaker virtually useless. On 14 April a group of them headed by Rory O'Connor, in a daring and provocative action, seized the Four Courts in the heart of Dublin and put the buildings into a state of defence. The occupying garrison claimed that the Four Courts now housed the seat of the rival republican government (i.e. the anti-Treaty IRA executive). Their action was a deliberate challenge to the authority of the provisional government, and it took all the political leaders by surprise—de Valera as much as Collins. For as long as they remained in the Four Courts they constituted a grave embarrassment to the provisional government, especially when the British government began to clamour for this ambiguous state of affairs to be speedily brought under control. But Collins made no move to oust the rebel garrison. He knew that any attempt to do so would spark off a general eruption of violence throughout the country, and he was particularly anxious that the general election, scheduled for June, should be conducted in peaceful conditions.

Even at this late stage Collins had not despaired of bringing the two sides together. He and Griffith even went so far as to draft a constitution which would placate the Republicans, but Lloyd George rejected it, pointing out that it contradicted the terms of the Treaty. Nevertheless, a meeting of army officers of both sides was held, and an 'Army Document' was prepared on 1 May calling for an 'agreed election' based on a general acceptance of the fact that the majority of the population supported the Treaty. This development led to a pact agreed between Collins and de Valera on 20 May, according to which they would resolve their differences by means of what would nowadays be called a power-sharing arrangement: all candidates for the Third Dáil would stand on the Sinn Féin ticket, and the number allowed to each side would be in exactly the same proportion to its existing strength in the Dáil, i.e. with Treaty supporters in a slight majority. This artificial arrangement was totally undemocratic, but in removing the Treaty as an election issue, it would enable Sinn Féin to remain intact and would reduce the likelihood of fighting during the election.

But even as this unlikely agreement was being concluded outbreaks of fighting were becoming more frequent throughout the country. Rail and post facilities were being disrupted, roads blocked, banks robbed, buildings bombed. Snipers were active in many towns. An ugly aspect of the growing disorder was an outbreak of sectarianism. Attacks on Protestants had taken place during the War of Independence, but they had been confined to a small area in Co. Cork. Now they became general. Many large country houses were burned by the irregulars, and there was a concerted campaign to intimidate Protestants and drive them out of republican-dominated districts. Collins's hopes for restoring peace between the warring factions were fading fast, and he eventually acknowledged the unreality of the circumstances created by his pact with de Valera. Two days before the election he repudiated the pact and advised the electors to vote simply for the Treaty.

The general election was held on 16 June and its result announced on 24 June: pro-Treaty Sinn Féin 58; anti-Treaty Sinn Féin 35; Labour 17; Farmers 7; Independents 7; ex-Unionists 4. The distribution of votes was: pro-Treaty Sinn Féin 239,000; anti-Treaty Sinn Féin 134,000; others 247,000. This result showed two important things: (1) Support for the Treaty was much greater than many politicians had suspected, especially since the Independents and minority parties were all in favour of the Treaty. In contrast to the almost even split in the Second Dáil, the general public had *decisively* expressed its acceptance of the Treaty. (2) The excellent showing of the minority groups indicated that a surprisingly large section of the population (approximately two-fifths) did not consider the Treaty settlement to be the *dominant* issues in Irish politics. It is also possible that, in the conditions which prevailed at the time of the election, they regarded their abstention on the Treaty question as a vote against anarchy and war.

But anarchy and war were every day looming nearer. On 22 June Sir Henry Wilson was assassinated in London by two IRA men who were captured and executed without revealing on whose orders they had acted. There is some evidence to suggest that the assassination had been authorised by Collins as part of his campaign to protect the nationalists in the six counties from the ruthless repressive measures advocated by Wilson. However, the British government was convinced that the assassination had been ordered by O'Connor and the Four Courts executive. Lloyd George and Churchill even considered using British troops to mount an attack on the Four Courts, but instead they issued an impatient ultimatum to the provisional government: 'If the occupation of the Four Courts was not brought to an end, the British government would regard the Treaty as having been violated.' Against this background of growing pressure from the British, the Four Courts garrison committed a final act of provocation on 27 June when they captured a high-ranking officer, General 'Ginger' O'Connell, deputy chief of staff of the national army. This was a deliberate affront to the provisional government which not even Collins could tolerate. Early on the morning of 28 June an ultimatum was issued to the anti-Treaty junta demanding its immediate surrender. This was ignored by O'Connor, and the shelling of the Four Courts, using heavy artillery borrowed from the British, began forthwith.

Causes of the Civil War

In investigating the origins of the Civil War it is first of all necessary to emphasise a number of points. (1) The Civil War was *not* the inevitable consequence of the split in the Dáil over the Treaty. The purely political struggle was sidetracked after the Dáil's decision, and subsequent events were determined by two groups of armed men who paid little heed to the politicians. Furthermore, until the early summer of 1922 there was a possibility that war would be headed off as the political leaders—both pro-Treaty and anti-Treaty—made desperate but increasingly vain efforts to bring about a reconciliation between the two sides. (2) The Civil War was *not* caused by partition or by the explosive situation in Northern Ireland. Both sides desired national unity, but both trusted in Lloyd George's assurances which seemed to indicate that unity was inevitable and imminent. A war was very nearly fought over the North in 1922—but it would have been a very different type of war to the one which actually occurred. (3) Apart from an insignificant minority of radicals whose aim was a 'workers' and small farmers' republic', the combatants on neither side were interested in bringing about social or economic reform. Whatever class divisions may have existed between the Free Staters and Republicans (the former tended to have more affluent backgrounds than the latter), they played little part in the war. (4) The Civil War was *not* caused by de Valera. Even if he had accepted the Treaty, he could never have placated the extreme republican element in the IRA. It is possible that the prestige of the former President encouraged individuals to share his firm stand against the Treaty, and his decision to throw his support behind the irregulars after June may have helped to protract the war longer than would otherwise have been possible; but his power to influence events in the crucial months before the war was negligible, and his genuine efforts to prevent the outbreak were therefore doomed to total failure.

The real causes of the Civil War were as follows:
Underlying causes (i.e. the irreconcilable ideals and interests which created a climate of potential conflict): The Civil War was caused by the clash of two completely contrasting ways of looking at political problems: pragmatism and idealism which in 1921-22 became polarised over the question of the Treaty. The point at issue was Ireland's continued connection, in a subordinate position, with Great Britain, as expressed through the oath of allegiance. How important was it? Was it more important than the considerable measure of practical freedom and independence which Ireland had won? The idealists answered that it was of supreme importance—that freedom qualified by the oath was worthless. The pragmatists argued that such abstractions were irrelevant—that practical benefits were what really counted. There could be no compromise between these two positions, no middle-of-the-road solution. You could take the Treaty, or you could leave it—that was the agonising choice facing everyone in the twenty-six counties. Many years later de Valera accurately analysed the alternatives facing the country after January 1922: 'The conflict between the two principles, majority rule on the one hand and the inalienability of the national sovereignty on the other, that was the dilemma of the Treaty.'

Proximate causes (i.e. the developments which gave rise to an evolving set of circumstances in which a general outbreak of violence became increasingly likely): The Civil War was a direct result of the split in the IRA. The presence in early 1922 of two armed and resolute bodies of men, theoretically forming a unified army but in practice mutually hostile, created a situation fraught with immense potential danger. If this state of affairs had not existed, the Civil War would have been impossible.

Worse still, the IRA, with its history of independent guerilla action, had never been fully under the control of the Dáil government, and as the crisis of 1922 developed it grew increasingly uncontrollable. The British withdrawal left a military power-vacuum throughout the country and led to the two factions scrambling for the vacant strategic positions and the available supplies. The resulting confrontations inevitably led to friction, acts of aggression and retaliation, and eventually to shooting.

Two actions taken by the bellicose anti-Treaty IRA were intended as deliberate acts of defiance to the provisional government: the establishment of the military junta known as the irregular executive, and the seizure, in the name of the executive, of the Four Courts. Yet the provisional government was extremely reluctant to respond firmly to the worsening situation, and Collins in particular was anxious to do everything possible to reconcile the two sides and ward off 'fratricidal strife'. With the benefit of hindsight, it is easy to criticise Collins for not taking more vigorous action at an early stage; but as head of the provisional government he considered it his duty to make every effort to bring about a settlement, even at the last minute. Hence the possibly unwise decision to postpone the general election, and hence too the absurdity of the Collins–de Valera pact. These arrangements merely preserved the myth of unity and peace. Instead of averting conflict, they only postponed it. Collins was banking on a last desperate hope, and he lost. Moreover, as well as not having the inclination to act swiftly and firmly against the irregulars, the provisional government in the early months of 1922 did not have effective power to do so. In this early phase of sporadic hostilities the irregulars were in the majority, and Collins, Cosgrave and O'Higgins in Dublin had little control over what was happening in some parts of the country, particularly in Munster.

In contrast to the soft-pedalling tactics of the provisional government, the British government was loudly calling for strict enforcement of the Treaty settlement throughout the twenty-six counties. These pressures added an extra complication to the situation and perhaps also played a part in bringing about the Civil War.

Immediate causes (i.e. the incidents which touched off large-scale conflict and which caused the war to break out when it did): The assassination of Sir Henry Wilson brought a stern warning—virtually an ultimatum—that the rebel garrison in the Four Courts could no longer be tolerated. It was against this background of urgent pressure from the British that the capture of General O'Connell occurred, this was the final act of provocation by Rory O'Connor and his comrades-in-arms which convinced the provisional government that an attack on the Four Courts could no longer be put off.

The Civil War, June 1922-May 1923

In addition to the preliminary violence between the end of February and the end of June 1922 which has already been described, the course of the Civil War falls into three distinct phases.

(1) The Republican Rising, 28 June-5 July 1923. The national army attacked the Four Courts early on the morning of 28 June. The offensive action had the immediate effect of driving de Valera and the more moderate 'anti-imperialist' opponents of the Treaty into the arms of the out-and-out republican irregulars, whom de Valera now hailed as 'the best and bravest of our nation'. But by 30 June the Four Courts buildings were untenable because of shelling by provisional government forces and the irregular garrison surrendered. The fighting then spread to O'Connell Street, where the Republicans occupied a number of prominent buildings. The result was a repeat of Easter Week, ending with the total defeat of the insurgents and the destruction of much of O'Connell Street. Many of the Republican politicians joined the irregular forces, though they held no positions of high command. One of these was Cathal Brugha, who, inflexible to the last, was shot to death as he fought his way out of a burning building.

(2) The Fall of the Munster Republic, July-August 1922. After their defeat in Dublin, the irregulars fell back south of a line stretching from Limerick to Waterford. It was in this area, the so-called 'Munster Republic', that they could count on the sympathy of a large proportion of the population. After the capture of Rory O'Connor, Liam Lynch, chief of staff of the irregulars and commandant of a Cork brigade, rapidly emerged as the leading figure on the Republican side.

A period of large-scale military engagements now ensued as the Free State forces attacked the Republican line. At the outset of the campaign they were at a severe numerical disadvantage, but, unlike the irregulars, they possessed the sophisticated field weapons lent by the British. A massive recruiting campaign for the national army was also started, and soon 1,000 men were enlisting each day, so that the army's strength was rapidly built up to 60,000—far in excess of the irregulars. (The speed with which this target was reached is an indicator of what ordinary people over most of the country thought of the irregulars.) The crucially strategic city of Limerick was taken by this new army on 20 July, and Waterford fell a day later. Encountering fierce resistance at every step, it pressed on into the 'Munster Republic'. At the beginning of August an outflanking deployment of troops by sea was carried out, so that the stronghold of resistance in the extreme south came under attack from two fronts. Cork was captured on 12 August, and by the end of the month all the major towns in Munster were in Free State hands.

The month of August saw the death of the two leading figures on the Free State side. On 12 August Arthur Griffith, whose sound common sense had guided the infant state through its early troubles, died suddenly at the age of fifty, worn out by the strain and fatigue from which he had been suffering since the Treaty negotiations.

Ten days later Michael Collins, on an inspection tour of mopping-up operations in Co. Cork, was ambushed and shot dead. He was only thirty-two. The removal of this magnanimous realist at such a critical juncture destroyed the last chance of an early conclusion to the war and an amicable and honourable settlement between the two sides. Griffith and Collins were succeeded by Cosgrave and O'Higgins, who were determined to enforce a policy of law and order and to stamp out what they regarded not as a soldierly resistance movement but criminal subversion. Collins had seen the struggle as a tragic conflict of former comrades; Cosgrave and O'Higgins saw it as a clash between civil law and gun law. Their succession to the leadership of the government coincided with the start of the third and most horrific phase of the Civil War.

(3) Guerrillas in retreat, September 1922-May 1923 The hard-pressed Republicans now attempted to fall back on the old technique of guerrilla warfare. But conditions during the Civil War were not so suitable for such tactics as they had been during the War of Independence. In the first place, the guerrillas did not enjoy widespread sympathy throughout the rural community. Furthermore, their opponents had as sound a knowledge of local terrains as they had themselves. As a result, the irregular columns did not hover in the vicinity of country towns, but retreated into remote mountain and bogland areas. Although the fight had clearly gone against them, their principles would not allow them to betray the visionary republic, but strengthened their determination to resist to the bitter end.

The Third Dáil, which held its inaugural sitting on 9 September, was equally determined to put down lawlessness with a firm hand. Cosgrave and O'Higgins brought in an Emergency Powers Act, which established a special military tribunal and authorised the death penalty for a wide range of offences. Under this new legislation a number of republicans were executed, one of the first being Erskine Childers. A new element of bitterness now entered the war. In their determination to crush the irregulars once and for all, the national army mercilessly hunted down Republicans, and stories of atrocities worse than any that had been committed by the Black and Tans began to leak out. Prisoners were tortured or were blown to pieces by landmines, and by the end of 1922 over 12,000 persons had been interned. The irregulars reacted by carrying out a policy of reprisals, including a campaign against members of the Dáil and Senate, particularly against wealthy Protestant members of the latter body. Perhaps the lowest point was reached with the ambushing and assassination of a Dáil deputy, Seán Hales, in a Dublin street on 7 December. On the following day four Republican prisoners of war, including Rory O'Connor and Liam Mellows, who had been in custody since the summer, were executed in a cold-blooded act of vengeance. The new state, which had only just come formally into being when the provisional government was dissolved on 6 December 1922 (the first anniversary of the Treaty), had not got off to a very auspicious start.

Meanwhile the irregular executive and the Republican politicians had set up a rival state of their own in October when they elected a government with de Valera as President. But whatever influence 'Dev' may have had over his civilian followers, he cut no ice at all with the anti-Treaty IRA and was never anything more than a puppet President. The real power on the Republican side was in the hands of the indomitable Liam Lynch, operating from his secret headquarters in the mountain fastnesses of Co. Waterford. De Valera, who had long since realised the hopelessness of their military situation, repeatedly urged Lynch and his fellow-officers to give up the struggle and come to terms with the enemy, but they obstinately refused to consider his advice.

In the early months of 1923 the war dragged wearily on, the Free State army remorselessly closing in on the beleaguered irregulars. On 10 April Lynch was killed in action and was succeeded as chief of staff by Frank Aiken, a commander more amenable to de Valera's suggestions. After some heartsearching the Republicans decided to terminate hostilities, and on 24 May de Valera issued a proclamation to all who had fought for the Republic:

> Soldiers of the Republic, Legion of the Rearguard: The Republic can no longer be defended successfully by your arms. Further sacrifice of life would now be in vain and continuance of the struggle in arms unwise in the national interest and prejudicial to the future of our cause. Military victory must be allowed to rest for the moment with those who have destroyed the Republic.

There were no formal negotiations, no peace talks, no agreed terms between the two sides. There was no surrender, conditional or unconditional, and no amnesty. The Republicans simply stopped fighting, hid their arms and went 'on the run'. Neither was there any surrender of principle: the Republic was defeated, but in the eyes of its supporters it still lived. The new state was thus faced with the problem caused by the existence of thousands of disaffected citizens who refused to recognise its legitimacy and whose only official status was that of wanted criminals. In this muddled and unsatisfactory manner the Civil War came to an inglorious end.

Effects of the Civil War: The Civil War was the greatest single tragedy in modern Irish history since the Great Famine of 1845-49. No one really *won* the war. It produced no positive effects, except to confirm the authority of the Free State government throughout the twenty-six counties—and even so, the Cosgrave administration had to face a massive internal security problem for many years to come.

The negative effects of the Civil War were far more apparent. First of all, it had been responsible for a terrible waste of leadership and talent. The death of Michael Collins is the most obvious example: had he survived the war, Irish history would undoubtedly have taken a very different course for at least a generation. But there were other irreplaceable losses: the country was all the poorer for the deaths of men like Griffith, Childers, O'Connor, Mellows and Brugha.

The spiritual cost is more difficult to assess. By world standards, the Civil War was a microscopic affair. The total number killed may have been as low as 600 but the bitterness with which the war was fought and the savage atrocities and reprisals that were committed on both sides left a deep psychological wound on the whole nation which continued to fester in the forms of cynicism and resentment.

The Civil War also shattered the unity of Sinn Féin and put an end to the second and most glorious phase of its existence between 1917 and 1922, when it had been synonymous with Irish nationalism as a potent and progressive force. The magic name 'Sinn Féin' was far from dead and had a long history in front of it, but it was as an extremist minority group hovering uncertainly on the fringes of politics and legality. The forefront of the political scene was now dominated by the new parties which were formed in the 1920s on the basis of the divisions created by the Civil War.

The tragedy of the Civil War was that it meant another new beginning. Already there had been the challenge of making a start in January 1919, when the First Dáil met. Then in 1921-22 there had been the challenge to meet the new situation brought about by the end of the War of Independence and the question of the Treaty. Now, when the Free State government met in the aftermath of the Civil War, they had to make another start. And this time they had the prospect of a shattered and divided country brought to its knees. The economic recession, bad enough before the war, was now considerably worse; thousands of acres of land were lying uncultivated; there was widespread unemployment and poverty, and the early Free State had one of the lowest standards of living in Europe. The new government was also confronted with grave social problems, a heavy debt for the conduct of the war, and a population well-versed in lawlessness. The situation called for courageous and principled statesmanship tempered with humanity, understanding and patience, for firmness tempered with restraint. The all-important question in the years following the Civil War was whether the new leaders of the Free State could provide these vital qualities in exactly the right proportion.

Talking Points

Chapter 8: The Treaty and the Civil War, 1921-23

1. Compare the attitudes and approaches to the Treaty negotiations from the British and Irish sides, prior to the signing on 6 December 1921.

2. What were the main arguments put forward for and against the Treaty, during the debates from December 1921 to January 1922?

3. What do you consider were the main causes of the Civil War? Was there any moment when hostilities could have been avoided?

4. Outline the main features and events of the Civil War from June 1922 to May 1923.

5. Comment on the statement: 'No one really won the Civil War'.

6. What were the main effects of the Civil War upon the Irish political and economic scene?

Chapter 9
THE IRISH FREE STATE, 1923-32

The Irish Free State (Saorstát Éireann) came into existence officially on 6 December 1922, one year after the signing of the Treaty or 'Articles of Agreement'. The powers and responsibility of the provisional government expired and henceforth the government of the Irish Free State was entrusted to a parliament, or Oireachtas, with two houses, Dáil Éireann and Seanad Éireann (the Senate or upper house). The Sinn Féin Dáil of 1919 had met in the Mansion House, Dublin, but in September 1922 the Royal Dublin Society offered Leinster House to the Dáil as temporary accommodation. Subsequently Leinster House was purchased from the Royal Dublin Society, and it was there that the Dáil met for its first session under the new constitution of the Irish Free State. Leinster House has been the seat of the Irish parliament ever since.

The Constitution

When, in January 1919, the 'Constitution of Dáil Éireann' was published, the document was not intended to provide a complete blueprint for a sovereign independent state. In fact, it reflected the republican and democratic nature of the Irish independence movement. The constitution was short and was itself supplemented by two other documents, a 'Declaration of Independence' and a 'Democratic Programme'. The constitution of the Irish Free State (1922) was, however, a long document, providing for an effective sovereign state, but a state which had a special relationship with Great Britain. The new constitution was basically a document 'for implementing the Treaty between Great Britain and Ireland signed at London on 6 December 1921' and was meant to give force of law to the Treaty. Articles 1 and 2, defining the Free State's constitutional status, were as follows:
1. The Irish Free State (otherwise hereinafter called or sometimes called Saorstát Éireann) is a co-equal member of the Community of Nations forming the British Commonwealth of Nations.
2. All powers of government and all authority legislative, executive, and judicial in Ireland are derived from the people of Ireland and the same shall be exercised in the Irish Free State (Saorstát Éireann) through the organisations established by or under, and in accord with this Constitution.

All members of the Oireachtas were obliged by Article 17 to take the oath of allegiance to the king of Great Britain which had been included in the Treaty (See page 163). Disagreement over this oath had been responsible for the Civil War, and it continued to be a bone of contention for many years after the war was over.

De Valera and his Republican supporters refused to take the oath, and by this very act refused to recognise the authority of the constitution or the Oireachtas. 'As it stands', said de Valera, 'it will exclude from the public service and practically disenfranchise every honest Republican'. The Republicans also objected to the new constitution, because it not only recognised but also ratified the Anglo-Irish Treaty of 6 December 1921. The withdrawal of de Valera and his followers from the Dáil until 1927 when he said he would be prepared to take the oath because by then it had become 'an empty formula', and also the non-co-operation of the Republicans in the running of the country, left the field open to the pro-Treaty party, under W. T. Cosgrave. It must also be remembered that the introduction of the 1922 constitution came at the height of the Civil War. It was impossible to expect complete normality under the circumstances, although the takeover by the new government in December went smoothly. The Third Dáil reconvened for the first time under the new constitution on 12 December 1922. The governor-general, T. M. Healy, read the address from the king, and the deputies then proceeded to deal with ordinary business.

Cumann na nGaedheal

The Sinn Féin organisation was shattered by the Treaty issue. Although both the pro-Treaty group and the anti-Treaty group continued to call themselves Sinn Féiners while the debate on the Treaty was in progress, by early 1922 the name had lost its original significance. The Civil War ended all hopes of salvaging Sinn Féin. It became necessary to find new names for the two major parties, the anti- and pro-Treaty groups.

In January 1923, a convention of pro-Treaty supporters met in Dublin to form a new party. They drew up a programme and issued a policy. In April this new party was officially launched under the title Cumann na nGaedheal, a name which had belonged to a Sinn Féin-type group early in the century. Cumann na nGaedheal was not just a political party, nor was it meant merely as a type of umbrella organisation for all those who took the Treaty side during the Civil War. It was hoped that it might become the rallying point for men of different classes, origins and creeds, prepared to help build a new Ireland on the basis of the new constitution. Cumann na nGaedheal was well established by the time the Civil War ended in May 1923 and the first general election held under the new constitution was in August 1923. The result of the election gave Cumann na nGaedheal 63 seats, Sinn Féin (i.e., de Valera's anti-Treaty party who had no intention of taking their seats) 44, Independents 16, Farmers

15, and Labour 14. The voting was on a proportional representation basis. Although Cosgrave's party had only 63 of the 153 seats, the absence of de Valera's party from the Dáil meant that in practice Cumann na nGaedheal had a safe overall majority. The role of official opposition was taken by the Labour Party, led by Thomas Johnson and Cathal O'Shannon. The new government was made up of W. T. Cosgrave (President of the Executive Council, i.e., the Dáil cabinet), K. O'Higgins (Vice-President and Home Affairs), R. Mulcahy (Defence), D. FitzGerald (External Affairs), J. McGrath (Industry and Commerce) E. Mac Néill (Education), E. Blythe (Finance), etc. They had many pressing problems to deal with, the first being that of restoring law and order.

Law and Order

As Minister for Home Affairs, the responsibility for maintaining law and order fell on the shoulders of Kevin O'Higgins. Although only thirty-one years of age in 1923, O'Higgins had been in public life for many years. He had some of the qualities of Michael Collins, and possessed great courage and powers of work. A man of strange contrasts, he was loved by some and hated by others, being reputed to have 'a temper like the wrath of God'. One of his first decisions was to create an unarmed police force. The Garda Síochána, or Civic Guards, were founded early in 1923. Special care was taken that they knew the law well as their main job was to uphold it and protect people from criminals. The Garda Síochána replaced the old semi-military RIC and proved themselves one of the more stabilising influences in the Irish Free State during the next few years. Once the Civil War ended, the guards were able to take up residence in the local barracks. They wore a special uniform which at first made them objects of curiosity, but were soon accepted among the community where they lived.

O'Higgins then turned his attention to the problem of setting up courts of law. The state of legal justice in Ireland at the time was confusing. The so-called 'Dáil Courts' had been set up by Sinn Féin in 1919, but there were still some courts functioning under the old British system. By the Courts of Justice Act (1924) all these former courts were set aside and a completely new system introduced. District Courts superseded the former Petty Sessions, while District Justices took the place of the Justices of the Peace and Resident Magistrates. Likewise the County Court was abolished and replaced by Circuit Courts. At the top of the legal ladder were the High Courts, Courts of Criminal Appeal and Supreme Courts. As a result of these reforms, justice was henceforth dispensed more quickly and was also less costly. The Irish Free State retained the common law as it had evolved over the centuries, and also the traditional training and dress of the legal profession. In this way, the changeover was far from revolutionary and guaranteed an element of continuity and stability where law and justice were concerned.

At the time when the Free State government began to function, a very large number of anti-Treaty prisoners were in jail. By mid-1923, the number of prisoners had risen to 12,000. Under the Public Safety Act of 1923, the Minister for Home Affairs (O'Higgins) was empowered to keep in internment without trial any prisoners the government considered as representing a danger to public peace and order. De Valera was arrested in Ennis on 15 August 1923, and not released until July 1924. However, as order was restored to the country, the political prisoners were freed, and returned to civilian life. Many of them found it difficult to settle down or even to get a job and were forced to emigrate.

The Army Mutiny, 1924

Perhaps the most pressing problem of the young state was how to guarantee the loyalty of the army. Within the first year of the new government's life a crisis arose in the armed forces, which for a time threatened to explode in a full-scale mutiny or even a further outbreak of civil war.

Owing to the Civil War situation, the army had grown to some 60,000 men. Obviously such a large number could not be kept under arms in peacetime, so in March 1924 the government decided to order the demobilisation of nearly 2,000 officers and 35,000 men. These dismissals were resented by army veterans, many of whom had been in service since the early days of the Volunteer movement; they referred to themselves as the 'old IRA' in order to distinguish themselves both from the 'new IRA' (i.e., the Republican section of the army which had fought against the Treaty) and the new recruits, including many former British soldiers, who had enlisted in the national army during the Civil War. Most of these 'old IRA' men had learned no other trade but that of soldiering, and they had little liking or aptitude for civilian jobs.

The 'old IRA' also had a more serious political grievance. They had supported and fought for the Treaty largely out of a sense of loyalty and devotion to Collins, sharing his belief that the arrangement was not a permanent one, but a stepping stone to something more desirable. But after the death of Collins, this aspect of the Treaty seemed to have been forgotten, not only by the government, which initiated no new moves towards a republican settlement, but also by the IRB, which had come to dominate the army's internal controlling body, the Army Council. Furthermore, the Minister of Defence, General Mulcahy, was himself a strong IRB man.

These dissatisfactions led the 'old IRA' to produce an ultimatum, dated 6 March 1924 and signed by two officers, Liam Tobin and C. F. Dalton, which was sent to the government. It demanded (1) an end to demobilisation, (2) the removal of the Army Council and (3) some guarantee of the government's intention to achieve an Irish Republic. Referring specifically to Collins's ideals, the document declared: 'the [old] IRA only accepted the Treaty as a means to achieving its objects—namely to secure and maintain a Republican form of Government in this country. After many months of discussion with your Government it is our considered opinion that your Government has not these objects in view and that their policy is not reconcilable with the Irish people's acceptance of the Treaty.'

On receiving this ultimatum the government acted promptly. The signatories were arrested, and General Eoin O'Duffy, the Commissioner of the Civic Guards, was brought in to take charge of the army. A number of officers thereupon deserted, and there was a serious confrontation between them and soldiers loyal to the government which seemed likely to end in shooting. However, this disaster was prevented by the timely intervention of Joseph McGrath, whose sympathy for the 'old IRA' had already led to his resignation from the Executive Council. Through the mediation of McGrath an agreement was reached whereby (1) an enquiry into army administration was promised; (2) the existing members of the pro-IRB Army Council were to be replaced by neutral officers; (3) there would be no victimisation, and those deserting officers who refused to return to their posts would be held to have 'retired' from the army; (4) an army service pension scheme was guaranteed. These arrangements were made under the direction of Kevin O'Higgins, who had taken overall responsibility for the government during President Cosgrave's absence through illness. O'Higgins handled the whole incident with firmness and impartiality. As well as redressing what he felt were genuine grievances, he also insisted on the resignation of three senior officers and he was about to make the same demand of Mulcahy when the latter resigned of his own accord. The mutiny was thus nipped in the bud, and the old question of who had ultimate control in the state—the civil authorities or the army which had brought them to power—was finally settled; in O'Higgins's words, 'Those who take the pay and wear the uniform of the state, be they soldiers or police, must be non-political servants of the state.'

The Boundary Commission, 1925

By the Anglo-Irish Treaty of 6 December 1921, the existence of Northern Ireland as a separate entity on a temporary basis was recognised. However, articles 11 and 12 contained special provisions, whereby if Northern Ireland refused to become part of a United Ireland, a Boundary Commission was to be set up, which would determine the boundaries between Northern Ireland and the rest of Ireland 'in accordance with the wishes of the inhabitants, so far as may be compatible with economic and geographic conditions'. After the First World War such boundary commissions were very much a pattern of the Treaty of Versailles arrangement in Europe, but the wording of the Irish arrangement was particularly vague and ambiguous.

A number of factors helped to complicate the situation still further. First of all, the Civil War began early in 1922 and was still in progress when on 6 December 1922 the Free State Act ratifying the Treaty came into existence. On 7 December 1922, Northern Ireland exercised its right of opting out of a united Ireland. Secondly, the political instability in England during the years 1922-24 led to a serious problem of communication between the Dublin and London governments. Lloyd George fell from power in 1922 and the Conservatives came back into office under Bonar Law, who was of Ulster descent. However, owing to ill-health Law had to retire and was succeeded by Stanley Baldwin, also a Conservative, a man who had distrusted Lloyd George and would have little respect for any arrangement made by him. The Conservatives lost the general election in 1923 and a Labour government was formed under Ramsay MacDonald. When the Labour government arranged a loan to Russia and this became public, the famous 'Red Letter' election of 1924 was held, MacDonald defeated, and Baldwin returned to power at the head of a Conservative government which remained in office until 1929. During the years 1922-24, England had too many internal problems of her own, political, economic and social, to pay much attention to Ireland. Both British and Irish ministers hesitated to raise the Boundary Commission question, fearing the fall of their respective governments on the issue. Finally, the Northern Ireland government refused to consider itself bound by an article of a Treaty to which it had never assented.

When the Civil War was over, and the Free State government surveyed the general situation in Ireland, they could not overlook the question of partition and especially the position of the Catholic minority in Northern Ireland. In October 1924, Cosgrave and Baldwin finally agreed to set up the Boundary Commission, under a neutral chairman, Mr Justice Feetham of the South African Supreme Court. J. R. Fisher, a well-known Ulster Unionist, was appointed by the British government to represent Northern Ireland, while Eoin Mac Néill, the Minister for Education in the Free State government and an Ulster Catholic, represented the Dáil. The Commission spent most of 1925 taking information and preparing a report, but their meetings were in private. It was agreed that all three commissioners would sign a report approved by any two of them.

There was much speculation about the commissioners' findings and especially that large parts of Counties Fermanagh and Tyrone would be given to the Free State. But before the report was due for release, the *Morning Post* of 7 November 1925 published a statement (which probably had its origins in a disclosure from Fisher) to the effect that the commission would leave the border very much as before, save for a portion of Donegal which would go to Northern Ireland, and portions of South Armagh and South Fermanagh which would go to the Free State. Although the gains for the South were far in excess of those for the North, they were very far from the wholesale transference of huge areas of land into the Free State—which would have made the continued existence of Northern Ireland doubtful—which Mac Néill and everyone else in the South had been expecting.

The rumour of the commission's findings caused an immediate outcry in Dublin, and Mac Néill, acutely embarrassed and disappointed by the whole affair, resigned from both the Boundary Commission and the Executive Council.

It was now vitally urgent for Cosgrave to prevent the report from being implemented, and even published, since feelings about it in the South were so high that it would almost certainly lead to the fall of his government. Cosgrave and his fellow-ministers rushed to London, where they hurriedly worked out an agreement with MacDonald and Craig which maintained the status quo of the border and suppressed the troublesome report (it was not published until 1968). The tripartite agreement contained two further articles: (1) The Irish Free State was released from its obligations and liabilities in relation to the public debt of the United Kingdom. (2) The powers of the Council of Ireland relating to Northern Ireland were transferred to the Northern Ireland government although a vague provision was made for meetings between the two Irish governments to discuss matters of common concern.

The removal of financial pressures on the Free State was generally welcomed by all, for the government was finding it very difficult to meet the financial obligations imposed on it by the Treaty. But the parts of the agreement dealing with North-South relations had very unsatisfactory long-term results for the Free State government. The virtual demise of the Council of Ireland and the estrangement of the two regimes meant that all official communication between them was in effect ruled out, and no meeting took place between the two heads of government until 1965. The Free State government's connivance in maintaining the border and consolidating partition played into the hands of the Republicans, who claimed that Cosgrave and his ministers had bartered away a portion of the national territory; this argument hit home, and after 1925 Republican sentiment on the Ulster question began to win over a number of disillusioned Free Staters. It also gave a boost to the IRA, focused their attention on the unsolved Ulster question and confirmed them in their belief that a united Ireland would never be achieved except by force of arms.

Economic Recovery

Cosgrave's government adopted a conservative and protectionist policy in dealing with the national economy during the first few years of the new state. There was an almost panic situation in 1924 when they failed to balance the budget, so much so that one shilling a week was taken off old-age pensions. A great deal of responsibility for the improved situation as the years passed by was due to the hard work of dedicated civil servants. It has been estimated that some 21,000 civil servants who had worked under the pre-1921 British government in Ireland, transferred over to the new state.

But the greatest problem facing the young state was that of providing enough jobs for everyone, in spite of the fact that some Dáil deputies felt it was not the responsibility of the government to provide employment at all. But to many people it had become painfully obvious that Ireland could never become a modern state without improving her sources of power. There was also a serious lack of capital in the country to initiate even light industry. Something had to be done, if the Irish Free State was not to remain a poor and undeveloped country. Many centres such as Sligo, Drogheda, Kilkenny, Tralee and Athlone had no electricity in 1923, while even in the cities, only one out of every three houses in Dublin had electricity and the ratio was one in every four in Cork. The total output of privately operated generating stations in the country in 1923 only came to forty million units.

The greatest revolution in Ireland during the 1920s from the economic point of view was the state-sponsored Shannon Scheme to provide electricity by harnessing the flow of the country's longest river a few miles from Limerick. The scheme was the brain-child of Dr T. A. MacLoughlin, an Irish engineer who had worked in Germany, and who made a thorough investigation of Ireland's electrical capacity in a tour of the country in 1923. He approached the Minister for Industry and Commerce, Joseph McGrath, who introduced the plan to the Dáil. There was considerable opposition, mainly on the grounds of expense. The total cost was estimated at £5 million and many Dáil deputies thought the scheme would never pay for itself. After McGrath's resignation in 1924 on the army mutiny issue, his ministerial post was taken by Patrick McGilligan, who gave the scheme his full backing. McGrath, however, was one of the principal driving forces behind the scheme and became director of labour at Shannon. German engineers and machinery were used and 4,000 Irishmen found work for four years. They were only paid 17/6 a week, but it was constant and regular work—not so easily found in Ireland at the time. The Free State government set up the Electricity Supply Board in 1927 and the Shannon Scheme began to go into operation in October 1929. Electricity, especially in rural areas, was to be one of the more powerful factors in bringing about social changes in Ireland, and was of special benefit to the farming community. It is almost impossible to imagine how Ireland would have developed in the years ahead without the Shannon Electrical Scheme. Joseph McGrath, who had brought such energy and skill to this matter, later founded the Irish Hospitals Sweepstake in 1930 and helped provide funds for the building of hospitals throughout the country.

The government also applied itself to the job of promoting recovery in the largest sector of the Irish economy—agriculture. A Land Act passed in 1923 helped to complete the process of compulsory land purchase and the revolution in land-ownership that had been initiated under Gladstone. Schemes for regulating standards in farm produce and making marketing techniques more effective were also introduced. The government established a large sugar-beet factory in Carlow, which developed into an important national industry giving employment to many hundreds of people. In 1927 an Agricultural Credit Corporation was set up to make loans to farmers, however small their farms, in order to carry out improvements. Although such reforms did not bring about instant spectacular results, they served to halt the economic recession in which Ireland had been plunged in the early 1920s and by 1929 it seemed as if the Free State was advancing slowly towards greater economic prosperity.

The Founding of Fianna Fáil, 1926-27

Eamon de Valera was released from jail on 16 July 1924. He made his first public appearance outside Dublin at Ennis on 14 August exactly a year after his arrest in the same place, beginning with the famous words: 'Well, as I was saying to you when we were interrupted . . .'. In his speech, he reiterated well-worn Republican principles: 'The aim of Sinn Féin is to secure the international recognition of an Irish Republic.' De Valera and his Republican followers were still operating under the Sinn Féin umbrella. Following a policy of non-attendance at Dáil Éireann, their role was a purely negative one and, up to 1926, they played no effective part in the development of the new state.

Towards the end of 1925 de Valera and the IRA found their viewpoints so different from each other that Sinn Féin, as it then stood, was split in two. De Valera even made some remarks which suggested that if the oath were removed, he would be prepared to sit in Dáil Éireann. Thus in March 1926 he resigned as President of Sinn Féin over this issue and decided to launch a new party. In May 1926, at a meeting in Dublin, de Valera founded a new political party called Fianna Fáil. Sinn Féin had been on the decline ever since the Treaty, and the Civil War had caused it to lose many of its original supporters. The name Fianna Fáil was chosen because it indicated a continuity with the movement that had started with the founding of the Irish Volunteers in 1913. The Volunteers' badge had the initials 'F.F.' on it, and members of the Volunteers were often called 'Fianna Fáil' by Irish speakers. De Valera outlined the principal aims of his new party in a press statement intended for his American supporters:

The new Republican organisation, Fianna Fáil, has for its purpose the re-uniting of the Irish people and the banding of them together for the tenacious pursuit of the following ultimate aims, using at every moment such means as are rightly available:

1. Securing the political independence of a united Ireland as a Republic.
2. The restoration of the Irish language, and the development of a native Irish culture.
3. The development of a social system in which, as far as possible, equal opportunity will be afforded to every Irish citizen to live a noble and useful Christian life.

4. The distribution of the land of Ireland so as to get the greatest number possible of Irish families rooted in the soil of Ireland.

5. The making of Ireland an economic unit, as self-contained and self-sufficient as possible, with a proper balance between agriculture and other essential industries.

In November 1926 Fianna Fáil held its first *árd-fheis* and de Valera was unanimously elected president of the new organisation. Fianna Fáil was in many ways *the* de Valera party. His name attracted to its side many who might not otherwise have joined. However, he was ably supported by such political veterans as Sean T. O'Kelly, Frank Aiken, James Ryan and Sean Lemass, all of whom had been prominent in the previous Sinn Féin parties. Fianna Fáil were able to take over some of the machinery of Sinn Féin, especially its clubs, with their experienced party workers. And above all, its declared Republican policy was certain to make it popular among those who were becoming disillusioned with Cosgrave's Cumann na nGaedheal. Fianna Fáil seemed to many to represent a 'new departure' and adopted a more moderate tone in its Republican programme.

The first real test of the new party came with the general election of June 1927. De Valera fought the election on the Oath of Allegiance issue, as well as pledging himself to establish a Republic. His party won 44 seats, which was the same number they had gained in the 1923 election. However, the Cumann na nGaedheal party only won 47 seats, as compared with their 63 seats after the 1923 election. The Labour Party won 22 seats, Independents 14, and Farmers 11. When de Valera and his fellow Fianna Fáil deputies arrived at Leinster House, they were refused permission to take their seats unless they first took the oath. They then retired and Cosgrave's Cumman na nGaedheal party was able to form a government.

On 10 July 1927, Kevin O'Higgins, Minister for Finance and Vice-President of the Executive Council, was assassinated as he walked to Mass. His killers were never brought to justice. His death at the age of 35 was a very considerable loss to the Cumann na nGaedheal party. Another potential leader was thus removed from Irish life. As a result of his murder, the government introduced a new and more stringent Public Safety Act to counter lawlessness. At the same time an Electoral Amendment Act was passed which provided that every candidate for election to the Dáil or Seanad should, when nominated, swear he would take the oath, if elected; otherwise he would be disqualified from holding his seat. In this way it was hoped to put an end to the abstentionist policy of Fianna Fáil. It presented de Valera and his followers with a dilemma: they must either give up political action altogether or take the oath and enter the Dáil. De Valera decided to enter the Dáil. On 10 August 1927, the Fianna Fáil party took their seats in the Free State Dáil. De Valera took the oath, but he did so in a way which made of the oath 'an empty political formula' and he made it clear that he 'was not taking any oath nor giving any promise of faithfulness to the king of England'. The entry of Fianna Fáil in force to the Dáil altered the balance of power in the Free State, especially as it seemed that Fianna Fáil would be supported by Labour and some of the minority deputies. The supremacy of the Cosgrave government had thus been confronted with its first serious challenge.

Cosgrave decided to call a general election, the second within one year, which was held in September 1927. The results were Cumann na nGaedheal 67, Fianna Fáil 57, Labour 13, Farmers 6, Independents 12. The increase in the Cumann na nGaedheal vote was due to the widespread revulsion at the murder of O'Higgins. Most of the minority parties were wiped out during the election as they had not sufficient funds to fight a second general election in three months. But de Valera and his party were firmly established as the second largest party in the Dáil. It gradually organised itself both within and without the Dáil, perfecting a machinery of constituency organisation through local *cumainn* which was far superior to that of Cumann na nGaedheal. In 1931 de Valera founded *The Irish Press* as the party's newspaper. *The Irish Press* soon had a circulation of 100,000, which indicated the extent of Fianna Fáil support in the country.

The Statute of Westminster

The history of Ireland in the 1920s contains so many events of a 'domestic' character that it is easy to overlook the wider world context. At no stage in the years 1922-23 was Ireland isolated, cut off from what was happening in England, Europe or the rest of the world. The Irish Free State was particularly involved in the process of Commonwealth evolution and the transformation of the old British Empire which occurred between 1923-31. A series of Imperial Conferences were held in London almost annually and Ireland sent a representative to each of them. The country's constitutional position did not depend solely on what was said or done in Dáil Éireann. Under the terms of the Treaty, the Irish Free State had a unique international relationship with Great Britain, a country which was itself adjusting to changing world situations. Developments in India, Canada, Australia and New Zealand impinged on Irish affairs as well, because all these countries formed part of the British Commonwealth. During the 1920s the term 'empire' began to go out of fashion, and the expression 'British Commonwealth of Nations', which had first been used officially in Article 4 of the Anglo-Irish Treaty, was now accepted and used in all British constitutional documents.

When Michael Collins told Dáil Éireann during the debate on the Anglo-Irish Treaty that the Treaty gave Ireland 'freedom, not the ultimate freedom that all nations desire and develop to, but the freedom to achieve it', he was expressing a view which was not prophetic but realistic. The Irish Free State government under Cosgrave worked towards the long-term goal of full and unrestricted sovereignty. In 1921 Dominion status fell far short of complete independence, but, thanks to agreements reached at Imperial Conferences in the years ahead, it became possible for the Irish delegates to help achieve a peaceful transformation, a more complete measure of freedom in domestic and foreign affairs.

Ireland had reached Dominion status through revolution and so the new nation was considered by many British politicians as 'a problem child'. The Civil War only seemed to demonstrate that the Irish were incapable of ruling themselves. However, having achieved a position within what Kevin O'Higgins called 'this miniature League of Nations', the Free State government was determined to reach full independence. On paper the great issue was that of changing an apparent status of subordination, i.e., less than full nationhood, to that of equality with England. Ireland's position was watched with great interest by South Africa, Canada and the other Dominions. The barely camouflaged Republican ideals of the Irish delegates at the Imperial Conferences made them the most outspoken and intransigent. And when in 1924 the Free State government brought the Anglo-Irish Treaty formally to the attention of the League of Nations at Geneva, it was clear that they were acting as a sovereign independent nation.

In fact, by 1927, the Oath of Allegiance had become an empty formula. The oath had never been the same as that taken in Britain and the other Dominions. The Dáil deputies at no time were asked to swear direct allegiance to the king, but rather swore 'true faith and allegiance to the Constitution of the Irish Free State as by law established'. They then swore to be faithful to the king and his successors 'in virtue of the common citizenship of Ireland with Great Britain and her adherence to and membership of the group of nations forming the British Commonwealth of Nations'.

The final stage came when the Imperial parliament enacted the Statute of Westminster on 11 December 1931 and gave co-equal relationship to the Dominions and the United Kingdom. More important still, it laid down that 'the parliament of a Dominion shall have power to repeal or amend any existing or future Act of Parliament of the United Kingdom in so far as the same is part of the law of the Dominion'. The Statute of Westminster was the outcome of lengthy discussions at the Imperial Conferences of 1926, 1929 and 1930. Kevin O'Higgins had played a prominent role in the 1926 Conference, and Patrick McGilligan was the chief Irish delegate at the later Conferences. They were responsible for helping to untangle many of the confused constitutional anomalies which existed between Great Britain and the Commonwealth of Nations. The Statute of Westminster was later described as having 'put the goblet of freedom into Ireland's hands, to be drained at her discretion'. McGilligan had succeeded in persuading the British government to stop using British Seals on Irish legal documents. The Irish Free State was given its own Great Seal on 10 March 1931. Thus, by the end of 1931, the Cosgrave government had achieved a great deal in strengthening Ireland's international position as an independent country. But Cumann na nGaedheal were not to be given an opportunity of reaping the benefit of their newly-won free status. A general election was held in Ireland in 1932, and de Valera's Fianna Fáil party won a substantial victory. They now had 72 seats as against Cumann na nGaedheal's 57. With the help of the seven Labour deputies, Cumann na nGaedheal's alliance with minority parties and independents was outnumbered, and de Valera was able to form the first Fianna Fáil government.

Reasons for the defeat of Cumann na nGaedheal

There were many reasons for the defeat of Cosgrave's party: (1) the appearance of de Valera and his party in Dáil Éireann in 1927 brought the first really organised 'opposition' into public debates. As an opposition party, Fianna Fáil were quite ruthless and kept up a constant bombardment of objection and criticism. They found plenty of useful ammunition for their attacks in the apparently pro-British policy of Cosgrave; and, by proving themselves die-hard Republicans, won the sympathy of those who wished to see Ireland entirely free of the English connection.

(2) The years 1929-31 were years of great economic depression all over the world. The Wall Street crash of 1929 affected Ireland as well as other European countries. Remittances home from the emigrants in America almost ceased and there was great suffering and poverty among the old and the unemployed. Ireland's finances were linked 'for better or for worse' with England, and when England abandoned the gold standard in 1930, the pound lost nearly one-third of its value. At home, Cosgrave's government was blamed for these setbacks.

Ireland was predominantly an agricultural country and, owing to the world situation, she could not find an outlet for farm produce. Between 1928 and 1931 exports of bacon and butter fell by almost half, while egg exports fell by a third. Cattle and sheep prices fell. Unemployment soared from 21,000 in April 1929 to 31,000 in April 1932. Factories were forced to close down and the country was almost in a state of emergency. Cosgrave's government could find no way out of the difficulty, and some of the measures they adopted, such as reducing police and teachers' pay only made the public more hostile and critical. De Valera's newly-founded *Irish Press* used its pages for anti-Cosgrave propaganda and to call for a change of government.

(3) The Public Safety Act which had been passed after Kevin O'Higgins' death in 1927, was repealed at the end of 1928. This gave an opportunity for some extreme Republican and revolutionary groups to reappear and create difficulties for the Cosgrave government. One of these was called Comhairle na Poblachta, the Council of the Republic, which proceeded to publish a newspaper called *An Phoblacht*. In issue after issue, this paper criticised Cosgrave's government, and preached extreme republicanism. Two other organisations, Saor Eire (Free Ireland) and the IRA also began

campaigns of anti-government propaganda, and by 1931 there was a considerable amount of illegal drilling throughout the country. A number of serious shooting incidents took place, at a time when extreme left-wing and right-wing movements were active all over Europe. The growth of the IRA was extraordinary. Peader O'Donnell, Sean Russell and others organised a parade of the Dublin brigade on 7 June 1931. The IRA held their first congress in Dublin on 26 and 27 September 1931, which drew up a draft constitution and declared itself socialist in its policy. It made a special appeal to the agricultural community and claimed to be working for a 'Peasants' Republic'. When, therefore, the government rushed a ferocious Public Safety Bill through the Oireachtas in October 1931, these groups were further incensed. Fianna Fáil strenuously opposed the Bill, but it eventually became law on 17 October as the Constitution (Amendment No. 17) Act. Military tribunals were set up to try political offences and this only helped to bring the IRA closer to Fianna Fáil. Some members of the militant IRA emigrated to America and returned later to Ireland as wealthy men. Cosgrave's government was slowly losing whatever popularity and following it had. It came as no surprise that Fianna Fáil attracted over 160,000 new supporters in the general election of 1932.

(4) The Dáil was legally not required to call for a general election until October 1932. But partly because of the threat of continued disorder and partly because Cosgrave wanted to have a positive expression of public support before attending the forthcoming Commonwealth Conference later in the year, it was decided to hold a snap election in February 1932. It is difficult to say if this hurried and precipitate election played into the hands of Cosgrave's critics, but the government's decision to prosecute the *Irish Press* before the military tribunal early in 1932 certainly alienated Cumann na nGaedheal's more lukewarm supporters. In any case, Fianna Fáil came out of the election with the largest number of seats. When the Dáil convened, Cosgrave could only muster a total of 74 supporters, as against de Valera's 79. He had to step down and de Valera became the leader of the new government.

During the years 1922-32, the Cosgrave government brought Ireland out of the chaos which followed the War of Independence and through the bitter days of the Civil War. It restored order to the country and established the Irish Free State as an internationally recognised independent country. It had ruled for ten years, and given some form of stability to the new state, by establishing a solid tradition of democratic constitutional government, backed by an efficient and dedicated Civil Service. It passed on all of these achievements to Fianna Fáil, who held the reins of government in Ireland for the next sixteen years.

Talking Points

Chapter 9: The Irish Free State, 1923-32
1. What was the general attitude adopted by the Cumann na nGaedheal government to the problem of law and order during the years 1923-25?
2. What was the reason for the Army Mutiny in 1924? Show how the Irish army had certain inherent difficulties, born out of its origins and antecedents.
3. Analyse the problems surrounding the Boundary Commission. How do you account for its ultimate failure?
4. In what way did the Cosgrave government cope with the various economic problems facing the new state between 1923 and 1929?
5. Why did de Valera decide to found a new party in 1926? In what way did the Fianna Fáil party go from strength to strength between 1927 and 1932?
6. How do you account for the defeat of the Cosgrave government in 1932?

Chapter 10
DE VALERA IN POWER, 1932-48

The New Government

De Valera came to power at a time when great political changes were taking place all over Europe. Although the Treaty of Versailles had tried to make the world 'safe for democracy', the early 1930s produced a spate of dictatorships and military governments. Mussolini was well established in Italy at the head of a Fascist regime; Stalin was supreme ruler in Russia; Hitler was about to launch his Nazi party and establish a dictatorship in Germany, while Salazar was in control of Portugal. In each case, one strong personality succeeded in getting complete control of power within his country. Many people thought that de Valera would establish a kind of dictatorship in the Irish Free State. Just before the 1932 election, Dublin pubs were ringing with a parody of Percy French's 'Phil the Fluter's Ball', describing conditions in Ireland under de Valera's rule:

Och! We'll shoot and we'll loot and with bullets we will riddle oh!
We'll keep the whole land sizzling like a herring on the griddle oh!

However, de Valera's reign, during the first few years, was anything but an easy supremacy of power. Although he came to power as an apparent revolutionary, he introduced not dictatorship but government based on a new constitution which was both democratic and conservative. Just as the first Free State government had taken over the administration of the country from the British, and retained most of the original trappings of Dublin Castle and the civil service, so de Valera's government took over from Cumann na nGaedheal, without causing any radical disturbance. In 1932, Fianna Fáil inherited a functioning apparatus of government and ran the country by the same means and often through the same personnel as the Cosgrave administration.

When de Valera and his party attended the first meeting of the seventh Dáil on 9 March 1932, some of them carried revolvers in their pockets. They feared a *coup d'état* by disgruntled soldiers of the Free State army. However, all went peacefully. Thanks to the support of Labour and three Independent deputies, de Valera was elected Prime Minister of the Irish Free State by 81 votes to 68. A few days later, de Valera said in the Dáil: 'We heard of frightful things that would happen the moment the Fianna Fáil government came into power. We have seen no evidence of these things. We have had a peaceful change of government.' Taking the portfolio of External Affairs for himself, he then proceeded to appoint his new cabinet: Sean T. O'Kelly (Local Government and Public Health), Sean

MacEntee (Finance), Thomas Derrig (Education), Sean Lemass (Industry and Commerce), Frank Aiken (Defence), James Ryan (Agriculture). Because of the persistent economic depression the new government was determined to reduce the running expenses of the state as far as possible, and above all to achieve economic self-sufficiency for Ireland.

The Oath

Above all, however, de Valera was eager to dismantle the Treaty. His first attack was on the Oath of Allegiance, pointing out that the oath was not mandatory, and calling it an intolerable burden on the people of the Irish Free State. He maintained that the election of Fianna Fáil had indicated a desire on the part of the Irish people to remove the oath. He insisted that he only wished 'to bring about the friendliest relations between Britain and Ireland ... but there can be no normal relations between us so long as one side insists on imposing on the other a conscience test which has no parallel in Treaty relationships between states'. Despite the objections of J. H. Thomas, British Secretary of State for the Dominions, and the danger of a major crisis in Anglo-Irish relationships, de Valera introduced a bill in Dáil Eireann on 20 April 1932, to abolish the oath. It was approved the following month. Thus was article 17 of the Anglo-Irish Treaty removed from the statute book. De Valera scorned all the opposition from London by arguing that the oath was a purely domestic matter. Quoting from the recently ratified Statute of Westminster, he declared that he was acting even within English law in repealing the hateful Oath of Allegiance.

The office of governor-general was also a relic of British domination in Ireland, and de Valera decided to do away with this position of the king's representative in Ireland. In June 1932 de Valera's government received the principal guests at the International Eucharistic Congress, whereas the crown representatives were either ignored or kept in the background. This affront, along with other official insults led to the removal of governor-general James MacNeill by order of King George V on 1 November 1932. De Valera then asked one of his supporters, Domhnall O'Buachalla, a 1916 veteran who ran a shop in Maynooth, to accept the post in a purely nominal sense. O'Buachalla never took up residence in the Viceregal Lodge, but lived in a small suburban house in Dublin. By taking no part in public life, O'Buachalla, with the connivance of the Irish Free State government dealt a death blow to the office of governor-general. The post was formally abolished in 1937, with the introduction of de Valera's new constitution (see below). Thus, by the end of 1932, after less than a year in power, de Valera removed the oath, one of the causes of the Civil War, and showed how he too could make good use of the Statute of Westminster, which empowered the legislature of the Irish Free State to amend or alter British Acts of Parliament including the Treaty and the Irish Constitution of 1922.

De Valera encountered a good deal of opposition to his proposed measures relating to the constitution and a number of other controversial matters from the Senate (the upper house of the Oireachtas), which was dominated by Cumann na nGaedheal and a group of former Unionists who did everything in their power to delay Fianna Fáil bills. Exasperated beyond endurance, de Valera eventually succeeded in passing legislation abolishing the Senate altogether in 1936.

Economic Policy and the Economic War, 1932-38

The keynote of Fianna Fáil's economic policy was the ideal of national self-sufficiency. A self-sufficient Ireland, it was argued, would generate its own economic growth and would be able to extricate itself easily from the crisis caused by the world depression. Fianna Fáil hoped that its objective would be achieved primarily by means of industrial expansion and a vigorous and forward-looking industrial programme was devised by the Minister for Industry and Commerce, Sean Lemass. In 1933 an Industrial Credit Corporation was established to advance capital for new industries. The government's new industrial plan was designed to operate side by side with a new scheme intended to revive the depressed agricultural sector of the economy.

Looking at the Irish farming scene in 1931, there could be little doubt that Irish agriculture was in dire need of stimulation. The total agricultural area of the twenty-six counties was just under twelve million acres, and the figures showed that only 12 per cent of the land was under tillage, 20 per cent in hay, whereas 68 per cent was pasture. There were some 45,000 farms under one acre, while farms between one and thirty acres accounted for 58 per cent of all holdings. Most farms were run on a family subsistence basis, and only 19 per cent of the labouring force on farms were paid employees.

Fianna Fáil's aims were (1) to encourage a return to tillage; (2) to break up the larger ranch-type farms and destroy the 'rancher' class; (3) to divide the big farms among small farmers and landless labourers; (4) to expand the scope and powers of the Land Commission, which had taken over responsibility for land distribution on a formal state-sponsored basis; (5) to improve farming methods by providing technical advice and educational facilities; (6) to impose modern marketing regulations; (7) to introduce a general policy of protection, and break the country's commercial dependence upon Britain; (8) to discontinue the payment of land annuities to the British government. The last of these aims had far-reaching political implications, for it was to involve the Free State in a costly six-year 'economic war' with Britain.

The 'land annuities' were the sums of money to be paid annually to the British government by tenants who had purchased their holdings under the Land Acts with British state assistance before independence. The annuities were in effect repayments for the original purchasing loans advanced by the British government. The Cosgrave government had honoured this financial commitment to Britain and had undertaken to collect and pay directly to the British government the land annuities due from tenant-purchasers, under agreements of 1923 and 1926 between the two countries. De Valera, on coming to power in 1932, decided that the Irish Free State government would retain all future payments of land annuities.

The Fianna Fáil government's principal argument for the non-payment to England of the land annuities rested on the fact that the agreements of 1923 and 1926 had never been ratified by Dáil Éireann and were, therefore, invalid. It was also pointed out that, when in 1925 the Irish Free State was released from the liability of contributing to the United Kingdom public debt, land annuity payments were covered by this agreement. However, the British government took a different view, and when the Irish government withheld the annuity payments due on 1 July 1932, imposed duties of 20 per cent on the selling value of all Irish cattle and other agricultural exports to the United Kingdom. Britain hoped by this means to recoup the lost annuities. The Free State government retaliated by imposing 5 per cent duty on certain goods exported from England to Ireland: cement, coal, machinery etc. Thus began the economic war which lasted until 1938.

The result of the economic war was disastrous for Ireland. It is difficult to estimate the complete cost to the country, but it ran to something like £50 million in six years. Cattle exports to Britain fell from 750,000 in 1930 to 500,000 in 1934. Irish agriculture exports fell from £35.8 million in 1929 to a mere £13.9 million in 1935. The economic war meant (1) a serious depression of agriculture throughout the country: (2) the almost complete destruction of the cattle industry; (3) a considerable reduction in the incomes of farmers; (4) an increase in emigration to England; (5) an increase in the number of unemployed (in 1931, the total number of unemployed was 29,000; in 1933 it had risen to 96,000; in 1935 it was 138,000); (6) wages of agricultural labourers dropped to as little as 8s. a week for a seven-day week, which was barely a living wage.

Although the Irish government tried to counter the effect of the economic war by distributing free meat and giving loans to farmers, the farming community as a whole suffered very considerable hardship during the years 1932-38. The prices of tea, petrol and coal increased and many farmers found themselves in debt for even the necessities of life. The government realised the hardships they were enduring and de Valera tried to console the farmers by saying: 'We are all brothers in this, that no one of us can suffer for any length of time without their suffering reflecting on the rest of us. It is our duty to stand together.'

By 1938 both governments agreed that the time had come to patch up their differences, particularly in the light of the grave international situation and the threat of another world war. Thus in March 1938, the two countries signed an Anglo-Irish agreement: (1) the Irish government was to pay Britain £10 million in settlement of outstanding claims between the countries; (2) the special duties imposed by each side, during the economic war, were to be withdrawn, although there was to be provision for protection of certain goods; (3) the British government undertook to evacuate the Irish naval bases occupied by their troops under the 1921 Treaty. This last point was a diplomatic triumph for de Valera. It strengthened his contention that Éire (the new name given to the Irish Free State by the 1937 Irish constitution) was a sovereign independent state, and meant that she could adopt an independent foreign policy. When the Second World War broke out in 1939, de Valera was able to opt for a policy of neutrality, which would not have been possible had England still retained control of Irish ports as military naval bases.

The IRA and the Blueshirts, 1932-36

Although de Valera's election manifesto had been couched in relatively moderate terms (avoiding all mention of a 'republic'), he made it clear that he intended to release the political prisoners detained by the Cumann na nGaedheal government. Accordingly, within a few days of coming to power, he ordered all the prisoners to be set free. On 18 March 1932 the Public Safety Act of 1931–the Constitution (Amendment No. 17) Act–was suspended and the military tribunal abolished. These changes, in effect, lifted the ban on a number of organisations, including the IRA. Some of those now released from Arbour Hill jail had been in prison since 1922. They had been sentenced under the Cumann na nGaedheal government, and after their release they pursued a campaign of unrelenting hostility against Cosgrave and his party. There were many cases of intimidation, attacks on persons, breaking up of Cumann na nGaedheal political meetings in the ensuing months. Recruitment for the IRA grew by leaps and bounds and open drilling was reported by the police. Many joined the IRA in the belief that de Valera would give them a pension or a living allowance. An IRA Council requested that 'the Fianna Fáil government will provide payment out of public funds, of the legitimate debt contracted by the IRA in the prosecution of the war of defence of the Republic since the Treaty'. Others joined in the belief that Fianna Fáil was about to send the army into Northern Ireland in an attempt to end partition. But the IRA made itself felt principally by harassing Cumann na nGaedheal speakers and heckling with slogans such as 'No Free Speech for Traitors'. Cumann na nGaedheal supporters soon began to feel the need for an organisation to protect them from such intimidation.

The IRA were to cause much embarrassment and trouble to the de Valera government. Not only did they show a spirit of unrest as many found it difficult to readjust to a normal peaceful life, but they showed themselves to be trigger-happy when opportunity arose. They won most of their support among the smaller farmers and working classes. The IRA held an important General Army Convention early in 1933, at which it expressed its Republican view and strongly criticised the Fianna Fáil government. Despite their apparent allegiance to de Valera and all that he stood for, by February 1933 the leaders of the IRA had come to a parting of the ways with the Fianna Fáil government. The IRA represented full-blooded Republicanism and set themselves the following programme: (1) the securing of a Republican form of government, (2) the establishment of a united thirty-two country Ireland, (3) the elimination of British armed forces from both the north and the south, and (4) the achievement of all these aims by force rather than by constitutional means. Between 1932 and 1936, its leaders included Peadar O'Donnell, Frank Ryan, Maurice Twomey, the Gilmore brothers, Sean MacBride and Michael Price.

To combat the increased activities of the IRA a new association, calling itself the Army Comrades Association, was founded early in 1932. As its name suggests, it was designed for ex-officers and men of the Free State Army. In August the Army Comrades Association (ACA) was reorganised by Dr T. F. O'Higgins, a brother of Kevin O'Higgins, and it soon had some 20,000 members. An ancillary of Cumann na nGaedheal, it developed into a kind of defence force, supporting Cosgrave's party against the intimidations and attacks from the IRA. In its declaration of enrolment, the ACA opened its ranks to 'all who feel the need for the existence of a powerful, steadying, moderate body of opinion in the country'.

Thus within a few months of de Valera's coming to power, two military-style extra-parliamentary bodies, the IRA and the ACA were facing each other. It seemed to some observers that the Civil War was about to recommence with the ACA or 'Free Staters' on one side and the IRA or 'Republicans' on the other. The fact that the ACA was under the leadership of Dr O'Higgins, a Cumann na nGaedheal TD, meant that the Association could hardly claim to be non-party. O'Higgins assured his listeners at a rally of the ACA: 'Our objects are peace. We are an army of peace.' But the IRA newspaper *An Phoblacht* described its rival as 'the new Fascist force'.

In January 1933, de Valera decided to hold a general election, to see if the country was really behind him, and also to strengthen his hand in dealing with the British government over the abolition of the oath, the downgrading of the office of governor-general and the land annuities. The result of the election was an overall victory for Fianna Fáil, who gained 5 new seats and could act within the Dáil independent of Labour party support. Cumann na nGaedheal lost 9 seats and thus suffered a second electoral defeat in less than a year. The election was marked by clashes between enthusiastic Fianna Fáil supporters and the ACA.

On 22 February 1933, General O'Duffy, Commissioner of the Civic Guards, was dismissed from his post by the Fianna Fáil government. In July, he was offered the leadership of the ACA which had begun to adopt as their uniform a blue shirt. Under O'Duffy the movement changed its name to the National Guard and began to advocate a number of political objectives, the chief of which was the formation of a corporate state inspired partly by Mussolini's Italy and partly by the social teachings of Pope Pius XI. The Blueshirts (as they now came to be called) were part of a general European trend in the 1930s, having something in common with Hitler's Brownshirts in Germany, Mussolini's Blackshirts in Italy and Mosley's Blackshirts in England. All were forceful right-wing movements, strongly nationalistic in tone, whose members were vigorous opponents of left-wing tendencies in the government, revolutionary subversion and, most of all, communism. They believed that such manifestations had been encouraged by a too lenient democracy, and they therefore preferred a strictly enforced authoritarian system of government, even is this meant a dictatorship backed up by military might. In Ireland, the Blueshirts were additionally characterised by rigid Catholicism. The Irish movement was less ruthless or militaristic than the great fascist combinations on the continent; instead of the bomb and gun of the IRA, its weapons, allegedly carried only for self-defence, were the blackthorn cudgel and the knuckleduster. But its development alongside the IRA (still at this stage a legal organisation) created a potentially explosive situation in Ireland and posed an awkward problem for the government. Fianna Fáil found itself hemmed in by two rival bodies of hardliners on extreme ends of the political spectrum, with one of which it had old ties of friendship, while the other seemed to be adopting an ever more defiant attitude towards the government's authority.

On 14 July 1933, de Valera warned that 'we are not going to permit people to parade in uniform'. In spite of this, O'Duffy decided to hold a march of the National Guard on 13 August 1933 and all members were instructed to wear their blue shirts. The government, fearing lest O'Duffy become a second Mussolini and attempt a *coup d'état* by marching on Dublin, banned the march and revived the provisions of the Public Safety Act of 1931, including the military tribunal which Fianna Fáil had once denounced so vehemently. The parade was called off and we shall never know what would have happened had O'Duffy gone ahead with his plans. Certainly there would have been some bloodshed as the IRA, who had arms, had threatened to make an attack on the Blueshirts, and the latter were unarmed.

After this incident, the National Guard changed its name to Young Ireland and later became known as the League of Youth, probably in imitatation of the Hitler Youth movement. Every member of the new movement was automatically enrolled as a member of Fine Gael, the new party which had replaced Cumann na nGaedheal towards the end of 1933 (see below). O'Duffy, posing as a kind of pseudo-fascist leader, was head of the new party with Cosgrave as one of his vice-presidents. He loved demonstrations, speeches and public applause and was an enthusiastic military organiser. W. B. Yeats, the poet, was attracted to O'Duffy and wrote a marching song for the Blueshirts.

The Blueshirts began to disintegrate by mid 1934. The local elections to the County Councils were a trial of strength between O'Duffy, supporting Fine Gael, and Fianna Fáil. When Fine Gael won only 6 out of 23 local elections, O'Duffy lost much of his authority and prestige. The Blueshirts floundered also on the plight of the farmers during the economic war. They failed to provide a solution to the immediate problems of rural Ireland. They tried to get the farmers to withhold the payment of land annuities to the de Valera government. This apparently unconstitutional action marked the end of the road for General O'Duffy and the Blueshirts. In a curious epilogue to the Blueshirt story, O'Duffy and 700 of his followers sailed to Spain in 1936, where they fought on the side of General Franco in the Spanish Civil War.

The whole Blueshirt affair had lasted only two years. It had not helped Fine Gael in its political struggle for power (see below). The Blueshirts provided a welcome scapegoat for the IRA element, who found in O'Duffy and his movement an enemy with whom to contend. Had it not been for the Blueshirts, the IRA may well have turned all their force against Fianna Fáil.

The Blueshirt movement was born out of mistrust of Fianna Fáil and had some of its roots in the Civil War of ten years before. At its height, the Blueshirts never counted more than 20,000 members. It was very much O'Duffy's personal organisation and when he began to lose his authority and power, the Blueshirts disintegrated. The alliance between the Blueshirts and Fine Gael was always a difficult and strained relationship, and in any case O'Duffy did not have a seat in the Dáil, so that his political influence was limited to extra-parliamentary meetings. Whenever the Blueshirts seemed to go beyond the limits of the law, the Fine Gael politicians began to object. Finally, O'Duffy did not provide a personal attraction for the mass of Irish people in the same way as de Valera did so successfully. The defeat and failure of the Blueshirts helped to enhance the prestige and ascendancy of de Valera and his party.

After the disappearance of the Blueshirts from the political scene the IRA fell increasingly out of favour with the de Valera administration which it criticised for being far too slow-moving on the question of partition. Furthermore, disagreements began to arise within the IRA and it eventually divided into two wings. One group (including O'Donnell, Ryan and the Gilmores) were socialist republicans who tried to set up a Republican Congress, but without any lasting success. The other group (including Twomey and MacBride) followed a more traditionalist line; its alleged involvement in some particularly cold-blooded killings in 1935-36 lost it most of its support and forced even its former friends in the government to turn against it. De Valera went so far as to make full use of the military tribunal to combat IRA subversion and finally in 1936 he declared the

IRA an illegal organisation. After this date Fianna Fáil never renewed its association with the IRA.

The Emergence of Fine Gael, 1933-38

Cumann na nGaedheal or the Cosgrave party, which had ruled Ireland from 1922 to 1932, found itself shorn of all its strength and prestige once Fianna Fáil came to power. Its second defeat in the general election of 1933 dealt it a severe blow and many of its supporters began to feel that its days were numbered. Something more dynamic—especially in leadership—was needed to face up to de Valera. Already in October 1932, a new party had been formed, the Irish Centre Party, under the joint leadership of James Dillon and Frank MacDermot. The Centre Party claimed to represent the interests of the big farmers (traditional Cosgrave supporters), and included in its programme the ending of partition by peaceful means as well as burying the Civil War hatchet and cultivation of friendly relations with Britain and Northern Ireland.

In September 1933 the Centre Party merged with Cumann na nGaedheal to form a new party called the United Ireland Party, or Fine Gael (Tribe of Gaels). It also drew into its ranks the Blueshirts, and General O'Duffy became the leader of the new group. Cosgrave, Dillon and MacDermot represented the parliamentary interests of Fine Gael, since O'Duffy had no seat in the Dáil. Fine Gael, through its association with the Blueshirt movement, established branches all over the country and relied very much on its youth organisation. The party set itself the following aims: (1) to establish a thirty-two county Ireland as a single independent state, as a member, without abatement of Irish sovereignty, of the British Commonwealth of Nations in free and equal partnership; (2) the setting up of economic and agricultural corporations; (3) the abolition of the election system of proportional representation in its existing form; (4) the conclusion of the economic war. However, O'Duffy did not prove an efficient leader of this new party, principally because of his involvement in the extra-parliamentary activities of the Blueshirts. When he failed to bring Fine Gael to victory in the local government elections of July 1934, he came under fire from the other influential members of Fine Gael. In September 1934, O'Duffy resigned his leadership. The split in the party over control of the Blueshirts, and the lack of support from many of its former sympathisers, caused Fine Gael to sink into decline until 1935. After the disappearance of the Blueshirts, the party was once more revived under the leadership of W. T. Cosgrave, but it still had to live down its O'Duffy interlude and connections. When a general election was held in 1937, Fine Gael gained only 48 seats, whereas Fianna Fáil won 69 seats. The 1938 election was just as disastrous, since Fianna Fáil got more than 50 per cent of the total votes cast, while Fine Gael lost 3 more seats and was reduced to 45 TDs.

The 1937 Constitution

The Irish Free State based its constitutional existence on the Anglo-Irish Treaty of 6 December 1921. In 1922 the Southern Ireland parliament, which had been summoned under the terms of the Treaty, passed the constitution of the Irish Free State (Saorstát Éireann) Act. There were several articles in the 1922 constitution which were repugnant to Irish Republicans, especially the oath of allegiance and partition. On coming to power in 1932, de Valera introduced a series of amendments to the constitution, principally the abolition of the oath. In 1936 on the occasion of King Edward VIII's abdication, de Valera took the opportunity to pass another constitutional amendment, by which all references to king and governor-general were deleted from the Free State constitution. By this act the Irish Free State ceased to consider itself one of His Majesty's Dominions.

At this time de Valera was at work on a new constitution for the Irish Free State, which was to be Republican in everything but name. Owing to constant clashes with the former Senate, (abolished in 1936), which had used all its power to hold up legislation, de Valera considered it necessary to curtail the powers of the second house under the new constitution. Having already stripped down the Anglo-Irish Treaty article by article, the 1937 constitution was simply a restatement of the progress that had been made in this direction. It contained no reference to the dominion status of the country, and changed the name to 'Éire' (Ireland). The title of the constitution in Irish was 'Bunreacht na h-Éireann'. It was enacted on 1 July 1937 and came into force on 29 December 1937, after a referendum, or popular vote of the people, had approved it. Its preamble and first six articles were as follows:

> In the Name of the Most Holy Trinity, from Whom is all authority and to Whom, as our final end, all actions both of men and States must be referred, We, the people of Éire, humbly acknowledging all our obligations to our Divine Lord, Jesus Christ, Who sustained our fathers through centuries of trial, gratefully remembering their heroic and unremitting struggle to regain the rightful independence of our Nation, and seeking to promote the common good, with due observance of Prudence, Justice and Charity, so that the dignity and freedom of the individual may be assured, true social order attained, the unity of our country restored, and concord established with other nations, do hereby adopt, enact and give to ourselves this Constitution.

1. The Irish nation hereby affirms its inalienable, indefeasible, and sovereign right to choose its own form of Government, to determine its relations with other nations, and to develop its life, political, economic and cultural, in accordance with its own genius and traditions.
2. The national territory consists of the whole island of Ireland, its islands and territorial seas.

3. Pending the re-integration of the national territory, and without prejudice to the right of the Parliament and Government established by this Constitution to exercise jurisdiction over the whole of that territory, the laws enacted by that Parliament shall have the like area and extent of application as the laws of Saorstát Éireann and the like extra-territorial effect.
4. The name of the State is *Éire,* or in the English language, *Ireland.*
5. Ireland is a sovereign, independent, democratic state.
6. 1. All powers of government, legislative, executive and judicial, derive under God, from the people, whose right it is to designate the rulers of the State and, in final appeal, to decide all questions of national policy, according to the requirements of the common good.
6. 2. These powers of government are exercisable only by or on the authority of the organs of State established by this Constitution.

The constitution provided for the election of a President who was to take precedence over all other persons in the state and hold office for seven years (Article 12). The President was also held to be 'above politics', and to avoid confusion the old title of President of the Executive Council was replaced by that of taoiseach. The first President of Ireland was Douglas Hyde, elected on 4 May 1938. Power of making laws for the state was vested in the Oireachtas, i.e., Dáil Éireann and Seanad Éireann (Article 15). The Senate was only allowed to delay the enactment of a bill by ninety days, after which it became law (Article 23).

The new constitution was based on the doctrine of popular sovereignty. It owed much to a series of papal encyclicals issued by Pope Pius XI, 'The Christian Education of Youth' (1929), 'Christian Marriage' (1930), and it also reflected Catholic thinking of the time on social questions. As a result, the constitution outlined certain 'fundamental rights' (Articles 40-44) to which the citizen was entitled, and also laid down 'directive principles of social policy' (Article 45). These articles combined liberal principles with Catholic social teaching and tried to strike a balance between the two.

The constitution made no direct reference to Ireland as a 'Republic'. Its importance as a document of both domestic and international value became clear after its publication. At home, it gave new life and stability to the young state. Abroad the 1937 Irish constitution provided a model for some of the emerging countries (India, Pakistan and Burma). It can be considered as one of the most important and lasting achievements of de Valera. Qualified by a few subsequent amendments, it is still in force.

Ireland and The Second World War

Britain and France declared war on Germany on 3 September 1939. The Dáil and the Seanad rushed through an Emergency Powers Bill, which gave the Irish government almost dictatorial powers to secure public safety and the preservation of the state. Later that same day, de Valera broadcast to the nation, declaring the intention of his government to adopt a policy of neutrality between the belligerent powers. Neutrality had been made possible by the 1938 Anglo-Irish Agreement, whereby the British government unconditionally handed over to the Irish government the ports retained by them under the terms of the 1921 Treaty.

This decision by de Valera to remain neutral was no sudden or unpremeditated act. He had already made his position clear in 1936, when he said at Geneva that 'all the small states can do, if the statesmen of the greater states fail in their duties, is resolutely to determine that they will not become the tools of any great power, and that they will resist with whatever strength they may possess every attempt to force them into a war against their will'. He knew that there would be some opposition to this decision, as indeed there was from Winston Churchill, who was appointed cabinet minister in command of the British navy at the outbreak of the war. Churchill was concerned that German U-boats might operate from Ireland, or at least 'be succoured by Irish malcontents (i.e. the IRA) in West of Ireland inlets'. He went so far as to declare Irish neutrality 'illegal', but did not receive support for this view from his cabinet colleagues. Any attempt on the part of Britain to seize the ports by force would have brought disapproval from the still neutral but powerful United States. Nor did Britain wish to lose the goodwill and sympathy of the Irish people by any high-handed action over the ports. In practice it was generally accepted in both Ireland and England that 'neutrality' would be a one-sided affair, allowing for considerable co-operation between Britain and Ireland during the war. In fact, the Irish government took immediate steps to guarantee that no part of the country would be used as a base for German or IRA attacks against England.

De Valera's government took certain steps so that the country could adapt to its novel position of neutrality. The government set up a new department, that of Supplies, headed by Sean Lemass, and for the first time since the foundation of the state, the people of Ireland faced rationing. Clothing, tea, sugar, butter—even bread for a short period in 1942— were all restricted, and each person was issued a special ration-book, with coupons for the amount of each item allocated to each individual or family. Rigid controls on the use of fuel and sources of power were introduced; gas and electricity could only be used for limited periods on each day. The war years became commonly known in Ireland as 'the emergency'. Despite the vigilance of the police, a considerable black market flourished. Items such as petrol, tea, sugar, rubber boots and coal could be obtained, usually at exorbitant prices, if a person had the money to pay for them. But for the most part the public adopted a grin-and-bear-it policy and most people managed to survive the war years without excessive hardship. In comparison with war-torn Britain and Europe, Irish people led sheltered lives.

They still went for their summer holidays to the seaside, and cinemas and dance-halls were filled to capacity week after week.

The problem of unemployment was one which caused much concern to the Irish government. It became immediately clear that some of the accepted forms of employment in Ireland, especially those entirely dependent on imports, would suffer because of the war. Thus the number of people engaged in such activities as motor-car assembly, or soap and candle-making, fell considerably. On the other hand there was a constant demand for Irish labour in England, and this reached such a high figure that emigration had to be controlled, at least for agricultural workers. However, the agricultural boom which had come to Ireland during the 1914-18 war was not repeated in the Second World War. Irish farmers had not recovered sufficiently from the 'economic war' of the 1930s to benefit from the sudden demand for foodstuffs. An outbreak of foot-and-mouth disease in 1941 proved disastrous for the cattle market. Despite government subsidies and an increase in the acreage under wheat, supplies of fertilisers remained low and the fertility of the land was affected. All-in-all the wartime economy was a stagnant one and the standard of living in Ireland fell as the war progressed.

Another outlet for employment lay in the British army. It has been estimated that some 50,000 Irishmen were serving with the British forces by the end of the war. De Valera used the emergency to increase the regular Irish army to about 14,000 men. This move had a double advantage: it gave employment to young men who could not find work in any other occupation, while at the same time it proved to Britain that Ireland was determined to defend its own independence and neutrality. The Irish government was forced to deal rigorously with the IRA, which it had already condemned, and it introduced the Offences Against the State Act of June 1939. A crisis occurred when the IRA raided the magazine fort in the Phoenix Park on 23 December 1939 and got away with over one million rounds of ammunition. Following intensive army activity, most of the ammunition was recovered. The incident was used to make the Emergency Powers more strict, in that internment was extended to Irish citizens as well as aliens. A special camp was set up in the Curragh, in which some fifty republicans were eventually interned, as well as certain captured German air-force personnel and spies.

Ireland retained its diplomatic relationship with Germany throughout the war, and Dr Hempel, the German Minister to Ireland, remained at his post in Dublin. The attitude of the Irish government towards Hempel was friendly. There is no evidence to show that Hempel was using Dublin as a centre for spying. Neither was he in league with the IRA. His dispatches show that he considered the IRA unreliable, and only interested in Irish unity, not a German victory in the war. De Valera caused something of a stir both at home and abroad, when on 2 May 1945, he called on Hempel at the German legation in Dublin to express his condolences on the death of

Hitler. He had made a similar courtesy call to the United States embassy a few weeks previously on the occasion of the death of President Roosevelt, but most people in Ireland and abroad (especially after the revelations of German concentration camps) felt that de Valera's visit to Hempel was a blunder.

The war years saw very little change in the government's general attitude towards Britain. Sir John Maffey, the United Kingdom Representative in Ireland, remained in Dublin and friendly diplomatic relations were maintained. However, the war years brought up the question of partition again. It seemed that the British government might be prepared to consider making a bargain over Northern Ireland and certain proposals were presented to the Irish government by Sir John Maffey in June 1940. The suggestion was for a package deal between the two countries, in which Ireland would enter the war on Britain's side and Britain agree vaguely to Irish unity after the war. It was an attractive offer—but de Valera was a realist, and turned down the plan. In reply to the British Cabinet he stated that 'the plan would commit us definitely to an immediate abandonment of our neutrality. On the other hand it gives us no guarantee that in the end we would have a United Ireland, unless concessions were made to Lord Craigavon opposed to the sentiments and aspirations of the great majority of the Irish people'.

For most of the war Irish newspapers were censored rigidly by the government. Among the duties of Frank Aiken, Minister for the Co-ordination of Defensive Measures, was the supervision and control of all publications. Most Irish people listened eagerly for war news on the radio and even followed the anti-British propaganda broadcasts on German radio which were read in English by an Irishman, William Joyce (Lord 'Haw-Haw'). Joyce's sense of humour appealed to Irish people who took no offence when he informed the world that 'the Irish army could not beat the tinkers out of Galway'.

As the war continued, the economic situation and the disruption of regular trade called for new means of bringing supplies of essential goods to the country. In March 1941, the Irish government set up an ocean-going shipping line, Irish Shipping, under the chairmanship of John Leydon, secretary of the Department of Supplies. In its first year, Irish Shipping bought eight vessels and chartered five others, bringing in badly-needed supplies from the United States. By the end of the war the company had fifteen ships. which had carried over one million tons of cargo to a country which was virtually blockaded. Ireland's merchant navy played a significant role in keeping the economy going and in maintaining supplies of essential items such as wheat and coal.

Even after America entered the war in December 1941, de Valera maintained his rigid policy of neutrality. Misunderstandings between de Valera and the American Minister to Ireland, David Grey, did occur especially after American troops were based in Northern Ireland prior to D-day in 1944, but these all passed off without any serious rifts.

Churchill, however, who had become British Prime Minister early in the war, never forgave the Irish government for its policy of neutrality, and gave vent to his bitterness during his victory speech on 13 May 1945, in which he said:

> This was indeed a deadly moment in our life and if it had not been for the loyalty and friendship of Northern Ireland we should have been forced to come to close quarters with Mr de Valera or perish forever from the earth. However, with a restraint and poise to which, I venture to say, history will find few parallels, His Majesty's government never laid a violent hand upon them though at times it would have been quite easy and quite natural, and we left the de Valera government to frolic with the Germans and later with the Japanese representatives to their hearts' content.

De Valera waited four days before replying to Churchill's accusation. He also knew that Irishmen had served with honour and distinction in the war, winning a total of 780 decorations, including eight Victoria Crosses. On the night of 17 May 1945 de Valera at last broadcast his reply to Churchill:

> Mr Churchill makes it clear that, in certain circumstances, he would have violated our neutrality and that he would justify his action by Britain's necessity. It seems strange to me that Mr Churchill does not see that this, if accepted, would mean that Britain's necessity would become a moral code and that when this necessity became sufficiently great, other people's rights were not to count . . . Mr Churchill is proud of Britain's stand alone, after France had fallen and before America entered the war. Could he not find in his heart the generosity to acknowledge that there is a small nation that stood alone, not for one year or two, but for several hundred years against aggression; a small nation that could never be got to accept defeat and has never surrendered her soul?

De Valera's answer to Churchill was applauded by everyone who had been stung by the bitterness of the British Prime Minister. It also helped to make amends for his ill-advised visit to Dr Hempel on the occasion of Hitler's death. However, nothing that de Valera said could bridge the widening gap which the war had created between the two parts of the country. The unionist people of Northern Ireland came to depend as much, if not more, on Britain, after the war. Once again they had sealed their friendship with Britain with their blood by joining in the UK war effort. Nationalist Ireland had taken a lone neutral path during the war years, and her isolation and apparent insularity became even more accentuated.

Despite his successful defence of Irish neutrality, the war years had brought some dissatisfaction with de Valera's government. In the general election of 1943, Fianna Fáil lost ten seats. In 1944 W. T. Cosgrave retired as leader of the Fine Gael party and was succeeded by General Richard Mulcahy. At the general election of 1944, Fine Gael won only thirty seats, though among the successful Fine Gael deputies was John A. Costello, who was destined to take a leading part in Irish political life as taoiseach in 1948-51 and again in 1954-57.

The Fall of de Valera

The Fianna Fáil government, therefore, emerged in a relatively strong position and it was hoped that peace would soon put the economy back on the road to prosperity. However, the post-war years brought continued economic depression instead, with rising prices, emigration, growing unemployment and even a continuation of rationing and other austerities. The summer of 1946 was very wet and was followed by a very severe and prolonged winter. Bread had to be rationed and de Valera was forced to announce in the Dáil on 22 January 1947 that the country was still in a state of emergency: 'The position regarding supplies essential to the life of the community is in some respects worse than at any time since 1939, and the possibility is that a period of even greater difficulty may occur.' All this did not make for popular appeal, and the government was further embarrassed by a series of strikes in both the public and private sectors.

The emergence of a new political party, Clann na Poblachta, under Sean MacBride, in 1947, caused the government further alarm, as it was composed of many IRA veterans. It advocated a radical republican programme, social reform and the end to partition. When a sudden general election was called by de Valera in 1948, Fianna Fáil gained only 68 seats out of 147 and the possibility arose of the anti-Fianna Fáil parties coming together to form a coalition government. Agreement was reached and John A. Costello, of the Fine Gael party became the new taoiseach. Other ministers were Sean MacBride (External Affairs), Patrick McGilligan (Finance), James Dillon (Agriculture), Noel Browne (Health) and T. F. O'Higgins (Defence). De Valera and his government had ruled the country from 1932 to 1948 without a break. There was now considerable public sympathy and support for the new Coalition government, whose first job would be to restore the country to a condition of prosperity.

Talking Points

Chapter 10: De Valera in Power, 1932-48
1. In what way did de Valera begin to dismantle the Anglo-Irish Treaty during the years 1932-37?
2. What role did the Blueshirts play in Irish history during the 1930s? Did they succeed or fail in their aims?
3. How and why did the de Valera government allow itself to become

involved in the economic war? What were its consequences for the country up to the beginning of World War Two?

4. Analyse the content and ideology of the 1937 constitution.

5. What were the main problems facing the Irish Free State during the War years (1939-45)?

6. Give a general assessment of de Valera's political performance during the years 1932-48.

Chapter 11
COALITION GOVERNMENTS AND THE NEW FIANNA FAIL, 1948-66

The period 1948-66 can be considered a turning point in modern Irish history. In its opening year it was declared that the country was formally to become an independent Republic. The then taoiseach, John A. Costello, in proclaiming the Republic of Ireland announced: 'We now stand alone, a nation of our own.' The declaration of the Republic took Ireland out of the British Commonwealth and set the twenty-six county state clearly on its own path, although this meant further widening the gulf with Northern Ireland.

Secondly the period marked a new departure for the Irish economy. Until the mid 1950s, the forces holding back progress and prosperity seemed to dominate Irish society. International events such as the Korean War (1950) and the Suez crisis (1956) also hampered growth in output and employment. In the 1950s, however, Irish economists became more determined to take positive action to improve the country's position. Old 'hit and miss' methods, the products of conservative and backward-looking economic policies were replaced by more enlightened and forward-looking plans. These led to a series of programmes for economic recovery, the foundation of which was mainly associated with one of the country's leading civil servants, Dr T. K. Whitaker.

A third feature of the period was political change. Alternative multi-party coalition governments to Fianna Fáil were in power in 1948-51 and in 1954-57. As a result, Fianna Fáil took a more critical view of its image and of its fitness for office. In 1959, on de Valera's retirement as taoiseach, the party found a new and very different leader in Sean Lemass. More than any other person, Lemass can be claimed as the architect of a new Ireland which was beginning to emerge in the early 1960s.

Fourthly during the period 1948-66 Ireland became more concerned to exert some influence in world affairs. The country was a founder member of the post-war Council of Europe (1949). In the beginning membership of the Council was used mainly for anti-partition propaganda. Eventually, however, Ireland became a more involved member of this European body and was the first country to accept the jurisdiction of the European Court of Human Rights. In 1955 Ireland joined the United Nations and since then has constantly sought to play an active part in its deliberations. On numerous occasions Irish soldiers joined UN forces in troubled parts of the world as a practical token of the country's contribution to international peace. Ireland, however, has never joined NATO (The North Atlantic Treaty Organisation, involving western Europe and the USA against the communist powers of Eastern Europe), since its governments have taken the view that such a commitment would reduce the chances of remaining neutral in any future war.

The Republic of Ireland declared (1949)

During the general election of 1948, the question of repealing de Valera's External Relations Act of 1936 and of declaring Ireland an independent republic was one of the principal issues raised by the new Clann na Poblachta party. Clann na Poblachta won ten Dáil seats in the election. It was vital for the new Fine Gael taoiseach, John A. Costello, to keep Clann support for his multi-party coalition government which had been put together to oust Fianna Fáil from office after sixteen years of uninterrupted rule. Sean MacBride, the republican Clann leader, became Minister for External Affairs in the new coalition and the question of the country's international status became a major government concern.

Since the end of the Second World War in 1945 Ireland's relationship with Britain and the Commonwealth was increasingly felt to be ambiguous. The External Relations Act and the 1937 Constitution had still left the king of Great Britain with a role in Irish foreign affairs. The relevant clause in the External Relations Act stated:

> So long as Saorstát Éireann is associated with Australia, Canada, Great Britain, New Zealand and South Africa, and so long as the King, recognised by those nations as the symbol of their co-operation, continues to act on behalf of each of those nations (on the advice of the government thereof) for the purpose of the appointment of diplomatic and consular representatives and the conclusion of international agreements, the King so recognised may, and is hereby authorised to, act on behalf of Saorstát Éireann for the like purposes as and when advised by the Executve Council to do so.

Although de Valera maintained that Ireland was a state *outside* the Commonwealth, under the 1926 Act Ireland could not claim unequivocally to be a republic with its own president as its highest authority in both domestic and foreign affairs. Costello, MacBride and their colleagues decided in principle in August 1948 to repeal the External Relations Act. This information was leaked to the press during a visit by the taoiseach to Canada the following month, and it was in Ottawa that Costello announced officially that his government intended to sever Ireland's connection with the Commonwealth.

On his return to Ireland, Costello introduced his Republic of Ireland Bill to the Dáil. Meetings were held with British ministers to discuss the practical implications of the new legislation. The bill was one of the shortest on record, consisting of less than one hundred words. It was accepted by all parties in the Dáil and came into force on Easter Monday (18 April) 1949.

On the occasion of the declaration of the Republic, King George VI sent Costello a message of goodwill and the title of the British diplomatic representative in Dublin was changed to 'UK Representative to the Republic of Ireland'. In an effort to minimise legal problems, particularly for Irish immigrants in the UK as a result of Ireland's leaving the commonwealth, the British government passed a new British Nationality Act in 1948. Under this legislation, Irish citizens would no longer be regarded as British subjects, but when living in Britain would be treated just as though they were.

Costello's bill implied that the area envisaged as the Republic of Ireland covered the whole island, a suggestion which aroused strong feelings in Northern Ireland. Ulster Unionists put much pressure on the British government to reassure them in the strongest terms that Northern Ireland would always remain part of the United Kingdom. Prime minister Atlee gave such an undertaking to Sir Basil Brooke, prime minister of Northern Ireland. The promise was put into legislative form by the British parliament's Ireland Act of 1949 which stated that Westminster

(a) recognises and declares that the part of Ireland heretofore known as Eire ceased as from 18 April 1949 to be part of His Majesty's Dominions; (b) declares that Northern Ireland remains part of His Majesty's Dominions and of the United Kingdom, and affirms that in no event will Northern Ireland or any part thereof cease to be part of His Majesty's Dominions and of the United Kingdom without the consent of the Parliament of Northern Ireland.

The declaration of the Republic did not seriously impair relations between Britain and Ireland, and Costello had the satisfaction of seeing Ireland's long-awaited status of a republic accepted internationally. He hoped in this way to put an end to the controversy which had divided Irishmen since the Civil War. But while the act may have given republicans a twenty-six county Republic, it did nothing to help solve the vexed question of partition and Northern Ireland.

The Economy under the Coalition, 1948-51

Trade as much as constitutional matters was of pressing importance for the coalition. Costello inherited a near-inflationary economy and the situation called for basic changes in policy as well as new approaches to old problems.

The general policy of the coalition government towards the Irish economy was a novel one of 'state-investment'. A long-term programme of capital investment and state finance was envisaged in an effort to apply in Ireland the latest principles of economic thought put forward by the most influential economist of the time, John Maynard Keynes, who insisted that government spending could play a vital direct role in post-war world economic recovery.

The minister for finance, Patrick McGilligan, set up two new Irish state-sponsored bodies. The function of the first of these, the Industrial Development Authority (IDA) was to plan and offer new state assistance for industrial growth, and also to adopt a traditional protectionist policy for Irish industry. Córas Tráchtála, the second body, was established to promote Irish exports to the USA and Canada. So successful was Córas Tráchtála, that it subsequently extended its activities to cover the promotion of Irish-made goods throughout the world. Between 1946 and 1953, 50,000 new jobs were created in Irish industries and industrial production was increased by sixty per cent.

The coalition government also sponsored a national programme of building. During the war years 1939-45 and immediately after, building materials were very scarce. By 1948 there was an urgent demand for the immediate construction of over 10,000 local authority houses. Two years later over 12,000 houses were being built annually, so helping to provide not just better homes for many families but more jobs in the building industry itself. In spite of such efforts, however, emigration remained as high as ever and about 24,000 people left the country every year during the coalition's term of office.

Agriculture was helped by a number of important new measures. A new trade agreement between Ireland and Britain was signed in June 1948, and covered all agricultural exports from Ireland to the UK for a four-year period. James Dillon, minister for agriculture, stated that through the better prices guaranteed to Irish farmers under the terms of the trade agreement, it was hoped to raise store cattle exports to Britain from 300,000 to 400,000 per year within two years, and double the annual export of fat cattle from 50,000 to 100,000. The government hoped that the trade agreement would remedy the adverse trade balance between the two countries. In 1948 British imports into Ireland were valued at about £80 million per year, while Irish exports to Britain were a mere £30 million annually.

A Land Rehabilitation Project started in 1949 was a nation-wide drive to bring back into full production some four million acres of land which had remained under utilised because capital and technical expertise were scarce. The government's intention was to spend £40 million over a ten-year period to bring land back into productive use. One writer said of the effects of this project:

> The face of Ireland is having deep furrows ploughed into it. They are not furrows of depression, but of hope. Giant machines, brought from the United States, are working on derelict bogland and swamps, draining useless territory that may yet be restored to productivity for the good of Ireland and the increased happiness of her people.

In September 1949 the British government devalued the pound sterling and Ireland was forced to do likewise, since most of the country's external assets, about £400 million, were in sterling. This devaluation was a severe blow to the Irish economy, since it increased the costs of imported goods without sufficiently benefiting exports. The following summer saw the start of the Korean War, which had serious inflationary effects throughout the world. The coalition government's economic policies were seriously undermined, at a time when it was seeking money to improve the country's inadequate health and welfare services. The controversy over the introduction of a national health service was to add to the difficulties of the coalition government.

The Mother and Child Scheme and the Fall of the Coalition, 1951

The minister for health in the coalition government was Noel Browne, who belonged to Clann na Poblachta. A doctor by profession, he had, as a young man, contracted tuberculosis, a disease from which both his parents, like many people in Ireland, died. Browne entered politics with the aim of raising public funds to help fight TB. An active campaigner, he was successful in the 1948 election and became minister for health on his first day in the Dáil.

Browne's first concern as minister for health was, not surprisingly, the disease which killed between 3,000 and 4,000 Irish people every year. The country lacked modern, properly-equipped sanatoria and no money had been earmarked to undertake the vast building programme necessary. Browne found the cash by liquidating the assets of the Department of Health (valued at about £20 million) and obtaining a £10 million mortgage from the Irish Hospitals' Sweepstake. Within a few years, TB in Ireland was well under control. In 1949 the death-rate from the disease fell below 100 per 100,000 of the population and, by 1952, to almost half that figure. The coming of the BCG vaccination, mass radiography and other modern treatments helped eradicate the dreaded disease, but Browne's personal dedication and his drive to build sanatoria were equally decisive factors.

As a socialist, Browne believed that the state had the right and duty to provide essential medical services for everyone. Ireland certainly lagged behind Britain and many European countries in its health services, but public opinion generally was wary about the government getting closely involved in medical matters which might be regarded as private. When Browne introduced a scheme for maternal and child welfare, which would have provided mothers with free maternity treatment and their children with free medical attention up to the age of sixteen, uproar broke out.

The 'Mother and Child Scheme' was challenged as unconstitutional and the Catholic bishops also voiced their objection. The proposed scheme also brought the government into direct conflict with the medical profession who did not relish the idea of 'socialised' medicine. Doctors feared that a free-for-all scheme would be impractical and even unworkable. They also regarded existing services as adequate, pointing out that in Dublin City three voluntary (i.e. not state-owned) maternity hospitals provided for 85.7 per cent of births in the city.

The Mother and Child Scheme also brought Church-State relations to a crisis. It was the Catholic bishops' opposition which ultimately wrecked Browne's scheme. The bishops maintained that the right to provide for the health of children belonged to parents and not to the state. They also objected strongly to government medical officers giving women and children information about sex and health. On 5 April 1951, Archbishop McQuaid of Dublin wrote to the taoiseach that:

> The Hierarchy must regard the Scheme proposed by the Minister for Health as opposed to Catholic social teaching. Firstly, in this particular Scheme the State arrogates to itself a function and control, on a nationwide basis, in respect of education, more especially in the very intimate matters of chastity, individual and conjugal. Secondly, the State arrogates to itself a function and control in respect of health services, which properly ought to be and actually can be, efficiently secured, for the vast majority of citizens by individual initiative and by lawful associations.

Costello as taoiseach could not ignore such strong opposition from the Church and he had his own doubts about the wisdom of Browne's innovations from a political and financial point of view. The issue came to a head when Costello and most of the government made it clear that they would not support the minister for health. Browne was openly disavowed by MacBride, his own party leader, and he resigned from the government on 12 April 1951. The proposed Mother and Child Scheme was abandoned. Browne's decision to publish the entire correspondence on the affair, including the letters from Archbishop McQuaid, made it a matter for heated public controversy and threw the coalition into disarray.

Clann na Poblachta was already suffering from internal dissensions and several members left the party. Thus the delicate balance of forces in the Dáil was upset and in May 1951 the taoiseach called a general election. Fianna Fáil won 69 seats, an increase of only one; but the coalition had disintegrated and could not be re-formed, and with the support of five independent deputies (including Browne) de Valera was re-elected taoiseach.

The years 1948-51 had shown the weaknesses as well as the strengths of a coalition government. A change of ministers had given political life a new impetus, but in a cabinet of widely differing parties and personalities, Costello acted more as a chairman than a chief. As matters turned out, he was to be given a second chance in power. In the meantime a Fianna Fáil minority government took over for the next three years.

Fianna Fáil in Power, 1951-54

The Fianna Fáil administration of 1951-54 was perhaps the least distinguished of that party's governments. Obsessed with the persistent deficit in the country's trade balance, and unable to solve the age-old problems of unemployment, emigration and rural depopulation, de Valera's government struggled simply to keep the Irish economy afloat. In the five-year period 1951-56 nearly 200,000 people left the country and the rate of emigration was three times as high as before the war.

Ireland was falling well behind British and European standards of living, especially where social benefits were concerned. In an attempt to correct the marked imbalance in social services between Ireland and its neighbours, de Valera passed a Social Welfare Act in 1952 which rationalised and increased the availability of widows' and orphans' welfare benefits, health insurance and unemployment benefits. Employers henceforth had to make weekly payments towards a compulsory government-sponsored welfare insurance system. Ireland, however, did not become a fully-fledged socialist welfare state, and private charity remained an important source of assistance for the large numbers in real need.

Ireland had yet to make the most of its tourist potential. But there was some progress in this area. Aer Lingus, the Irish airline formed in 1936, began to link with several continental cities and in 1951 ordered four Vickers Viscount aircraft. Negotiations were also started with British European Airways to induce them to provide new services between the UK and Ireland. April 1953 saw the holding of the first annual *tostal*, which was advertised as a festival of 'Ireland at Home' and intended as a means of boosting the country's tourist trade. The *tostal* had several beneficial side-effects: it led to the organisation of new local activities and efforts to clean up small towns and villages.

The Second Coalition 1954-57

Two by-elections in March 1954 were won by the principal opposition party, Fine Gael. Voting showed such a marked swing away from the Fianna Fáil government that de Valera immediately announced a general election. Fianna Fáil, as expected, saw most of its independent supporters defeated and itself lost four seats, leaving the party at its lowest strength for over twenty years. Fine Gael jumped from forty to fifty seats, while Labour also improved its performance from sixteen to nineteen seats. When the new Dáil met in June 1954, Costello was re-elected taoiseach and a second coalition government was formed.

Costello appointed several new figures to important ministries: from Fine Gael Gerald Sweetman (Finance) and Liam Cosgrave (External Affairs) and from Labour Brendan Corish (Social Welfare). Under the second coalition Ireland became a member of the United Nations. The country's first application for membership had been made as early as 1946, but Ireland had been excluded from the international body by Russia's veto. After being admitted in 1955, Ireland became one of the more active of the small nation members of the UN.

An important initiative was taken by Sweetman in 1955 when he set up a Capital Investment Advisory Committee to examine the best means of improving the future performance of the Irish economy. Dr T. K. Whitaker, the new secretary of the Department of Finance, was entrusted with this Committee's organisation. It took three years to complete its investigations and Whitaker's proposals for economic planning in the form of a 'Programme for Economic Development' were accepted, and followed through by succeeding Fianna Fáil governments.

The year 1955 also witnessed the foundation and rapid growth of a new farmers' organisation, modelled on the lines of farmers' unions in other countries. The National Farmers Association (NFA) became a pressure group with considerable power and influence in the years ahead. Farmers felt a strong need for more stability and security and for more effective relations with the Department of Agriculture. With the NFA a new agent for negotiating was born. It also served as a platform for farmers' opinions and later as a means of airing farmers' grievances. In response to farmers' demands, Costello's government set up an Angricultural Production Council in 1956 and also established The Agricultural Institute for research into better methods of farming and eradicating disease in cattle.

The second coalition government also had to cope with an upsurge of IRA activities. The sudden revival of republican militancy in the mid 1950s was in part due to the still-stagnant state of the Irish economy, as well as to a feeling of frustration over the continuance of partition and the decline of the most actively anti-partitionist political party, Clann na Poblachta. On 11 November 1956 six Northern Ireland customs huts on the border were destroyed and on the following day the IRA began a series of attacks on barracks of the Northern Ireland police, the Royal Ulster Constabulary, which lasted for several weeks and resulted in loss of life on both sides. On New Year's Day 1957 two young IRA militants, Sean South and Fergal O'Hanlon were killed during a raid on a barracks in Co. Fermanagh. These incidents caused Costello considerable embarrassment and the taoiseach warned: 'the government has now decided to take such steps as it deems necessary and appropriate against these organisations who have again arrogated to themselves powers and functions that belong to the duly elected representatives of the people, and to these representatives alone'.

Police and troops were moved to the border and a number of arrests were made. Relations between Ireland and the UK became somewhat strained. To the British prime minister's remark in the House of Commons that the safety of Northern Ireland was a direct British responsibility, Costello replied acidly that 'it would be in the interest of Britain as well as Ireland if the British government took the initiative in terminating partition, for the existence of which that government is primarily responsible'.

Inflation, unemployment and emigration continued to strike at the roots of Irish society. Ireland, in common with most European countries, suffered severe economic repercussions from the Suez crisis of 1956. Early in 1957 MacBride's party, Clann na Poblachta, withdrew its support from Costello's government. The Dáil was dissolved and a general election called for 5 March, the third in less than six years. In the election Fianna Fáil won 78 seats, a majority of ten over all other parties in the new Dáil, and returned once again to power. For the first time since 1927, republican Sinn Féin contested an election: four of its 19 candidates were elected but refused to take their seats in the Dáil.

Sean Lemass and the new Fianna Fáil, 1959-66

De Valera was re-elected taoiseach when the new Dáil met but remained in office for only another two years. In 1959, at the age of seventy-seven and nearly blind, de Valera left active politics and was elected president. His retirement from government marked the end of an era in modern Irish history. The new age of recovery which was just beginning was also the age of Sean Lemass, de Valera's successor as taoiseach and leader of Fianna Fáil.

Lemass had already proved himself an efficient and successful minister for industry and commerce in several Fianna Fáil governments ever since the party first came to power in 1932. An energetic minister for supplies during the Second World War, he had always shown himself a pragmatist rather than an idealist by nature—a man who liked to get things done.

Although Lemass was sixty when he became taoiseach, he achieved a great deal during his seven years in office. Some commentators would say that this brilliant organiser came too late to power, but in a few short years he not only changed the character of Fianna Fáil but also introduced a new direction into Irish politics emphasising the importance of proper economic management. He once described his decision-making technique in the following words: 'Generally I would agree that the quick decision is always better than the long-delayed decision.' He was an admirer of the forward-looking American president, John F. Kennedy, whom he welcomed to Ireland in 1963. Lemass was also a man who tried to break down old barriers and he paid a historic visit to Belfast in 1965 for talks with Captain Terence O'Neill, the Northern Ireland prime minister.

A refreshing feature of Lemass's period as taoiseach was his readiness to admit that he had made mistakes in the past. On coming to power in 1959, he turned his back on the protectionist policy which, more than any other man, he had advocated in the 1930s and 1940s. In the 1960s he set out to build up a country where the government would show positive leadership in economic matters.

Lemass looked on the civil service and state-run industries on one side and private enterprise on the other as complementary, not rival, sources of economic activity. He encouraged consultation and discussion at every level. Lemass's approach called for a revolution in civil service attitudes, especially when he put forward the view that government departments should look upon themselves less as purely administrative bodies and more as development corporations with their own ideas. He fully supported

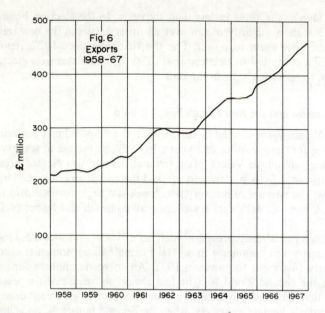

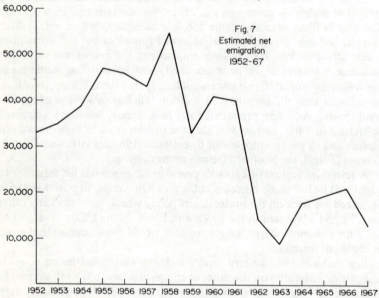

Whitaker's economic programme, and he was fortunate in that his period as taoiseach coincided with an upward trend in the Irish economy. By 1961 Ireland was on the road to economic prosperity.

In 1963 Lemass's government launched its Second Economic Programme, which provided an overall national plan and did much to challenge the mediocrity and parish-pump mentality which still prevailed in many government departments. A National Industrial and Economic Council was set up which called for co-ordination between trade unions, private enterprise and the civil service. The key word in Lemass's economic policy was 'planning' and private firms were urged to plan ahead for more output and employment over three-to five-year periods. Often the Dáil was by-passed in making decisions. Instead new powers to make both general and day-to-day decisions were given to state-sponsored bodies and organisations.

All this was far removed from the old Fianna Fáil philosophy of self-sufficiency and industrial protection. And it worked to the extent that unemployment fell by one-third, factories and new housing schemes were built throughout the country and most people's standard of living rose. For the first time since independence, the census of 1966 showed a population increase of 62,000. A further sign of better times was the lower level of emigration, which during the years 1961-66 fell to about forty per cent of its level in the preceding five-year period.

Lemass's confident outlook for the Irish economy's future was indicated in 1960 when he started the first steps in Ireland's application for membership of the EEC. He also played an energetic part in negotiations which led to the signing of the Anglo-Irish Free Trade Agreement in November 1956. He did much to improve Ireland's image abroad, and encouraged foreign businessmen to invest in Irish industry. It was aptly written of him: 'The shamrock for him was the symbol of Irish International Airlines and he insisted that the land of mists and bogs was no more.'

One obvious sign of the new Ireland of the 1960s was the setting up of the first Irish television service. In 1962 Telefís Éireann began transmissions. Some prophets of doom had predicted that Irish television would never pay its way, and others feared lest it suffer from over-supervision by the government of the day. In practice Irish television proved a boon to large numbers of people, especially those living in rural areas who were unable to receive English TV programmes. Television revealed to many people the life styles of a world beyond the small island of Ireland.

In 1966 Lemass decided to retire as taoiseach and leave the country in charge of a new generation of politicians who had not taken part in the 1916 Rising or the Civil War. But the effects of 1916 were still evident in 1966, as the celebration of the Golden Jubilee of the Rising indicated.

One of Lemass's final public acts before his retirement at the end of 1966 was to preside over the 1916 anniversary commemorations, with speeches, marches and ceremonies all over the country. But the celebrations brought to a head many conflicting ideas on national identity and purpose in modern Ireland. The revival of the memories of 1916 caused much resentment among Unionists in Northern Ireland, and once again the great gap between the two parts of the island was emphasised. It was clear that the Ireland of 1966 was different from the Ireland of 1916. Yet despite change and progress there had also been continuity. Fifty years is a short time in the life-span of a nation and the legacy of problems left unsolved by 1916 and independence for nationalist Ireland came to the surface in Northern Ireland and were to dominate Irish political life for many years.

Talking Points

Chapter 11: Coalition Governments and the new Fianna Fáil, 1948-66
1. In what way can it be said that the years 1948-66 marked a new era in Irish history?
2. Explain the circumstances in which the taoiseach, John A. Costello, announced his government's intention to declare Ireland a Republic in 1948? What was the general reaction to this in Northern Ireland and Britain?
3. How did the first coalition government deal with the many economic problems of the day? What special arrangements were made for coping with the agricultural depression?
4. Outline the various points at issue in the Mother-and-Child controversy.
5. What were Ireland's relationships with Europe and the rest of the world during the years 1948-66? In what way did the world economy and politics affect Ireland?
6. Give an assessment of the career of Sean Lemass, especially his contribution to the making of modern Ireland during his years as taoiseach, 1959-66.

Chapter 12

THE ULSTER QUESTION AND NORTHERN IRELAND, 1914-69

The Ulster Question emerged from Unionist opposition to Home Rule proposals during the years 1886-1914 and came to a head in the months preceding the outbreak of the First World War. The militant attitude adopted by the Ulster Volunteers, who in April 1914 smuggled a substantial cargo of arms into Larne, along with the proposal of the Ulster Unionist leaders to set up a provisional government, if necessary, indicated their continuing determination to resist Home Rule, no matter what the cost or whether pressure to force Ulster into a united self-governing Ireland came from London or Dublin. During the first half of 1914 it was the Ulster Unionists, not the Southern Nationalists, who appeared to outside observers as the Irish rebels. Indeed, Ulster Unionist build-up of open resistance to the Westminster parliament's Third Home Rule Bill served to hide the equally purposeful forces of anti-English feeling in the south. But in any case, the Ulster Unionists were prepared to make their point, and they were not bluffing.

On the eve of the First World War, Ireland was, therefore, divided between the mainly Unionist six northern counties of Antrim, Down, Armagh, Londonderry, Tyrone and Fermanagh and the remaining mainly Nationalist twenty-six counties. The majority of people in those six Ulster counties wanted to remain fully within the jurisdiction of the United Kingdom, whereas the vast majority in the twenty-six counties wished for self-government.

The typical Ulster Protestant's image of Southern Ireland was of a priest-ridden, poverty-stricken and backward country. He judged that he would be mad to exchange the economic advantages of union with Britain for a share in Irish Home Rule. The very thought of joining in a united Ireland, under a Dublin government, was frightening. For their part, the Nationalist Irish did little or nothing to allay such fears and for years had ignored the problem of Ulster Unionism (see Chapter 4). Most Irish Nationalists had the simple belief that when Home Rule became law, the Westminster parliament would force Ulster Unionists to drop their resistance to the idea of an all-Ireland Dublin government. Although the Third Home Rule Bill became law in 1914, because of the outbreak of the First World War it was agreed not to implement it until international peace was restored. In fact, Home Rule as conceived in 1914 was never implemented. By the time the war ended in 1918, the whole political situation in Ireland had changed. As a result of the 1916 Rising and its aftermath, Home Rule no longer satisfied the nationalist population's desire for self-government. But the Unionists of Ulster had no wish to see an end to British rule in Ireland. No mere Dublin rising could undo the ties of friendship which bound the Unionists of Ulster to Britain. Had they not recently sealed their covenant with Britain, once in the solemn oath to which they had subscribed in 1912, and once again, in their own blood, on the battlefields of France and Flanders?

The Irish Convention of 1917, which, as we have seen (Chapter 6), was boycotted by Sinn Féin, was a desperate attempt to solve the Irish question but it resulted only in deadlock and failure because of the intransigence of the Ulster Unionists. In 1918 strenuous nationalist opposition to conscription led to a twenty-four hour general strike, which was effective in most of the country, but not in Unionist Belfast. The government's decision to abandon conscription in Ireland was welcomed by Sinn Féin as a triumph, but was felt by Carson and Northern Unionists to be capitulation to gross disloyalty. They were all the more determined to hold out for the permanent exclusion of Ulster from any settlement between the government and the militant Southern Nationalists.

The Establishment of Northern Ireland, 1920-22

The declaration of an Irish Republic by the Sinn Féin MPs after the general election of 1918 proved no more acceptable to Ulster Unionists than did Home Rule. The 23 Ulster Unionist MPs attended the Westminster parliament and declared themselves opposed to any form of self-government for Ireland. They demanded that the province of Ulster should continue to be governed from Westminster.

The results of the 1918 election did however indicate that Unionists could not claim majority support in *all* of Ulster's nine counties. Late in 1919, Lloyd George, the British prime minister, produced his plan for partitioning the country and establishing two parliaments for local affairs in Ireland, one in Belfast for the six most strongly Unionist counties of Ulster and the other in Dublin for the remaining twenty-six counties. These ideas formed the basis of the Government of Ireland Act, 1920. The Act was rejected by Sinn Féin in the South (Chapter 7) and in the twenty-six counties was a dead letter. However, it was accepted by Ulster Unionists as a compromise. Although it established a form of Home Rule, providing for a 'Northern Ireland' government and parliament with control of domestic affairs, but none over foreign policy, defence and customs, the act firmly guaranteed to Unionists their position within the United Kingdom. There was the serious problem of a large Nationalist Catholic minority within the six counties of Northern Ireland who were bitterly opposed to a Unionist government. In fact, serious sectarian strife broke out in Derry in May and June 1920 when 20 people were killed, and further riots broke out in Belfast in August. In November 1920, recruiting began for the 'A' and 'B' Special armed auxiliary police forces, while the Orange Order claimed to have no less than 50,000 armed men ready to preserve the Union. The growth of such a large armed force in the North was considered necessary (1) to prevent any possibility of the setting up of a parliament for the whole of Ireland through the Council of Ireland, as provided for in the Government of Ireland Act 1920 (see page 144) and (2) to oppose any attempt on the part of Sinn Féin forces in the South to take over the North.

In May 1921 the first general election for the parliament of Northern Ireland was held, and Unionists won 40 out of 52 seats in the House of Commons. Sir James Craig was elected prime minister on 7 June and formed a Unionist government. On 22 June King George V attended the State opening of the Northern Ireland parliament and made his famous appeal for peace and reconciliation between all Irishmen which led, in the South, to the Truce (see Chapter 7) and subsequently to the Anglo-Irish Treaty of December 1921 (Chapter 8).

One significant feature of the Treaty was the fact that the representatives of the Northern Ireland government took no part in the negotiations. Yet the Treaty, which came into force in December 1922, contained several articles referring to Northern Ireland and in some instances superseding the Government of Ireland Act (1920). Northern Ireland could opt out of the conditons involved in the Treaty, and the jurisdiction of the Irish Free State, provided it made a request within a month to that effect. Craig and his cabinet acted immediately (December 1922) and thus continued to rule the six counties under the general terms of the 1920 Act. Northern Ireland remained part of the United Kingdom. There was neither a war of independence nor a civil war in the six counties in the 1920s.

Politics and Religion, 1922-39

Up to 1922 the Royal Irish Constabulary acted as the police force throughout Ireland. They were disbanded in June 1922 and a new force for Northern Ireland, the Royal Ulster Constabulary, was founded and limited by statute to 3,000 men. One-third of its members were supposed to be Catholics, but, in fact, they never reached this quota. The RUC, like its predecessor the RIC, was an armed force, equipped to cope with the violence and disorder both inside the six counties and along the border in the 1920s. Despite Collins-Craig pacts of January and March 1922, the IRA continued to operate in the North, since they refused to recognise the existence of the border. In fact, there were two complete IRA divisions which belonged entirely within the six counties. As many as 8,000 IRA men were in operation there, and they fought as vigorously to do away with the border as did their comrades in the South over the oath of allegiance. This IRA menace and its consequent violence was a considerable irritant for the new government in Belfast.

However, it was not the only menace or threat to peace and order. Provocation by Protestants against Catholics took place when the Northern government took control. By January 1922 over 9,000 Catholic workmen had been driven out of their jobs in factories and shipyards. The government promised to reinstate them but failed to do so. It became more and more difficult to prevent discrimination in jobs. In March 1922, the 'B' Specials wiped out a family of five Catholics, and as a reprisal Catholics killed a Protestant mother and child and wounded the father. To deal with this situation the Northern Ireland government passed the Civil Authorities (Special Powers) Act, 1922. Originally intended to be a temporary measure it was renewed annually until 1928, then for five years until 1933, when it was given permanent duration. The act empowered the Northern Ireland Minister for Home Affairs to 'take all such steps and issue all such orders as may be necessary for preserving peace and maintaining order. Persons may be arrested without warrant on suspicion of acting, or having acted, or being about to act in a manner contrary to the peace'. Sentences of death were to be given to those who caused an explosion likely to endanger life, and flogging could be imposed for a number of offences concerned with firearms, arson and menaces. Finally, the Special Powers Act gave the RUC authority to enter and search buildings without warrant and stop and search vehicles and persons. The armed RUC and the 'B' Specials, also armed, were symptoms of the insecurity of the new Northern Ireland state.

Under a Unionist government, wide scope existed for discrimination against those who did not profess the Protestant religion. Craig made no effort to disguise the fact that Northern Ireland was Protestant: 'Ours is a Protestant government and I am an Orangeman', he declared in 1932, and again in 1934, he said: 'I am an Orangeman first and a politician and a member of this parliament afterwards... All I boast is that we are a Protestant parliament for a Protestant people.' Owing to the overall dominance of the Protestant Unionists in the Northern Ireland parliament, the government represented only their interests and ignored those of other groups. Sir James Craig, created Lord Craigavon in 1927 was prime minister of Northern Ireland without a break from 1922 until his death in 1940.

The most outstanding opposition leader was Joseph Devlin. He had initially abstained from attending the Northern Ireland parliament but, after the Boundary Commission of 1925 failed to bring about the changes in the border which he had hoped for (Chapter 9), Devlin decided to take his seat and fight things out. He was a Nationalist (i.e. a member of the remnant of the old Irish Parliamentary Party) and by 1927 led a party of ten in the Northern House of Commons. His position was not unlike that of Redmond or Dillon in Westminster, and he never won over the Republicans to his side. Devlin was a member of the Ancient Order of Hibernians, an organisation which provided a rallying point for Catholics, much the same as the Orange Order did for Protestants.

Social and Economic Problems, 1922-39

The Northern Ireland economy is closely linked with that of Britain. The first twenty years of the Northern Ireland administration coincided with a series of world economic depressions. There was widespread unemployment and in 1925 nearly a quarter of all insured workmen were unemployed. Some improvement took place during 1927-29, but throughout the ten years 1930-39, the annual unemployment rate in Northern Ireland never fell below 20 per cent.

Northern Ireland covers some 5,000 square miles and in 1937 had a population of 1,280,000. More than 60 per cent of the population lived either in Belfast or within a radius of thirty miles from the city. Agriculture accounted for a quarter of all occupations. Farms were run on a family-subsistence basis, and in 1937 over 60 per cent of all farm holdings were between one and thirty acres in size. Sheep, pigs and poultry were more in evidence than cattle. Some of the long-established industries—shipbuilding and textiles among them—were badly hit in the 1920s and 1930s. Perhaps the worst single result of the economic depression was the closure in 1934 of Belfast's second great shipyard, Workman and Clark's. Owing to the tarriffs imposed on imports by the Irish Free State government, the market and trade connections between some Northern centres of industry and the South of Ireland were ruined. Derry, which had been a flourishing port serving north-western Ireland, found itself cut off from its natural sources of trade. There was also a tendency in Northern Ireland to encourage light rather than heavy industries, so that while jobs for women were plentiful, there was a great shortage of jobs for men. Unemployment reached its peak in July 1938, when over 100,000 people, or nearly 30 per cent of the insured population, were out of work.

Northern Ireland was seriously deficient in minerals and natural resources. Coal, oil, iron and steel all had to be imported from Britain. The cost of producing industrial goods increased according as the cost of transport and raw materials increased. Northern Ireland was at the mercy of world prices in steel, iron and other basic necessities, and her economy, especially in such areas as the ship-building industry, suffered as a result.

During the years 1922 to 1939 there was a serious shortage of houses in Northern Ireland, especially in rural areas. Between 1919 and 1936 the total of all types of houses built in Northern Ireland amounted to only 50,000. The majority of these were built by private enterprise. The local authorities were often to blame for neglect. Up to 1939 less than 4,000 labourers' cottages were built by order of the government and most of these were sub-standard, without gas or electricity or proper sanitation. In Co. Fermanagh, up to 1939, the rural district council had not built a single cottage. A survey of rural dwellings made before the war in 1939 showed that 87 per cent of them had no running water.

Alongside poor housing conditions went an inadequate medical service for those who could not afford private medicine. There was a serious shortage of hospitals, while dispensary doctors, nurses and midwives were badly paid and unable to cope with all the calls on their services. Tuberculosis accounted for a large percentage of deaths even as late as 1938, when the figures show that this disease alone accounted for 46 per cent of those who died between the ages of fifteen and twenty-five, and 38 per cent of those between twenty-five and thirty-five. Up to 1945 the local authorities had to shoulder the burden of looking after the very poor. More often than not, the only relief possible was in and through the workhouse. Northern Ireland retained the totally inadequate system of unions and boards of Poor Law Guardians, introduced into Ireland in 1838. Workhouses became overcrowded with the sick, the aged and the insane all sharing the same gaunt building as the able-bodied poor. A survey of social conditions made in Belfast in 1938-39 showed that 36 per cent of the people interviewed were living in absolute poverty. Unemployment, poverty, bad housing, all helped to drive young Catholics into the IRA, while young unemployed Unionists got grants by working as police auxiliaries in the 'B' Specials. Marches, demonstrations, riots, were all part of the social and economic scene and conditions in pre-1939 Northern Ireland.

In 1938, Lord Craigavon, fresh from yet another election triumph, entered into several important agreements with the British government. First of all, Northern Ireland farmers were to receive agricultural subsidies and the cost would be borne by the British exchequer. Likewise it was agreed that there should be parity of taxation and of social services between all parts of the United Kingdom. Thus, Northern Ireland won for itself a substantial financial boost, as the British treasury henceforth guaranteed to make good any deficit in the Northern Ireland budget. This subsidy was eventually to grow to some £100 million a year.

The War Years, 1939-45

The outbreak of the Second World War brought prosperity and new life to Northern Ireland. Despite the fact that conscription was never imposed (mainly owing to Catholic and Nationalist objections), Lord Craigavon placed all the resources of his government and people at the disposal of Britain for the duration of war. On account of de Valera's firm stand on neutrality for the Irish Free State, the importance of Northern Ireland as a direct link in the sea-lanes between Britain and North America became obvious. After the fall of France in 1940, the north Atlantic became too exposed to German attacks to make such English ports as Southampton and Bristol safe for use. Scottish and Northern Ireland ports provided much safer naval bases for British ships operating in or across the north Atlantic. When America entered the war after Pearl Harbour, Derry was used as a naval base for the American Atlantic fleet, and from 1942 to 1945 large numbers of American servicemen were stationed and trained in the six counties. Barracks had to be built, airfields laid down and roads kept in repair. Wages increased and since there was little to spend money on, many people managed to invest and save something. Work was provided for many of those who had been unemployed and by August 1944, the total number of unemployed dropped to 10,000.

Belfast shipyards benefited by the demand for new ships as well as for repair work. New aircraft factories were built, and engineering works flourished as orders poured in from the British government. Clothing and textile factories also were commissioned to turn out shirts, uniforms, sails, parachutes and tents for the armed services. Many Northern Ireland people went to work in munitions factories in England, while others found employment in the various branches of the armed forces. Agriculture was also to benefit by the war, as farm prices improved and there was a certain market for all farm produce.

The war years brought the people of Northern Ireland and Britain closer together, as they shared the hardships and dangers of modern warfare. In soldiering with the Allies during the war years, Northern Ireland won the right to continued protection from Britain and thus deepened its attachment to the United Kingdom. Belfast suffered four air raids in April and May 1941 and in one raid alone 700 people were killed and 1,500 injured. Catholics and Protestants forgot their differences in their common need, and relations with the Free State government improved when fire brigades from Dublin and Drogheda helped to quench the fires of Belfast. In such a crisis even the border ceased to exist. These raids on Belfast proved how inadequate its defences were. 100,000 people were left homeless, and the British government later had to provide funds for building new houses.

Hospital and general medical facilities improved during the war, as the numbers of wounded and sick increased. Many of those wounded in battle had to be cared for and a new National Health Service was eventually introduced into Northern Ireland as in Britain. Whereas Britain contributed only £3 million from the imperial exchequer to Northern Ireland in the year 1939-40, by the end of the war this sum had increased to £36 million a year. After the death of Lord Craigavon in 1940, John Miller Andrews, a Unionist of the same generation served as Prime Minister of Northern Ireland until 1943. A younger man, Sir Basil Brooke (later Lord Brookeborough) became Prime Minister in 1943 and remained in office for twenty years.

Post-war Recovery and the Welfare State, 1945-49

The war had proved a time of challenge, prosperity and involvement in international affairs. It had shaken the whole framework of Northern Ireland. After the war, people were less willing to accept poor housing, bad and inadequate schools, lack of hospitals, squalor, poverty and all the other ills of former days. Plans were drawn up, financial loans floated, and post-war reconstruction got under way. New jobs had to be found, new industries established, new overseas markets developed. In the circumstances some of the old established industries suffered.

Housing Acts of 1945 and 1946 provided the necessary legislation to tackle the building of 100,000 new homes. A Housing Trust was set up to build workers' houses and supervise building methods and materials. The Northern Ireland Health Services Act (1948) abolished the Poor Law infirmaries and a General Health Services Board was set up to provide medical and dental services for all the population. An Education Act (1947) raised the school leaving age to fifteen and funds were made available for new school buildings. Owing to the fact that grants of 100 per cent were available only for state schools, voluntary schools—most of them Catholic—received less help from the government.

Northern Ireland also profited from the introduction of the welfare state by the British Labour government after the war and within ten years, 1939-49, had risen from relative poverty and backwardness to prosperity. Many of the social and economic ills of the 1930s were forgotten. Despite higher taxation, the country became more and more an integral part of the United Kingdom and learned to depend on British state intervention and support to boost the economy and solve social problems.

Yet there was evidence that the new prosperity did not benefit all the people of Northern Ireland. Discrimination in regard to jobs continued, especially in the public services. A person's religion was considered of prime importance for senior executive positions in the civil service. In some departments, such as that of Home Affairs (which was responsible for internal security), no Catholic could be employed. In factories and offices, there was widespread evidence of (1) segregation, i.e., firms only employing Protestants or only employing Catholics, and (2) partial discrimination i.e., Catholics employed, but only in the lower-paid categories of work. A general feeling prevailed among Protestants in Northern Ireland that Catholics could not be trusted with business secrets, that they had little regard for truth and that they were educationally sub-standard. Furthermore, since the top rungs in the economic ladder were dominated by Protestants for so long they came to consider themselves naturally superior to Catholics. The social implications of this attitude were serious; it led many Catholics to develop an inferiority complex. And since the high rate of unemployment affected Catholics most, they began to suspect that they were only second-class citizens. Herein lies the sense of social insecurity among many Catholics in the North, which in turn generated a sense of political insecurity and suspicion among Protestants.

The Fateful Years, 1949-69

The advent of the welfare state meant an improvement in the standard of living for most Northern Ireland people whether by way of national assistance, family allowance, non-contributory pensions or free medical aid. However, the control of these services lay in the hands of local authorities. In practice this meant that politics and religion entered into the dispensing of social benefits. During the hungry 1940s most people were content with what little they had and inequalities between families of the same class were hardly noticed. But when prosperity came and government spending increased, the gap was more noticeable between those who had little and those who had more than enough. The result of the welfare state in Northern Ireland was to raise the expectations of the less well off. And this meant in practice the Catholic minority. Sectarian bigotry hurt more when Catholics were denied obvious civil rights—as in housing and schools. More and more they were made to feel less-favoured citizens. At local government level Catholics were even denied the basic right of 'one man, one vote'. If one were to seek a reason for the continued harassment of Catholics by the Protestant majority, it could be summed up in the words of Captain O'Neill, prime minister of Northern Ireland in the 1960s: 'The basic fear of the Protestants in Northern Ireland is that they will be outbred by the Roman Catholics. It is as simple as that.'

Unionists had been given fresh encouragement and hope by the British govenment's Ireland Act of 1949, which guaranteed Ulster's position within the United Kingdom. Westminster's Ireland Act seemed to set the seal on the Unionists' control of Ulster, and the Nationalist minority felt that they had no hope of ever influencing the Northern Ireland government. Catholic frustration built up and there was much wishful thinking that one day the Dublin government would help put an end to partition.

Northern Ireland Unionist politicians, for their part, boasted that the North was far better off than the South. The continued influence of the Orange Order, and especially its annual display of solidarity on 12 July accentuated Protestant intolerance, which made many nationalists bitter. There was no room for Catholics in the establishment, as Sir George Clark, the Grand Master of the Grand Orange Lodge of Ireland, said in December 1959:

> It is difficult to see how a Roman Catholic, with the vast differences of our religious outlook, could be either accepted within the Unionist Party as a member, or, for that matter, bring himself unconditionally to support its ideals.

The Unionists provided the main driving force, as well as the essential element of continuity, in Ulster political life. At every election for the Northern Ireland parliament since 1921, the Unionist Party won a comfortable majority. However, some dry rot had accumulated over the years, and calls for more enlightened and progressive attitudes in politics became louder in the 1960s.

During the premiership of Captain O'Neill in the years 1963-69 definite signs of a change in the style of government could be observed. O'Neill set his face against traditional sectarian bigotry and tried to instil his somewhat patronising and paternalistic brand of liberal Unionism into Northern life. He blandly defined the problem in basic socio-economic terms and presented his own remedy for the cure of Northern Ireland's troubles: 'If a Roman Catholic is jobless and lives in the most ghastly hovel, he will rear eighteen children on National Assistance ... If you treat Roman Catholics with due consideration and kindness, they will live like Protestants.' But the prime minister had underestimated the intensity and passion with which old political convictions were held on either side of the sectarian divide and his vision of a happy new breed of loyal Catholic Unionists was destined to remain an unrealised fantasy.

O'Neill also applied himself to the cultivation of more friendly relations with the Republic. A highlight of his premiership was the exchange of visits between himself and Sean Lemass in 1965, which were intended as a step towards ending the cold war with the South. O'Neill, however, met with much opposition from within the Unionist Party, even from among his own cabinet ministers. William Craig, Minister of Home Affairs, was particularly intransigent. O'Neill also had to face the criticism of the arch-Unionist, Rev. Ian Paisley, who was determined to play the role of a modern Moses, leading the Protestant children of Ulster away from the change and decay of the O'Neill government.

However, neither Craig nor Paisley could stop the exasperation and resentment felt by Northern Ireland Catholics against unjust laws and sectarian discrimination. O'Neill's attempts to assuage their fears only convinced them all the more that they must fight for their rights. Inspired by the non-violent civil rights movement in the United States of America, a Northern Ireland Civil Rights Association was set up and became active in 1968, drawing most of its support from the Catholic minority. A series of peaceful demonstrations was planned demanding 'one man one vote' and an end to discrimination in housing allocation and other areas.

The first civil rights march was held in Dungannon in August 1968 and it passed off without incident. However, on 5 October 1968 another demonstration in Derry was confronted by the police armed with batons. The latter were acting under the orders of William Craig, the minister responsible for law and order, who had banned the march two days previously. Many of the marchers were wounded in the baton charges but since the incidents were covered live by television cameras, the government could not avoid questions being raised about its policy, particularly in Britain. Some days later, a group which called itself the Derry Citizens' Action Committee was formed, pledged to pursue the non-violent aims of the Civil Rights Association. Its leaders were John Hume, Austin Currie and Ivan Cooper.

At the same time another protest group, mainly centred on the Queen's University in Belfast was formed and later became known as the People's Democracy. Its leaders were Bernadette Devlin, Michael Farrell and Eamonn McCann. The People's Democracy was basically a socialist organisation, and advocated the setting-up of a 'workers' republic' for the whole of Ireland. In January 1969 the People's Democracy organised a four-day march from Belfast to Derry. The marchers were viciously attacked at Burntollet Bridge by Protestant extremists.

These incidents marked the beginning of the contemporary Northern Ireland 'Troubles'. Despite O'Neill's dismissal of Craig in December 1968 and the promise of reforms, there were few tangible results to be seen. It was felt that O'Neill had granted concessions only in response to sporadic outbursts of violence. O'Neill also met with considerably more opposition and criticism from his own party than he expected. Diehard Unionists refused to allow O'Neill dismantle their 'heritage' through reforms. Unable to face the anger of the Civil Rights Association as well as opposition from his fellow-Unionists, O'Neill decided to resign as prime minister on 28 April 1969. He was succeeded in office by Major James Chichester-Clark.

A long road of bitterness and suffering lay ahead for the Ulster community; all the nightmares of the campaigns of violence waged by the two branches of the IRA, the Officials and the Provisionals. There would also be the introduction of internment in Long Kesh (the Maze Prison), and finally the hundreds of dead and maimed. The troubles spilled occasionally into the Republic and the Ulster problem became a triangular one, with Belfast, London and Dublin all playing their part. The peaceful image of modern Ireland became tarnished throughout the world, as a result of continuing violence. And what was more disturbing still, no one could see an end to the troubles, at least not in the immediate future.

Talking Points

Chapter 12: The Ulster Question and Northern Ireland, 1914-69
 1. Outline the reaction of the Ulster Unionists to (i) the outbreak of First World War (ii) the 1916 Rising (iii) the war of independence and (iv) the Treaty.
 2. How did Lloyd George's Government of Ireland Act (1920) set the seal on Ulster's destiny?
 3. How did Sir James Craig and the first Unionist government cope with (i) political difficulties and (ii) social and economic problems, in the years 1922-39?
 4. Give a general survey of life in Northern Ireland during the war years, 1939-45.
 5. What did the coming of the welfare state mean for the people of Ulster? In what way did it deepen the gulf between the North and South?
 6. Outline the attitude of the various governments in the twenty-six counties towards Northern Ireland between 1922 and 1969. What were the main arguments put forward by Irish Nationalists for abolishing the border?

INDEX

Aiken, Frank, 180, 192, 198, 211
Ashbourne Act (1885), 36, 48
Ashe, Thomas, 130, 133, 136
Asquith, H. H., 58-62, 117

Balfour, A. J., 37-8, 43, 56
Barry, Tom, 149, 171
Barton, Robert, 141, 156-7, 161-2, 165
Biggar, J. G., 45
Birrell, Augustine, 40, 57, 123
Black and Tans, 145-50
Blueshirts, 202-6
Blythe, E., 185
Boundary Commission, 187-9
Boycott, Captain, 32
Bracken, J. K., 90
Brooke, Sir Basil, 217
Browne, Noel, 213, 219-20
Breen, Dan, 143
Bright, John, 26-7
Brugha, Cathal, 132-7, 140-3, 156-7, 165, 178, 181
Butt, Isaac, 42-6, 72

Church of Ireland, Disestablishment of, 19-21, 42
Campbell-Bannerman, Henry, 57
Carson, Edward, 60-2, 80-4, 228
Casement, Sir Roger, 109, 116, 121, 125, 130
Cavendish, Lord Frederick, 36
Ceannt, Eamonn, 117, 122
Childers, Erskine, 157, 162, 165, 167, 181
Churchill, Lord Randolph, 51, 78, 82
Churchill, Winston, 159, 163, 175, 209, 212
Civil War, 173-81
Clann na Poblachta, 216, 220, 222
Clarke, Thomas J., 103, 114, 118, 121-3

Collins, Michael, 132, 138, 141, 148-9, 156-62, 165, 169-81, 186, 193, 195-6, 229
Congested Districts Board, 38, 40
Connolly, James, 104-9, 120-3, 130
Cosgrave, Liam, 221
Cosgrave, W. T., 100, 130, 141-2, 156, 165, 170, 173, 177, 179, 181, 184-5, 189, 212
Corish, Brendan, 221
Costello, John A., 215-22
Craig, James (Lord Craigavon), 80-4, 151-2, 161-2, 173, 189, 229-30, 232-3, 236
Craig, William, 236-7
Cullen, Cardinal, 14, 21-2, 44, 72
Curragh 'mutiny', 61-2, 84
Cusack, Michael, 90

Davitt, Michael, 30-5
De Valera, Eamon, 95, 109, 129-30, 134-5, 137, 152-3, 155-61, 165, 169, 172, 174-6, 178, 180, 184-5, 191-3, 198-213, 215-16, 220-1, 224
Devlin, Joseph, 230
Devoy, John, 18, 30-2, 93, 97, 118, 121, 123
Dillon, James, 206, 213, 218
Dillon, John, 34, 37, 42, 47, 55, 130, 137
Disestablishment of Church of Ireland see Church of Ireland
Duffy, George Gavan, 157, 162
Duggan, Eamonn, 157, 162

Economic war, 200-2
Emigration (after the famine), 3, 6, 8, 9
Encumbered Estates Act (1849), 8-9

Fenianism, 15-19, 34
Fitzgerald, Desmond, 185

Ford, Patrick, 32, 46
Forster, W. E., 33-5
French, Lord, 137, 144

Gaelic Athletic Association, 17, 89-92
Gaelic League, 17, 92-5
Gladstone, W. E., 18-19, 21, 26, 32-5, 44, 47-53, 55, 57, 74, 78
Gonne, Maud, 99, 111
Greenwood, Sir Hamar, 146, 148, 159
Griffith, Arthur, 58, 97-102, 106, 113, 132, 134-5, 137, 141, 148, 156-61, 165-7, 169, 173, 179, 181

Hawarden kite, the, 48-9
Healy, T. M., 55, 184
Hempel, Dr, 210, 212
Hobson, Bulmer, 99, 102, 109, 111, 117, 121
Home Rule, 35, 42-62, 71, 73, 77, 88, 93, 114, 115
Home Rule Bill (1886), 49-51
Home Rule Bill (1893), 55
Home Rule Bill (1912), 59-62, 80, 85
Howth gun-running, 116
Hyde, Douglas, 93-5, 208

Irish Agricultural Organisation Society, 39
Irish Convention, The (1917), 135-6, 228
Irish Transport and General Workers Union, 106-8, 110

Kickham, Charles J., 16-17, 22, 30-1
Kilmainham 'treaty', 32, 35-6

Ladies Land League, 33
Lalor, James Fintan, 9-12, 26
Land Act (1870), 26-8
Land Act (1881), 33-4, 40
Land League, 17, 30-5, 47
Larkin, James, 106-9
Law, A. Bonar, 60-1, 82, 159, 172
Lemass, Sean, 192, 198, 209, 215, 224-5

Lloyd George, David, 58, 132, 135-6, 141, 144, 150-53, 155-6, 166, 168, 174-6, 188, 228
Local Government Act (1898), 57, 97
Luby, Thomas Clarke, 15, 17
Lynch, Liam, 149, 171, 178, 180

MacBride, Sean, 203, 205, 213, 216, 222
McCullough, Denis, 99, 102-3, 121-2
MacDiarmada, Sean, 100, 102-3, 114, 119-23, 126
MacDonagh, Thomas, 117-22, 128, 131
MacEntee, Sean, 199
McGilligan, Patrick, 190, 194, 213, 217
McGrath, Joseph, 185, 187, 190
MacNeill, Eoin, 93-4, 109, 115, 117, 122, 124-6, 141, 185, 188-9
Macready, Sir Neville, 146-7, 153
MacSwiney, Mary, 111
MacSwiney, Terence, 148
Maffey, Sir John, 211
Manchester Martyrs, 18
Markievicz, Countess, 100, 111, 130, 141
Maxwell, Sir John, 129-31, 137
Mellows, Liam, 180
Moran, D. P., 89, 96, 100
Mother and Child scheme, 219-20
Mulcahy, Richard, 169, 172, 185-7, 213

Nally, P. W., 90
Nathan, Sir Matthew, 123, 127
'New Departure', the, 30-1, 35, 46

O'Brien, William MP, 34, 37, 46, 56
O'Casey, Sean, 104, 109
O'Connor, Rory, 172, 174, 178, 180-1
O'Donovan Rossa, Jeremiah, 19, 122
O'Duffy, General Eoin, 187, 203-6
O'Growney, Father Eugene, 93
O'Higgins, Kevin, 142, 165-6, 170, 173, 177, 179, 185-7, 192-5

O'Kelly, Sean T., 100, 192, 198
O'Leary, John, 16-17, 22, 96
O'Malley, Ernie, 149, 171-2
O'Mahony, John, 15-16, 18
O'Neill, Captain Terence, 224, 235-7
O'Rahilly, The, 109, 117, 124
Orange Order, 71, 73, 76-81
O'Shea, Katharine, 46, 52-4
O'Shea, Captain W. H., 52-3

Parnell, Charles Stewart, 31-4, 42-54, 62, 72, 74, 91, 101
Pearse, P. H., 12, 19, 94-5, 100, 109-10, 117-31
Phoenix Park Murders, 35-6
Plan of Campaign, 37-8, 42
Plunkett, Sir Horace, 39, 89, 99, 135
Plunkett, Joseph, 117, 121, 123-4, 126, 130-1

Railways, 23-5
Redmond, John, 55, 58-62, 116-17, 130, 136

Richardson, Sir George, 83-4
Robinson, Seamus, 143

Spindlar, Karl, 125
Stack, Austin, 156-7, 165, 168
Statute of Westminster, 193-5
Stephens, James (Fenian), 15, 16
Sweetman, Gerard, 221
Synge, John Millington, 96-7

Tenant League, 12-15
Treacy, Sean, 143, 149

Ulster Unionist Council, 80, 82
Ulster Volunteer Force, 83-5, 109

Whitaker, T. K., 215, 221-2, 224
Wilson, Sir Henry, 173, 175, 177
Wyndham Land Act (1903), 40, 79

Yeats, W. B., 96, 99-100, 131